'*The Political Economy of Conflict and Viole*[r] that neoliberalism and globalisation are a wa[r] time. The structural violence of economic sys and wars, which are not aberrations from the ......, but are a continuation of capitalist patriarchy's war against nature and women. Most important, this important book highlights how the feminist ethics and economics of care contributes to developing new economic models for feminist peacebuilding.'

Dr Vandana Shiva, author of *Who Really Feeds the World?*
and *Earth Democracy*

# POLITICAL ECONOMY OF CONFLICT AND VIOLENCE AGAINST WOMEN

# POLITICAL ECONOMY OF CONFLICT AND VIOLENCE AGAINST WOMEN

## CASES FROM THE SOUTH

*Edited by Kumudini Samuel, Claire Slatter and Vagisha Gunasekara*

**ZED**

*Political Economy of Conflict and Violence Against Women: Cases from the South*
was first published in 2019 by Zed Books Ltd, The Foundry, 17 Oval Way, London
SE11 5RR, UK.

www.zedbooks.net

Typeset in Plantin and Kievit by Swales & Willis Ltd, Exeter, Devon
Index by Dawn Dobbins
Cover design by Steve Leard
Cover photo © Ivor Prickett, New York Times, Panos Pictures
Printed and bound by CPI Group (UK) Ltd, Croydon, CR0 4YY

A catalogue record for this book is available from the British Library

ISBN 978-1-78699-611-4 hb
ISBN 978-1-78699-610-7 pb
ISBN 978-1-78699-612-1 pdf
ISBN 978-1-78699-613-8 epub
ISBN 978-1-78699-614-5 mobi

MIX
Paper from
responsible sources
FSC® C013604

To Vijay K. Nagaraj

Friend and colleague, creative and provocative thinker and strategist, free-spirited eclectic whose intellect and wisdom, grassroots activism and international work and above all humanity inspired so many in both the South and the North. He will forever be remembered and sorely missed.

*Keep walking on these paths*

*They have been laid for you*

*Holding your hand*

*Here I am walking*

*I am walking*[1]

---

[1] Lyrics from 'Chal Diye' by Zeb and Haniya and Javed Bashir, Coke Studio, Pakistan, translated from the Urdu – much loved by Vijay.

# CONTENTS

# ILLUSTRATIONS

## Graphs

## Figures

## Tables

# ABOUT THE EDITORS

**Kumudini Samuel** is an Executive Committee Member of DAWN, engaged in its cross-cutting work and concentrating on the domain of political restructuring and social transformation. She lives and works in Sri Lanka and is a co-founder and current Director, Programmes and Research at the Women and Media Collective. She has a Master's in Women's Studies from the University of Colombo and has written and worked on gender and politics, conflict and transitions, women's movements, and sexuality.

**Claire Slatter** is a founding member and current Board Chair of DAWN. A Fijian national, she has an MA (Political Studies) from the Australian National University and a PhD (Public Policy) from Massey University and taught politics at the University of the South Pacific for 23 years. She has written, engaged in advocacy and done consulting work on issues of regional concern including neoliberal reforms, trade liberalisation, democracy and human rights and gender and development.

**Vagisha Gunasekara** is a Sri Lankan researcher, and a Senior Lecturer at the Department of Social Studies of the Open University of Sri Lanka. She is affiliated with the Social Scientists' Association (SSA), Sri Lanka. She received her PhD in political science from Purdue University, USA. She takes primarily a political economy approach in studying particular entanglements of gender and conflict in rapidly changing situations in the South Asia region.

# ABOUT THE CONTRIBUTORS

**Yaliwe Clarke** is a Lecturer in the Gender Studies Section in the School of African and Gender Studies, Anthropology and Linguistics (Faculty of Humanities), University of Cape Town. She is also a Researcher in the African Gender Institute. Over the years Yaliwe has interacted with African women's rights activists and peace-builders/conflict resolution practitioners and gained extensive continental training experience in gender and peace-building.

**Elizabeth Cox** is an active contributor to Pacific regional and national networks of Ending Violence Against Women (EVAW) organisations, and has 40 years of experience and understanding of development and change across Melanesian communities in the region. She is a technical advisor and contractor in capacity development and knowledge production in Papua New Guinea.

**Roshmi Goswami** is from Assam and is a founding member of the North-East Network. She was Program Officer with the Ford Foundation in New Delhi for several years, programming on women's rights, before moving on to UN Women in New York. She pioneered work with women in conflict-affected regions of India, including documenting and analysing the impact of war and conflict on the lives of women.

**Fahima Hashim** is a women's rights defender and activist, researcher and trainer. She serves as the Director for Salmmah Women's Resource Centre, Khartoum, Sudan. She has over 25 years of experience in the area of gender and development, with a special emphasis on women's rights and sexuality, violence against women and peace-working with women and youth in conflict and post-conflict situations.

**María-Claudia Holstine** is an architect and political scientist with experience in international trade, enterprise administration and financial operation, gender and the Colombian conflict. She is Executive Director and Legal Representative of International Center for Social and Economic

Thought (CiSoe) Colombia, as well as Managing Director of the CiSoe Institute based in Washington, DC.

**Michelle Kopi** is a Development Programme Coordinator with the New Zealand High Commission in Papua New Guinea. She specialises in conflict security and development and has eight years' work experience in project management, research, social and community development in conflict situations, governance, organisational development, gender equality and social inclusion.

**Cecilia López Montaño** is an economist, researcher, lecturer and Colombian politician. One of her main legislative initiatives was the creation of the legal commission for the Equality of Women and Law 1413 of 2010. She currently serves as president and founding member of CiSoe.

**Vijay K. Nagaraj** was a researcher, writer, activist and teacher. He taught at the Tata Institute of Social Sciences in Bombay, India and a secondary school in Colombo. He worked with Amnesty International, India, the International Centre for Human Rights Policy in Geneva, and the Centre for Poverty Analysis and the Law and Society Trust in Colombo, Sri Lanka. He worked on a range of issues from rural community empowerment in Rajasthan to evictions and militarisation, constitutional reform and social, economic and cultural rights and housing rights in the North, in Sri Lanka. Sadly, Vijay passed away in 2017.

**Dr. Constance O'Brien** now retired, previously taught courses at both undergraduate and postgraduate levels at the University of Cape Town's Department of Social Development. She was also the postgraduate research coordinator for several years and presently supervises doctoral students. Her main interests lie in post-conflict peace-building and she is currently involved in a rural development programme.

# ACKNOWLEDGEMENTS

This book is dedicated to Vijay K. Nagaraj, co-author of the Sri Lanka chapter who died tragically in a road accident several months before the book was completed.

The book had its genesis in early 2015 when DAWN discussed the possibility of beginning a research process that could link gendered violence and the root causes of conflict to political economy. We felt the framing would be new and would give the tired narratives of wartime violence against women, in particular wartime sexual violence, a fresh nuance and understanding. Vijay was helping DAWN develop a research methodology for conducting peer-to-peer conversations and was one of the first people with whom we discussed this new idea. He was immediately interested and enthusiastic. He understood that the two framings – violence against women in war and conflict and feminist political economy – should not be kept separate, and so began a time of discussion and reflection that led to the initial conceptualising of this book. At the time, Vijay was not contemplating writing a chapter, but he gave generously of his time and his immense intellectual curiosity in developing its framework. The dedication of this book to Vijay comes with a deep appreciation for his contributions in various ways to the work of DAWN.

A book such as this develops out of a multitude of conversations and incurs many debts to the people who helped shape it. Among the first of the conversations within DAWN on the book were those held with Vivienne Taylor, Celita Eccher and Zenebewerke Tadesse, who were on the DAWN Board together with Claire Slatter. These conversations gave us insights to further sharpen our initial conceptualising, and for that we are deeply grateful. As the project progressed, DAWN had the support of two excellent coordinators – Ambika Satkunanathen, who saw us through the first phase of the work until the inception workshop with the authors, and Thakshala Tissera, who took on this work in 2016 and helped us get the first chapter drafts in. A project of this nature requires patient coordination to ensure that deadlines are met and quiet diplomacy to push those who tarry. We thank them both for this work. We also extend our sincere appreciation to Ayesha Imam, who contributed diligently to this project while she was on the DAWN Executive Committee, identifying potential authors, helping with the conceptualising and facilitating the inception workshop that led to the research and writing of the first drafts of the chapters. Hibist Kassa, of the DAWN Executive Committee, was initially to be a co-editor and made constructive comments on the chapter on Sudan/South Sudan before she had to withdraw to complete her doctoral studies. Vagisha Gunasekara very graciously accepted our invitation to join the editorial team after the first publisher reviews came in and worked tirelessly to see the book through to its completion. Her scholarly contribution to this endeavour was invaluable. We also thank Kamla Chandrakirana, Harini Amerasuriya, Dinushika Disanayake, B. Shanthakumar, Niyanthini Kadirgamar, Farzana Haniffa and Sarala Emmanuel who generously participated in the meetings we convened with the authors or reviewed the chapters to give us critical comments on their work. Our singular thanks to Sarala Emmanuel for helping us frame the final discussions and facilitate the second authors' workshop.

We are indebted to Seona Smiles, who undertook the technical editing of chapters and prepared the final manuscript for publishing, with the many editorial changes and time constraints this entailed. We are particularly grateful to her for working down to the wire as the final deadline loomed. Last but not least, we thank all our authors for their cooperation through the editing stage, with special appreciation to those who came on board later in the process and worked to a shorter timeframe. We extend our deep appreciation to Zed Books for publishing the book, and especially to Kim Walker, Editorial Director, who believed in this project, encouraged us and accepted the manuscript for publication. Our thanks are also due to Dominic Fagan, who worked with us in Kim's absence.

The support extended to DAWN, as always, by Ford Foundation made all of this possible – the research, the analysis, the writing and the publication – and we record our sincerest thanks to them. Finally, this book would not have been possible without the unstinting and invaluable assistance we received from the co-coordinators of DAWN, Gita Sen and Maria Graciela Cuervo, the DAWN Executive Committee, and the DAWN Secretariat staff – in particular Sharan Sindhu and Damien Gock, who supported the final coordination.

Kumudini Samuel, Claire Slatter and
Vagisha Gunasekara – Editors

# INTRODUCTION[1]: FRAMING A SOUTH FEMINIST ANALYSIS OF WAR, CONFLICT AND VIOLENCE AGAINST WOMEN – THE VALUE OF A POLITICAL ECONOMY LENS

*Kumudini Samuel and Vagisha Gunasekara*

This collection of essays builds on previous work by Development Alternatives with Women for a New Era (DAWN) in understanding violence against women in contexts of war, conflict and transition. In 2009, DAWN began a process of exploring women's activism and agency through a series of self-reflective case studies written by feminist activists from Indonesia, Sri Lanka, Nepal and India, which we published as a monograph titled *Women Transforming Peace Activism in a Fierce New World: South and Southeast Asia* (Samuel, 2012).[2] Weaving through these narratives was a common thread of women's everyday experience of wartime and conflict-related violence. Almost all the case studies recorded experiences of sexual violence, including through personal testimonies. However, as with recent research, the ubiquity of sexual violence in war, the nature of perpetrators and variations within and across conflict often belied simple explanations (Cohen et al., 2013). The analyses of sexual and other violence during war and conflict seemed to assume an imaginary 'border' between war and the temporal boundaries of 'pre-war' and 'post-war'. Therefore, violence against women during war and conflict tended to bear an 'exceptionalised' nature.

The narrations revealed, however, that women's experiences of violence and in/security were mediated through a range of constantly changing social and economic structures – culture, religion, family, sexual division of labour and power, inequalities in employment opportunities and incomes, development practices, identity, sexuality and gender – that thread through times before and after, as much as during, war and conflict. The referent of security was also not merely the individual but the social relations that mediated human life. The women in the narratives encountered and challenged this complex nexus as they tried to deal with everyday life in situations of war and conflict (Samuel, 2012). The case studies also reflected the many global/local processes that coalesced to create 'plural forms of gender power and control' over women, which shaped 'new risks' and forms of insecurity for them and their communities (Wieringa et al., 2006). 'These gendered risks for women were manifest not only in the brutalisation of the body and impunity in the domain of violence but also in the dislocation of everyday life and the increase in women's burden in the domain of care and women's exclusion from decision making in the domain of political life' (Samuel, 2012: 11).

What became clear was that war and conflict consist of complex, multi-layered internal and global political economic dimensions. This underlying web of political economic processes of conflict is tightly knitted to the nature of relations between the national and the global economy in postcolonial nation states in the global South. Hence, as much as these processes are deeply enmeshed in the causes and consequences of war and conflict, they also shape the aftermath of post-conflict transition, reconstruction, recovery and peace. These rich and varied insights compelled us therefore to interrogate existing frames of analysis that sought to understand violence against women in conflict and war. We realised that our very own ways of thinking about violence against women during war and conflict needed to be rattled in order to push beyond simple explanations. In many ways, this collection of case studies is a modest attempt to challenge ourselves to 'read' or 'map' how patterns of violence against women are produced and reproduced in the broader relations between national and global economy, as well as in the political (and military) relations of conflict shaped by prevalent internal and external ideological and political paradigms and geopolitical contentions. In doing so, we also wish to simultaneously complicate, as well as bring together, existing analyses of violence against women and conflict advanced primarily by feminist security studies and feminist political economy.

### Our point of departure: dominant views on violence in peacemaking and peace building[3]

We set off from our own experiences of formal peacemaking and transitional justice processes, where women's participation is restricted and violence against women often remains outside the patriarchal structures and terms of reference of negotiation processes. We also wish to note that, historically, neither national nor international courts, or the formal processes of justice and redress, have been able to provide adequate justice to victims of rape and sexual crime either in times of war and conflict or in times of peace (Fitzpatrick, 1994; Charlesworth et al., 1991). The feminist struggle to surface sexual violence and rape out of the private realm succeeded in politicising sexual violence as an act related to social power. The acknowledgement of violence against women as a crime at the UN World Conference on Human Rights in 1993 is one such moment of victory for transnational feminist activism. At around the same time, feminists – both scholars and advocates – grappled with the unprecedented brutality of rape in conflict following the genocides in the former Yugoslavia and Rwanda, compelling the international community through the Rome Statutes to recognise certain aspects of violence against women as 'crimes against humanity'; these included rape, sexual slavery, enforced prostitution, forced pregnancy, enforced sterilisation, and any other form of sexual violence of comparable gravity. As a result of victim and witness narratives that unfolded at the international criminal tribunals for the former Yugoslavia, Rwanda and elsewhere, sexual violence was established as an integral part of war, not merely an effect of it (Henry, 2014; Copelon, 1995; Charlesworth and Chinkin, 2000).

Feminist scholarship further unravelled links between processes of militarisation, globalisation and war and how gender relations are constituted within them (Elias, 2015; Moran, 2010; Enloe, 1989; 2000; Chenoy, 2004; Meintjes et al., 2002; Cockburn and Zarkov, 2002). This articulation and the exceptional attention to wartime sexual violence, despite its critical importance, within feminist and rights discourses and international criminal law (Lorentzen and Turpin, 1998; Skjelbæk and Smith, 2001; Moser and Clark, 2001; Manchanda, 2005; Giles and Hyndman, 2004) have had 'unintended consequences' (Henry, 2014: 97) that merit further study.

Concerted efforts by feminists at local and global levels to convince national and international policy bodies to acknowledge violence against women as a crime have also led to a developing critique of how violence is framed in the context of war and conflict. The continued fixation on sexual violence against women in conflict by international criminal law imputes a hierarchy of gravity to some crimes over others and silences 'alternate narratives' (Henry, 2014). It also results in sidestepping other types of direct physical and psychological violence and structural violence. Nicola Henry's critique of the increasing criminalisation of wartime sexual violence against women notes that the 'specific contexts', 'diversity of victims' and 'intersections of marginalisation' are not reflected in the fixation on rape as the 'universal experience' of women during wartime (ibid.).

The marking of women's sexuality as a root of oppression serves to reinforce the 'sexed body' as a predictable target of sexual violence. This critique is also concerned that women are reduced to passive victims of violence and objects that need the protection of the law, where their identities are 'defined rather than challenged by this subjugation'. Another critique is that there is a ceding of power and 'legitimacy to law as a source of knowledge and truth and the grantor and protector of women's equality, rights and liberty' (Henry, 2014: 97). In this process, too, the very critical problems associated with the possibility and impossibility of rape prosecution are left mostly unaddressed, while some forms of rape are exceptionalised by international law (Copelon, 1995) and a 'hierarchy of harm' is established (Henry, 2014). It has also been argued that ethical and political wrongs and systemic injustice within the broader socio-economic contexts of war and conflict, as well as the impact of global capitalism on the causes and consequences of war, are little recognised or dealt with by international criminal law and trials rarely administer substantive justice for women seeking postwar recovery (Bell and O'Rourke, 2007; Rees and Chinkin, 2016).

Further, this critique also reflects the philosophy underlying political economic arrangements promoted by neoliberal peacemaking and development models supported and introduced by states and by bilateral and multilateral donors (Rees and Chinkin, 2016). UN resolutions and national peace processes are often premised on an understanding of security as state-centric. This same concept becomes a key consideration in defining processes of conflict resolution and peacemaking in transitional and post-conflict situations. Hence the emphasis is centred on state and institutional reform. This often entails obscuring the adverse effects generated by neoliberal models of development, which tend to be the cornerstones of post-war reconstruction and peace-building efforts (Bergeron et al., 2017). This work is generally overshadowed by the somewhat overdetermined approaches to 'women, peace and security' in which security studies perspectives tend to hold sway and violence – often sexual violence in war, militarised sexualities and post-war gender-based violence – is addressed without much attention being paid to the underlying causes and consequences of war (ibid.). The women, peace and security discourse, which is premised primarily on UN Security Council Resolution (UNSCR) 1325 and subsequent thematic resolutions, does not address the challenge of political economic arrangements inherent in neoliberal peace building that seriously impede sustainable peace (Cohn, 2012; Duncanson, 2016; True, 2016; Turshen, 2016). Nor does it challenge the assumptions of post-war reconstruction and economic development that neoliberal peace models offer.

The women, peace and security agenda promoted by the UN Security Council has instead been charged as 'complicit in promoting neoliberal peacebuilding and post-conflict reconstruction' (Basu, 2017: 724). Veering away from feminist framings of 'positive and transformative peace' as not merely the absence of war (these provided the basis for concerted advocacy that led to the adoption of UNSCR 1325 in October 2000), current peace-building interventions sanctioned by the UN are ideologically premised on the 'neoliberal logic' that understands 'market-driven policies for economic development as the panacea for conflict as well as post-conflict reconstruction' (ibid.: 725).

Furthermore, the women, peace and security resolutions are politically linked to the UN Security Council agenda that frames the broader international approach to peace and security, and this approach relies on bolstering 'military strength and securitized states' (Otto, 2016: 10). Such a conception of peace is limited to 'seeking women's participation in the decision-making structures of the existing frames of war, supporting disarmament only at the local level in post-conflict communities, and urging legal and practical reforms aimed at making armed conflict safer for women' (ibid.). The UN global study reviewing fifteen years of implementation of the UN's women, peace and security resolutions found women's official participation in peacemaking temporary or symbolic rather than substantive, and that their influence was directly resisted by cultural norms (Coomaraswamy, 2015). Moreover, the resolutions do not in any way deal with either the role of the global political economic order or the gendered structures of economic discrimination and the manner in which they shape and impact violence suffered by women. Neither do they pay attention to gendered social, political and economic inequalities that shape women's vulnerability to violence (Rees and Chinkin, 2016). Fundamentally, the UN must make its priority the prevention of conflict rather than the use of force, and it must critically examine measures to address the root causes of war and structural drivers of conflict, such as 'exclusion, discrimination, attacks on dignity and structural inequality' (Coomaraswamy, 2015: 15).

Feminists have identified neoliberal economic interventions inherent in contemporary international peacemaking and post-war reconstruction as a critical challenge to sustainable peace, which must include a transformative gender agenda. In light of this, we must now nuance this analysis to include a political economy lens that is integral to how gendered security is viewed and addressed. Since post-war reconstruction is often framed around global reintegration of war-torn economies through a process of market reform and economic liberalisation, feminist political economists have noted that this serves only to exacerbate war-related poverty and increase economic marginalisation and burdens such as unpaid care and domestic work for women (Peterson, 2005; Ní Aoláin et al., 2011). Both protracted armed conflict and post-conflict economic recovery and development models spawn the accumulation of wealth and power resulting from various economic processes that include land grabbing, dispossession, extractivism and privatisation (Bergeron et al., 2017). Such forms of structural economic violence serve only to exacerbate gendered inequalities, marginalisation and exclusion and must be addressed together with direct physical violence (Ní Aoláin et al., 2011).

Feminists have ventured into consolidating this discussion more proactively by developing new economic models for feminist peace building (Bergeron et al., 2017). Alternatives to neoliberal economic models 'draw upon a feminist ethics of care and sustainability to challenge the market-centered logic of the mainstream and its claim that we are all beholden to an invariant capitalist logic; they highlight, instead, a diversity of economic forms such as cooperative practices, community economies, household and reproductive economies, and solidarity economy initiatives' (ibid.: 718). This research now needs to take into account the challenges of war-torn economies and post-war recovery that factors in women's lived realities, entrenched inequalities and survival strategies. Hence, the purpose of this book is to use a political economy framework or lens to study violence against women by taking structural inequalities into account, thereby contributing to a nuanced and better understanding of, and more effective responses to, gender-based violence against women in conflict and war.

## The need for a political economy framework of analysis

In order to push beyond the current impasse related to our understanding of violence against women during war and conflict, the first step is to think differently about war and conflict. Even today, there is significant consensus on the idea that war and conflict are an aberration from the 'normal', that these conditions indicate a 'disturbance' of otherwise smooth sailing and presumed *non-violent* political, economic, social and cultural processes. The thesis of war or conflict as an exceptional state, although it does have its exceptions, often fails to capture more entrenched legacies of violence and tends to mask the fact that violence against women and sexual violence are also ingrained features in societies not actively in conflict. Further, it fails to acknowledge that, as a consequence, such violence can and does endure post-war or post-conflict, and that productive (and non-productive) accumulation almost always involves coercion and is seldom free of force (Moore, 2015; Agamben, 1998; Petchesky, 2002). The failure to make these connections also leads to the consideration of conflict and war only as aberrations from the normal and does not account for the violence that also inheres in 'normal' economic and political arrangements. Rather, situations of violent conflict are simultaneously both a breach in the normal and part of a continuum of gender-based violence, both direct and structural. This view also often assumes that violence is confined to spaces of combat. With its black-and-white understanding of the time and space of war, it also readily categorises victims and perpetrators into mutually exclusive boxes, often based on an ahistorical reading that typically fails to account for the continuity of structural violence where these categories are not so clear-cut. When war and conflict are treated in this manner, 'post-conflict recovery' automatically entails achieving 'normal conditions of the economy', which are assumed to be non-violent.

At this point we draw from David Moore (2015) and Karl Von Holdt (2014), who offer a framing of war that takes into account the structural nature of violence. Their ideas are similar in that they conceive war and conflict as moments of eruption in 'an ongoing course of class, ideological and political formation in the context of accumulation processes' (Moore, 2015: 2). Moore (ibid.) reminds us that democracy as much as processes of accumulation can foster and reproduce violent conditions, offering a much-needed corrective to such notions of normality. Von Holdt (2013) further argues that 'democracy may configure power relations in such a way that violent practices are integral to them' (Von Holdt, 2013: 592). Taking South Africa as an example, Von Holdt (ibid.) argues that the country's very democracy coexists with many of the existing fault lines or fissures that deepen its already extreme inequality. And as these fractures are activated and expanded along the lines of ethnic, gender and other identities, the result is multiple forms of violence (Von Holdt, 2013: 591; also cited in Moore, 2015). The parallel process of primitive or primary accumulation, or 'the creation of capitalism out of feudalism or other "traditional" modes of production, has never been free of force' (Moore, 2015: 8). These processes of accumulation and the inherent coercion and violence are also deeply gendered.

Foregrounding political and economic relations by bringing to bear critical feminist political economic analysis on war and conflict helps us further explore how these relations both condition and heighten women's vulnerability to violence. In general, political economic narratives of conflict and wartime gendered violence have been positioned around the '*cheapness of wartime sexual violence*' (Kirby, 2012: 808) in the context of economic and resource accumulation strategies of one or more of the parties to the conflict. Kirby refers to Eve Ensler's comment that 'rape is a very cheap method of warfare. You don't have to buy scud missiles or hand grenades' to illustrate the point that wartime rape is used as an economic strategy of resource accumulation in the Democratic Republic of Congo (ibid.). This is particularly compounded by the fact that many wars and conflicts across the globe are also rooted in power struggles to control land or natural resources. The link between the causes of conflict and sexual violence is less discussed, however, in the context of structural inequalities mediated by patriarchy at the level of the household or the community, and in global political economies during or in the aftermath of war and conflict. It is crucial, therefore, to view conflict and wartime sexual violence as political violence with a range of political economic dimensions 'connected to both private patriarchy and the differential gender impacts of economic globalisation' (True, 2012: 45). Such an analysis can potentially further illuminate the dynamics of gender and social relations within war- and conflict-affected polities and develop strategies to transform them. This becomes extremely important as existing dominant international relations and feminist security studies also appear to be preoccupied with sexual violence in war and conflict but rarely concern themselves with other forms of violence, such as the endemic nature of domestic violence or economic violence, or even the ways in which violations of socio-economic rights in 'peacetime' are heightened in armed conflict and situate women in conjunctures of vulnerability to gender-based violence.

Feminist political economy is useful in unpacking the gendered nature of violence inherent in domestic and global political economic structures as they relate to war and conflict (True, 2012). To begin with, it interrogates the dominant position of labelling women as simply victims of war, viewing them rather as participants and actors negotiating within a context of a militarised political economic system with supra-local if not global dimensions (Nordstrom, 2004). Discussing the more recent research on women themselves as violent actors, or as supporters and enablers of violence, Ní Aoláin et al. write: 'Research examining the overlap between women's roles and war economies has started to explore the subterranean relationships that intertwine women's agricultural and industrial labour as well as their functioning within the shadow economy accompanying war as relevant to enabling the conditions conducive to the maintenance of cycles of violent interaction' (Ní Aoláin et al., 2011: 6). Also significant are gendered analyses of political economies of war highlighting the historical and contemporary, local and global, political and economic relations that form, produce and reproduce violence, as well as the way in which wars magnify and reshape gender identities (see Raven-Roberts, 2013).

Reviews of accumulation by dispossession by critical feminists invoke the contention that the globalisation of capital should be re-understood as a moment of primitive accumulation that is very significantly gendered (Mies, 1987; Federici, 2004; Hartsock, 2006; 2011; Keating et al., 2010; LeBaron and Roberts, 2010). Maria Mies (1987), for instance, identifies women, nature and people of impoverished countries as locations of extraction and dispossession. She argues that these groups make up the base upon which the processes of capitalist accumulation have been historically established, and their subordination and exploitation continue to be essential premises underlying the reproduction of the current model, and therefore it is crucial to understand the interactions, both historical and present, between the sexual, social and international divisions of labour. Important to this analysis is the understanding that violence is at the heart of social

organisation, and gender relations and violence are mutually constitutive (Confortini, 2006). Gender subordination and discrimination
also result in violence against women, as do vulnerabilities inherent
in multiple and intersecting identities such as class, ethnicity, religion,
sexuality and other socio-cultural belongings that also exacerbate such
violence. It therefore becomes exigent to study the political economy
of the everyday violence women experience, its normalisation and
continuities, prior to, during and beyond the cessation of war and conflict. As True (2012: 44) articulates, 'power operates not only through
direct coercion but also through the structured relations of production
and reproduction that govern the distribution and use of resources,
benefits, privileges and authority within the home and transnational
society at large'.

A political economy analysis compels us to understand how the
multiple crises generated by economic globalisation and development, resultant macro-economic policies, trade liberalisation and
economic deregulation, together with financial and climate crises and
militarisation, pose new challenges, particularly for women (Seguino,
2010; Sen and Durano, 2014). These realities of the global political
economic order are often absent or overlooked in analyses of violence
against women. It must be understood that women's security is also
inseparably linked to the material basis of relationships that govern the
distribution and use of resources, entitlements and authority within
the home, the community and the transnational realm (True, 2012).
A political economy analysis can also incorporate an understanding
of how women's political, economic and social subordination makes
them vulnerable to violence, and an understanding that violence
against women is not merely a consequence of men's aggression in
the private or public sphere. This complex nexus is reflected in examples where the violent act of rape results in women losing access to
property through the social stigma and moral panic associated with
rape and the consequent ostracism of rape victims, while perpetrators
often go unpunished.

Two leading feminist scholars – Yakin Ertürk (2009) and Jacqui
True (2012) – propose three elements of a political economy method
that could be central to analysing violence against women based on
the political economic structures that underpin gender inequality
and women's vulnerability to violence. The two they agree on are:
the **gender division of labour** within the family/private sphere and

the public sphere; and the **contemporary global macro-economy** in which capitalist competition fuels the quest for cheap sources of labour, which is often women's labour. Ertürk's third element focuses on the gendered dimensions of war and peace, which are connected to **patriarchy and the differential gender impacts of globalisation** (2009: 11–12). She further argues that violent conflict, which seeks to control power and productive resources, often 'normalizes violence and spreads it throughout society' (ibid.: 12). True's slightly different third element is the **masculine protector and feminine protected identities** associated with war and militarism and the division of the 'war front' and the 'home front' associated with armed conflict and its aftermath.

True also calls for the exploration of strategic sites where structural economic forces come into play, intensifying the conditions for and increasing the magnitude of violence against women. She draws attention to the exploitation inherent in the transnational migration of women workers from developing countries to the rich and upper-middle-class households in the developed world; the expanding sex trade around free trade zones; and heightened levels of violence against women during financial liberalisation and economic crises. In the context of armed conflict and war, we argue that these strategic sites could include, inter alia, neoliberal restructuring that intensifies the precarious nature of women's livelihoods; men's reaction to the loss of secure employment; displacement; the rise in female-headed households; the growth of a wartime sex trade; enforced transactional sex for survival; and the impact of post-conflict reconstruction efforts. The case studies that form the chapters of this book expand on and illustrate the violence embedded in political economic arrangements of some of these strategic sites and those discussed by True (2012), particularly in the context of war and conflict.

A feminist political economy framework argues persuasively that post-conflict recovery programmes cannot uncritically advocate a return to 'business as usual' economic and political arrangements that are inherently gendered and violent. As the authors note in this book, their approach to gendered violence during war, conflict and its aftermath is to see the continuities and discontinuities of the gendered dimensions linked to patriarchy and the impacts of differential political economic arrangements beyond the temporality of war. However, the application of political economy in understanding and mapping violence against women in war and conflict is not uniform in the chapters. Some authors lean towards thinking that is advanced by feminist peace and security studies, while others attempt analyses premised in feminist political economy. Some authors initially position their arguments under one approach but move between the two through the course of the chapter. Together, the chapters of this book make a case for nuancing and complicating these perspectives, which in turn would strengthen analyses on violence against women and conflict.

## This book

This book brings together the work of a group of feminists from the global South. The authors are diverse in their backgrounds, experience, and academic and disciplinary orientations. They work in different political, economic, social and cultural contexts and some have approached writing about the political economies of violence against women in their own countries as much (or more) from lived experience and experiential insights as from formal or scholarly research, which we consider entirely valid and in keeping with feminist epistemology.

Some of the authors have resisted the urge to project stereotypical images based on dominant approaches by external scholars onto their contexts – the formerly colonised world – when attempting to describe or interpret women's experiences of war and conflict. Some of the authors primarily operate in languages other than English, and while well versed in existing feminist literature, they read, think and articulate feminism in varied registers. This is because their narrations are informed by their own experiences, thinking, reflection, and years of activism in various feminist struggles. In a sense, this book reflects what Donna Haraway called 'situated knowledges', accounts of gendered violence through 'epistemology and politics of engaged, accountable positioning' (1988: 590). This is not to say that these authors' narrations are free of privilege, hierarchy or exteriority; rather, they take a relatively 'closer-to-home' perspective when looking at violence against women in war- or conflict-affected contexts.

The three-year exercise of putting this collection together has made us realise that there is much to be gained from acknowledging and engaging with alternative ways of knowing and producing knowledge. This is not to subscribe to the notion that knowledge is 'culture-bound' ('true' – or 'producible and reproducible' – in only a single society or regional set of societies). Rather than accepting an entrenched dichotomy between South and North in matters of knowledge production and emancipatory feminist politics, we seek to affirm the conditions of possibility for solidarity, both in the production of research and in feminist struggle.

The chapters in this book call for situating violence against women within historical and contemporary political and economic structures and relationships, both at the national/subnational level and at the global level. The chapter on Colombia provides a richly textured understanding of the political economy of the country's long-standing and complex war, its class dimensions and the marked differences among the three armed protagonists, shedding light on rural women's important yet unrecognised role as crucial actors during the war and as agents of change. The case study on Papua New Guinea focuses on the role of foreign-owned, environmentally devastating extractive industries in exacerbating gender and intra-community inequality and facilitating the build-up of arms and conflict, with terrifying implications for women. The chapter on Sri Lanka demonstrates that the 'icon' of the 'self-employed woman from the war-affected area' is part of the global drive towards financialisation and traces the violence inherent in gendered processes of 'responsibilisation' that in turn reinforce particular gender ideologies. The case of the North East Region of India highlights state repression, militarisation, 'othering' and cultural violence as modes of control and gendered violence in three subnational conflicts and their protracted peace processes. The case study on Sudan and South Sudan discusses the complexity imposed by multiple and overlapping religious and customary structures of social control. The chapter on Northern Ugandan women's community peace initiatives examines the gendered socio-economic and political shifts that occurred as a result of the war as well as the ways in which women's agency attempted to subvert patriarchal norms.

A number of themes emerge from the chapters, which are briefly discussed here.

### Militarisation: gendered violence in a 'state of exception'

In most case studies, the authors observe that patriarchal power and territorial prerogatives over women's bodies coalesce with salient modes of power and control inherent in struggles for territorial claims, which in turn produce and reproduce structural violence of a distinctly gendered form. Militarisation is one such mode of control. 'Conflict and attendant militarisation are also reinforced by juridical situations that suspend the normal rule of law with the introduction of emergency powers and repressive legislation' (DAWN, 2011: 2).[4] This creates a 'state of exception' in which citizens are reduced to 'bare life', or stripped of the ordinary rights of citizenship (Agamben, 2005), which impacts adversely in the long term on democratic rights such as freedom of expression, association and mobility, among others. 'In such militarised environments, law and order and accountable governance are suspended for military ends' by states and militant groups alike, who enforce their own codes of conduct and a state of exception is instituted as the norm (DAWN, 2011: 2). Militarisation is thus 'integrally linked to systemic violence' (Laurie and Petchesky 2007: 3). Together with armed conflict and civil war, militarisation has played a major role in shaping and changing women's lives. 'Contemporary wars occur in the sites of the most severe social divisions', concomitantly generating 'multiple forms of crisis' (ibid.).

In her case study of the Naga conflict in North East India, Goswami argues that sexual violence against women has been facilitated particularly by the operation of the Armed Forces Special Powers Act of 1958 (AFSPA). The Act grants extraordinary powers to any military officer to use lethal force if deemed necessary, to arrest without a warrant using such force as may be necessary, including killing, and, again without a warrant, to enter and search any premises on mere suspicion. This law also shields security forces from arrest and criminal prosecution through provisions of statutory immunity. Goswami argues that these legal provisions have given free rein to military personnel to employ rape as a weapon of calling Naga people into submission. In using rape, the Indian state and security forces have violated the rights of women and destroyed the sense of self and worth of the Naga community, trampled on the masculinity of its men and succeeded in othering people from the peripheries who differ from those living in 'mainland India'.

The chapter on Papua New Guinea (PNG) reminds us of the compatibility of militarisation, deployed as a mode of control within an extractives-driven economy, with the pursuit of national economic growth (Cox). The face of militarisation in PNG is not only the uniformed and armed soldier or the police guarding the mines; he is the private mercenary hired by an extractives company, or a gun-bearing young man in a tribal war. Similarly, the chapter on the Colombian conflict maps diverse forms of violence against women in a heavily militarised context where the guerrillas, paramilitaries and Colombian military were embedded in layered political economies (López Montaño and Holstine).

Intertwined with militarisation in some situations of conflict are patriarchal ideologies that frame women as the purveyors of a community's cultural purity and subject them to the most brutal forms of violence and control when they are perceived as transgressing certain personal and social boundaries.

### The sexed body and the 'other' in war and conflict

Many of the chapters discuss how war and conflict shape and reinforce historical and entrenched forms of sexuality. In PNG, 'big man' culture valorises men and armed violence remains the norm to resolve old and new conflicts. Perpetrated by warriors, enraged spouses and opportunistic hosts of displaced populations, rape persists as a weapon, and justice frameworks introduced by new norms of peace appear unable to deter entrenched practices of militarised masculinity that sanction the use of physical and sexual violence in the control of women (Cox). An extreme form of such control is reflected in gendered hate crimes of sexualised torture and mob killings of women perceived as transgressing bounds and accused of practising sorcery (ibid.). During the conflict in South Sudan, the lived reality of gender-based violence included rape, 'girl compensation', forced prostitution and sex slavery. Such violence is premised on masculine identity that is tied to cattle raiding, bride price and customary practices that demand compensation for rape.

The chapters on North East India and Colombia highlight the use of rape in wartime and the stigma attached to women raped during war by state or non-state perpetrators, ranging from tribal warlords to militant groups, privately financed paramilitary units to corporate bosses and men controlling markets and productive resources. The authors also discuss widespread impunity that shrouds such militarised sexual violence, often sanctioned by framings of honour, blaming of women's sexuality and 'transgression' and moral panic. In North East

India, rape is used as a weapon of dominance by state and non-state entities alike. Historically, the Nagas in the North East Region of India had in place a defence structure and hierarchy to protect women and children from warring tribes. Women were the most prized possessions as the keepers of the tribe's culture and identity, and protecting them from outsiders is a defining feature of Naga men's masculinity. Hence, the failure to 'protect their women' from rape has high psychological purchase in this context, with entrenched socio-cultural norms of male 'ownership' over the women of his household and strict surveillance of women's bodies. Raped women are blamed for giving out 'sexual signals'. Perpetrators of sexual violence are allowed to escape justice while their victims bear the punishment of stigma and ostracism (Goswami).

López Montaño and Holstine discuss how rape was used as a strategy for economic dispossession in Colombia. The Colombian government's 1990 globalisation initiative, *Apertura*, undermined *campesino* production, and big landowners mobilised privately financed paramilitary forces to dispossess *campesinos*. These paramilitary forces publicly raped rural women to demoralise and disempower the men. They note that the physical and sexual violation of rural women was used as an effective strategy of control to destroy male masculinity and pride, diminishing their respected role as protectors and making them weak and worthless in their inability to protect women from violence. As such, rape was effectively used within a distinct political economy to drive poor agricultural producer groups away from the rural countryside, so that the land was vacated for the utilisation of big landowners. Paramilitary groups subsequently benefited directly from the decentralisation programme (which accompanied *Apertura*), putting up candidates to take control of small towns and the decentralised funds, using their power to impose dress codes and other patriarchal controls on women. The authors argue that the 'machismo' rule that was a defining characteristic of decentralisation maintained cohesion among troops, and provided a clear demarcation between the notions of *my women* and *my enemies' women*. The paramilitaries reinforced archaic patriarchal and religious values through this systematic control over all aspects of women's lives.

The chapter on North East India turns our attention to violence directed against the sexed body of the 'other'. Goswami argues that the 'peripherality' of the Nagas in North East India was a reason for intense sexual violence against Naga women, particularly by the military. The 'othering' of the Nagas was easy, as they stood out in appearance, food habits, culture and religion from 'mainland India'. The author contends that the 'peripheral other' women continue to be the most vulnerable 'other'.

## Gendered economies of war

Some chapters move away from the overdetermined focus on sexualised, ethnicised and militarised violence against women, which is the predominant narrative of violence experienced by women in war and conflict. The authors draw attention to neoliberal globalisation, which has transformed processes of accumulation by dispossession, leading to multiple forms of gendered structural violence in times of war and peace. These chapters move the discussion away from the essentialist framing of women as victims of violence and war and men as the perpetrators.

Chapters on Colombia and Sri Lanka problematise the 'growth *amid* war' notion that seems to question the conventional wisdom that war debilitates economies. They demonstrate the role of economies that thrive *because* of war, and women's roles in them. López Montaño and Holstine discuss the seemingly paradoxical economic growth that maintained the war economy of Colombia. They discuss the decrease in poverty in the rural sector, albeit with widening economic disparities between urban and rural, and between rich and poor, and the centrality of drug trafficking in supporting the FARC in its fight against the Colombian military in the last thirty-five years of the war. They note that this was a struggle that rural women voluntarily joined, often to escape verbal and physical aggressions within their families and to enjoy newfound freedom. The promise (by the FARC) of equal rights and tasks for men and women combatants also opened their minds to new possibilities. The chapter on Sri Lanka (Gunasekara and Nagaraj) maps how women's productive labour has supported and maintained the country's war- and post-war economies. The authors argue that women's labour drives modes of accumulation by dispossession, providing examples of women's contributions to the economy as plantation workers, garment factory workers in free trade zones, domestic workers, sex workers and home-based self-employed 'entrepreneurs'.

Chapters on Sudan (Hashim) and Uganda (Clarke and O'Brien) detect gendered violence in labour arrangements in the context of displacement. They highlight women's economic contributions to the production of subsistence crops, as farmers, gardeners, food producers and market sellers, despite insurmountable risks associated with displacement. Hashim discusses the precarious work of displaced women from the south of Sudan, Darfur and the Nuba mountains who are compelled to work informally in food selling and resort to the brewing of alcohol or sex work to ensure the survival of themselves and their families, falling prey to punishment under Sharia laws that ban both occupations. She further discusses the significant contribution Darfuri women make to the market and the economy, including as agricultural and construction workers, and points out that women have larger fields and grain storage facilities than men and that they grow stable crops for the upkeep of war-torn communities.

The chapter on Northern Uganda discusses how war destabilised women's socio-economic reliance on subsistence agriculture, particularly in rural areas, where forced displacement and the threat of abduction and sexual violence reduced women's activity in subsistence farming (Clarke and O'Brien). In Colombia, too, there was a mass exodus of rural men, women and children to towns and cities unprepared to receive them. While this was not an easy transition for the rural families, women rose to the occasion and engaged in care services. These working women then confronted new forms of violence at home, when frustrated and unemployed displaced rural men saw empowered *campesinas* gaining economic autonomy, and swiftly taking on the role of providers, leaving men behind.

Many of the authors discuss how oppression and domination is produced in both licit and illicit economies that continue even after armed violence is officially over. They demonstrate that national and global illicit economies are intertwined with formal economies, impacting adversely on women ensnared in an economy of survival. This nexus is illustrated through narratives of women who engage in transactional sex when they are not able to repay loans taken (from formal lenders) for self-employment, the most commonly available avenue of income generation for women in war-affected areas (Gunasekara and Nagaraj). The Sri Lanka chapter traces violence in moral economies that put women in a double bind: they are expected to support families financially through self-employment while not compromising on their duties as caregivers, nor transgressing sexual boundaries. Meanwhile, those surviving on precarious loan-driven livelihoods are 'responsibilised' as compliant, malleable and dutiful debtors, while they continue to be entrapped in poverty. Maintenance of such moral economies are often ensured through spatial, economic, subjective and sexual relations of violence.

Weaving through all the chapters, explicitly and implicitly, is that accumulation continues to be buttressed by gendered ideologies that maintain women's unpaid care work in the home, which is a prerequisite for the productivity of the male in the public sphere. Such gendered structures and processes produce and reproduce violence by restraining women's public participation and promoting their subordination and inequality both in the home and in society, thereby making them more vulnerable to both direct and structural violence.

*The sexual division of labour, family and household and the male provider*

It is well known that during conflict and war the status quo of families and communities is dismantled, bringing about shifts in power and status as women assume roles and responsibilities conventionally perceived to be the preserve of men. As women become de jure or de facto heads of household, assuming new economic and social responsibilities to ensure the survival of their households, they are forced to confront entrenched patriarchal values that are resistant to accepting their new situation as economic providers and heads of families. This is particularly the case as men see their masculine 'provider' role eroded and perceive a powerlessness that runs counter to normative behaviour. The chapter on Uganda discusses the multiple vulnerabilities of women as well as the destabilisation of masculine dominance and the opening up of spaces of partial power to women as conflict-related shifts in roles and responsibilities reconfigured family structures and created agentive spaces for women. Abducted women with children born in captivity returning to their communities challenged patrilineal family networks as they were compelled to replace men's (previously) dominant role as material providers and protectors of the family (Clarke and O'Brien).

In South Sudan, where 45 per cent of girls are married before the age of eighteen and polygamy is practised widely, women are rarely able to file for divorce in a culture where men arrogate to themselves the right to end marriages and a wife's family is expected to pay back bride price, making women economically dependent on husbands and vulnerable to violence and exploitation (Hashim). Traditions such as the bride price bind women in distinct labour contracts, particularly in the confines of their own homes. For the husband's family, a wife (or a wife-to-be) is a source of unpaid labour, something that has already been paid for in bride price. Violence within the home therefore is often kept under wraps by familial ideology that compels silence and normalises violence against women with impunity. The norms of the male protector and the female protected also play out in insidious ways during war and conflict, and occasion yet other multiple and intersecting forms of violence and discrimination against women. While war-related sexual violence is better documented and formal and informal initiatives that seek to deal with justice and accountability for rape now inform some post-conflict transitional processes, there is less attention paid to the long-term structural impacts of this violence on women. Critical among these are the stigma and disowning women face from families and communities due to conflict-inflicted rape, sex slavery, or the mere perception of transgression, such as women entering male spaces of combat, as illustrated in the chapter on Uganda. This stigma often results in families disinheriting women, refusing to accept them into households and communities, divorcing or abandoning them, and thereby forcing them into impoverishment and further exacerbating their vulnerability to violence (Clarke and O'Brien).

In Naga communities, despite the significant number of war-induced woman-headed households, the position or perspectives of both women and men remain unchanged as patriarchal mores are stronger than ever before. Men resent the powerlessness this change in role implies, and are often unable to come to terms with their perceived diminished worth as the primary providers and protectors of women and families. This in turn leads to heightened violence against women in the home (Goswami). Similarly, in Papua New Guinea, violence proliferated by the political economy of extractive industries has turned men against men in local conflict and men against women in family and spousal violence (Cox). Some chapters discuss issues stemming from the reinforcement of customary laws, which are often given primacy over general laws, particularly regarding land ownership and affairs related to the family. For example, the Indian constitution allows states such as Mizoram and Nagaland to frame their own laws in a manner that aligns with their patriarchal customary laws. This has meant that women are denied equal inheritance rights and a role in decision making, justifying and legitimising structural violence (Goswami). In PNG, women's rights to own, access and use land are not codified in law. Patriarchal practices recognise only men as landowners and therefore exclude women from the direct receipt of rents and royalties for customary land that has been appropriated or leased by extractive industries. In addition, women are the last and the least paid in male-controlled distribution systems of cash payments (Cox). Authors signpost the danger of overlooking changes to family structures and household economies during war and conflict. They argue that reinforcing customary laws and practices (which assume traditional family structures based on the male provider) during and after conflict pushes women to the brink of vulnerability. In mutually constitutive ways, the sexual division of labour in the private domain has served to constrict women's public participation as gender ideologies burden women with the responsibility of unpaid care work in the home and force them into poorly remunerated, precarious home-based employment. This prevents their access to better economic opportunities, resulting in uneven bargaining power and a greater risk of violence both within and outside the home (True, 2012; Gunasekara and Nagaraj).

### Women, violence and peace building

Several case studies in this book discuss peace-building processes in which violence is given a meaning beyond sexual violence against women. The chapter on Papua New Guinea discusses women's peace initiatives in the Highlands province of Jiwaka, detailing how women have challenged chauvinistic traditions of conflict mediation, negotiation and planning for future development. Refusing to contribute to the payment of effective war taxes appropriated by men, women have secured their savings against the constant demands of husbands for the purchase of weapons and ammunition to continue tribal warfare. Through 'smart and home-grown gender strategies', women have begun to control their own incomes, prioritising 'spending to pay for justice in village court cases, pursuing divorce from violent husbands, [and] paying back bride price to end men's control over their lives and bodies' (Cox). Linking violence against women to political economic arrangements that maintain conflict through the distorted cash flows of extractive industries, women have moved into facilitating informal conflict mediation by ensuring that compensation payments demanded for family and sexual violence are not exorbitant, that IDPs can return to their homes and land, and that full-scale tribal violence is prevented. Thus, women have made significant breakthroughs into exclusively male-managed conflict mediation and have stopped or prevented fresh outbreaks of tribal war (ibid.).

In Northern Uganda, the complexities that accompany women's peace initiatives are reflected in their efforts to establish community support groups that address the socio-economic and psychological fall-out of war rather than ethnic tensions, a strategy that is interpreted as a response to immediate needs. Far from unimportant, these initiatives dealt with the reconfiguration of families – where women returned pregnant with children who had no known or acknowledged fathers or clan ties and women had to take on responsibilities for new familial configurations, negotiate ethnic and clan boundaries and enable 'peaceful masculinities' while providing for the material needs of their families and caring for the most vulnerable. These were solutions more readily available to women, while challenging ethnic tensions or women's ownership of land remained non-negotiable according to continuing inflexible clan systems and customs. Thus, 'while [women] made some gains in occupying previously masculinised spaces such as by being material providers, they were blocked from shifting power dynamics inherent in land ownership' (Clarke and O'Brien). It would appear, therefore, that women's community peace-building efforts, while leading to some economic and political shifts, provided them with the opportunity to subvert patriarchy and contest some patriarchal spaces. In Northern Uganda, women's peace-building efforts, with their accompanying economic and political shifts, provided them with an opportunity to contest various patriarchal spaces. Yet the 'tension between agency and structure is once again evident. Agency is constantly being subverted by structural realities that may give the impression of shifting at the surface level but remain deeply immovable and ingrained at other levels' (Clarke and O'Brien). López Montaño and Holstine make a strong argument for the recognition of the agency of women in wartime, when their new roles – and in particular 'their needed, but often ignored, involvement in war and peace' – are often overlooked. The chapter contrasts the near absence of women in the negotiation process and on the 'front line' of post-conflict reconstruction with their critical contributions, especially those of rural women, to winning land right reform through mobilisations and struggles outside the formal peace process. The chapter celebrates their activism on many levels – the building of 'complex networks or pro-peace movements' against violence; the enactment of progressive laws, in particular on land reform and redistribution; and the resilience of rural women in securing economic livelihoods in the context of displacement into cities. Thus, the chapter situates women as important political actors both during the war and in post-conflict recovery, something that has been largely underestimated and ignored in formal peacemaking and peace building.

## Conclusion

This book places special emphasis on the centrality of violence in social organisation and its role in producing and reproducing the gender order, and conversely how the gender order in turn justifies and reproduces unequal and violent power relations in society, which are firmly anchored in overlapping patriarchies. The chapters set out a context for political and economic relations that span historical modes of accumulation and dispossession, centring on those that buttress contemporary war and conflict and continue in the aftermath of war, to argue that conflict and war cannot be treated simplistically as a deviation from the 'normal'. Some of the authors also argue persuasively that post-conflict recovery cannot advocate a return to 'normal' economic and political arrangements that are inherently gendered and violent. As the authors note, their approach to gendered violence during conflict and its aftermath is to see the continuities of the gendered dimensions as linked to patriarchy and the impacts of differential political economic arrangements beyond the temporality of war. In turn, as noted by Ní Aoláin et al., the authors echo the view that the second-class status of women endures post-conflict with little reference in peace agreements and transitional structures, which are deeply gendered and masculine, 'drawing on existing cultural, legal and political practices that are strongly embedded across societies and cultures' (2011: 7). This is precisely why the authors writing on Sri Lanka are concerned with how 'violence' is discussed in the ongoing transitional justice processes of the country. They argue that a fixation on sexual violence within transitional justice processes invariably leads to individualising responsibility and victimhood and risks fragmenting the 'possibility of collective political struggles' that should address the structural conditions producing such violence (Gunasekara and Nagraj). All authors point to the inadequacy of thinking about a 'transition' in people's lives from war to 'post'-war if the violence continues under different circumstances. They instead call for a kind of justice that is transformational, and strategies and mechanisms that can contribute to the reconfiguration of power beyond individual accounts or experiences.

In many ways, this book is an attempt to challenge ourselves as Southern feminists to employ different ways of thinking about gendered violence in war and conflict. Certain modes of power and control are dominant in each context, and this is where the author's vantage point is fixed. In some cases, the more salient mode of control is militarisation; in others it is financialisation. Each feminist writer pegs her/himself to a particular mode of power and control, and this determines how they 'read' and 'map' violence. The chapters do not all claim to carry out feminist political economy analyses. They do, however, engage with certain elements of a 'political economy method' in analysing violence in key 'strategic sites' (Ertürk, 2009; True, 2012). The authors discuss how conditions of war and conflict change the gender division of labour within the family and communities, as well as the violence associated with such transformation. By looking at post-war livelihoods and self-employment of women, they demonstrate not only how women's labour is exploited, but also how their social reproduction role is effectively maintained by the financialisation of the contemporary global economy. Many of the chapters also frame contemporary wars and armed conflicts as intrinsically connected to control over productive resources (Ertürk, 2009), which in turn reproduces and normalises gendered violence inherent in economic relations. Hence, a case is made for a feminist political economy analysis of war and conflict as it enables us to understand how political economic relations both produce and perpetuate the continuum of violence faced by women before, during and after war. The case studies unpack relations of violence in certain strategic sites, all with war and conflict in the background, and produce rich, contextually grounded accounts that depict multiple inequalities controlling women's sexuality and status in society and entrenching their political and economic marginalisation. The thick accounts offered by the case studies not only enrich the broader body of literature on gender and conflict but also challenge, with empirical evidence, the conventional notions that women are merely victims of war. The chapter on Colombia, for example, in its analyses of 'women in arms' (within the FARC), challenges the globally accepted notion that labels all women in war-torn societies as 'victims'. The authors problematise the assumption that women are often 'forced' into combat roles. Instead, they argue that most women in the FARC willingly participated in combat and proactively negotiated for their rights in the aftermath of the conflict. Similarly, most chapters move away from categorising women in war-affected contexts as 'victims'. The authors instead contribute towards a more complex positioning of women who are constantly negotiating within changing political and militarised configurations at global and local level, and within concomitant economic arrangements and gender relations (True, 2012). Critically, therefore, the authors argue that the significance of structural violence, long-term oppression, discrimination and impoverishment in the lives of women – the hallmarks of structural violence – cannot be ignored. Nor can the reality that the end of conflict and war rarely marks an end to these complex forms of violence against women.

## Notes

1 We acknowledge with gratitude the contribution made to the first drafts of this chapter by Ambika Satkunanathan and Ayesha Imam. Ayesha Imam helped coordinate the early stages of this project and participated in the inception workshop that discussed the framework for the research on which this book is based.

2 The monograph, edited by Kumudini Samuel (2012), was published by DAWN as an e-book.

3 Peacemaking generally refers to peace processes, and peace building generally refers to post-accord/agreement peace work. For UN definitions in the context of peacekeeping, see https://peacekeeping.un.org/en/terminology: 'Peacemaking generally includes measures to address conflicts in progress and usually involves diplomatic action to bring hostile parties to a negotiated agreement', while 'Peacebuilding aims to reduce the risk of lapsing or relapsing into conflict by strengthening national capacities at all levels for conflict management, and to lay the foundation for sustainable peace and development. It is a complex, long-term process of creating the necessary conditions for sustainable peace.' The chapters in this book refer to both processes.

4 See DAWN (2011).

## References

Agamben, G. 1998. *Homo Sacer: Sovereign Power and Bare Life.* Stanford: Stanford University Press.

Agamben, G. 2005. *State of Exception.* Chicago: University of Chicago Press.

Basu, S. 2017. 'The UN Security Council and the Political Economy of the WPS Resolutions', *Politics and Gender* 13 (4): 721–7.

Bell, C. and O'Rourke, C. 2007. 'Does Feminism Need a Theory of Transitional Justice?', *International Journal of Transitional Justice* 1 (1): 23–44.

Bergeron, S., Cohn, C. and Duncanson, C. 2017. 'Rebuilding Bridges: Toward a Feminist Research Agenda for Postwar Reconstruction', *Politics and Gender* 13 (4): 715–21

Charlesworth, H. and Chinkin, C. 2000. *The Boundaries of International Law: A Feminist Analysis*. Manchester: Manchester University Press.

Charlesworth, H., Chinkin, C. and Wright, S. 1991. 'Feminist Approaches to International Law', *American Journal of International Law* 85: 613–45.

Chenoy, A. M. 2004. 'Gender and International Politics: The Intersections of Patriarchy and Militarisation', *Indian Journal of Gender Studies* 11 (1): 27–42.

Cockburn, C. and Zarkov, D. (eds). 2002. *The Postwar Moment: Militaries, Masculinities and International Peacekeeping. Bosnia and the Netherlands*. London: Lawrence and Wishart.

Cohen, D. K., Green, A. H. and Wood, E. J. 2013. 'Wartime Sexual Violence: Misconceptions, Implications, and Ways Forward'. Washington DC: United States Institute of Peace, www.usip.org/sites/default/files/resources/SR323.pdf

Cohn, C. 2012. *Women and Wars: Contested Histories, Uncertain Futures*. Cambridge: Polity Press.

Confortini, C. 2006. 'Galtung, Violence, and Gender: The Case for a Peace Studies', *Feminism Alliance, Peace and Change* 31 (3): 333–67.

Coomaraswamy, R. 2015. *Preventing Conflict, Transforming Justice, Securing the Peace: A Global Study on the Implementation of United Nations Security Council Resolution 1325*. New York: UN Women.

Copelon, R. 1995. 'Gendered War Crimes: Reconceptualizing Rape in Time of War' in Peters, J. S. and Wolper, A. (eds), *Women's Rights, Human Rights: International Feminist Perspectives*. New York: Routledge.

DAWN. 2011. 'Submission to the CEDAW Committee: Day of General Discussion on General Recommendation on Women in Armed Conflict & Post-conflict Situations, 18 July 2011'. Manila: Development Alternatives with Women for a New Era (DAWN), www.ohchr.org/documents/HRBodies/CEDAW/Womenconflictsituations/DevelopmentAlternativesWomenNewEra.pdf

Duncanson, C. 2016. *Gender and Peacebuilding*. Cambridge: Polity Press.

Elias, J. 2015. 'The Everyday Gendered Political Economy of Violence', *Politics and Gender* 11 (2): 424–9.

Enloe, C. 1989. *Bananas, Beaches and Bases: Making Feminist Sense of International Politics*. Berkeley: University of California Press.

Enloe, C. 2000. *Maneuvers: The International Politics of Militarizing Women's Lives*. Berkeley: University of California Press.

Ertürk, Y. 2009. 'Promotion and Protection of All Human Rights, Civil, Political, Economic, Social and Cultural Rights, Including the Right to Development. Report of the Special Rapporteur on Violence against Women, its Causes and Consequences'. Human Rights Council, Eleventh Session, Agenda Item 3, A/HRC/11/6/Add.6, 23

June, www2.ohchr.org/english/
issues/women/rapporteur/docs/A.
HRC.11.6.Add.6.pdf

Federici, S. 2004. *Caliban and the
Witch: Women, the Body and
Primitive Accumulation.* New York:
Autonomedia.

Fitzpatrick, J. 1994. 'The Use of
International Human Rights Norms
to Combat Violence against Women'
in Cook, R. (ed.), *Human Rights of
Women: National and International
Perspectives.* Philadelphia: University
of Pennsylvania Press.

Giles, W. and Hyndman, J. (eds). 2004.
*Sites of Violence: Gender and
Conflict Zones.* Berkeley: University
of California Press.

Haraway, D. 1988. 'Situated Knowledges:
The Science Question in Feminism and
the Privilege of Partial Perspective',
*Feminist Studies* 14 (3): 575–99.

Hartsock, N. 2006. 'Globalization
and Primitive Accumulation: The
Contributions of David Harvey's
Dialectical Marxism' in *David Harvey:
A Critical Reader.* Oxford: Blackwell.

Hartsock, N. 2011. 'A New Moment of
Primitive Accumulation'. Inaugural
Inkrit Conference.

Henry, N. 2014. 'The Fixation on Wartime
Rape: Feminist Critique and
International Criminal Law', *Social
and Legal Studies* 23 (1): 93–111.

Keating, C., Rasmussen, C. and
Rishi, P. 2010. 'The Rationality
of Empowerment: Microcredit,
Accumulation by Dispossession,
and the Gendered Economy', *Signs:
Journal of Women in Culture and
Society* 36 (1): 153–76.

Kirby, P. 2012. 'How Is Rape a Weapon
of War? Feminist International
Relations, Modes of Critical
Explanation and the Study of
Wartime Sexual Violence', *European
Journal of International Relations* 19
(4): 797–821.

Laurie, M. and Petchesky, R. 2007.
'Gender, Health, and Human Rights
in Sites of Political Exclusion', www.
who.int/social_determinants/
resources/gender_health_human_
rights_wgkn_2007.pdf

LeBaron, G. and Roberts, A. 2010.
'Towards a Feminist Political
Economy of Capitalism and
Carcerality', *Signs: Journal of Women
in Culture and Society* 36 (1): 19–44.

Lorentzen, L. A. and Turpin, J. (eds). 1988.
*The Women and War Reader.* New
York: New York University Press.

Manchanda, R. 2005. 'Women's Agency
in Peace Building: Gender Relations
in Post-conflict Reconstruction',
*Economic and Political Weekly* 44/45:
4737–45.

Meintjes, S., Pillay, A. and Turshen,
M. 2002. *The Aftermath: Women
in Post-conflict Transformation.*
London: Zed Books.

Mies, M. 1987. *Patriarchy and
Accumulation on a World Scale.*
London: Zed Books.

Moore, D. 2015. 'Conflict and After:
Primitive Accumulation, Hegemonic
Formation and Democratic Deepening',
*Stability: International Journal of
Security and Development* 4 (1): 1–21.

Moran, M. 2010. 'Gender, Militarism,
and Peace-building: Projects of the
Postconflict Moment', *Annual Review
of Anthropology* 39: 261–74.

Moser, C. and Clark, F. (eds). 2001.
*Victims, Perpetrators or Actors?
Gender, Armed Conflict and Political
Violence.* London: Zed Books.

Ní Aoláin, F., Haynes, D. F. and Cahn, N.
R. 2011. *On the Frontlines: Gender,
War and the Post-conflict Process.*
Oxford: Oxford University Press.

Nordstrom, C. 2004. *Shadow Wars:
Violence, Power and International
Profiteering in the Twenty-first
Century.* Berkeley: University of
California Press.

Otto, D. 2016. 'Women, Peace and
Security: A Critical Analysis of the
Security Council's Vision'. London:
LSE, https://blogs.lse.ac.uk/
wps/2017/01/09/women-peace-and-
security-a-critical-analysis-of-the-
security-councils-vision/

Petchesky, R. P. 2002. 'Phantom
Towers: Feminist Reflections on the
Battle between Global Capitalism
and Fundamentalist Terrorism',
*Development* 45: 40–5.

Peterson, S. 2005. 'How (the Meaning of)
Gender Matters in Political Economy',
*New Political Economy* 10: 499–521.

Raven-Roberts, A. 2013. 'Women and the
Political Economy of War' in Cohn, C.
(ed.), *Women and Wars: Contested
Histories, Uncertain Futures.*
Cambridge: Polity Press.

Rees, M. and Chinkin, C. 2016. 'Exposing
the gendered Myth of Post-conflict
Transition: The Transformative Power
of Economic and Social Rights',
*New York University Journal of
International Law and Politics* 48 (4):
1211–26.

Samuel, K. (ed.). 2012. *Women
Transforming Peace Activism
in a Fierce New World: South
and Southeast Asia.* Philippines:
Development Alternatives with
Women for a New Era (DAWN), www.
dawnnet.org/sites/default/files/
articles/analyses_final_full_prst_
book_2012-mar.pdf

Seguino, S. 2010. 'The Way Forward
in the Wake of the 2008 Global
Economic Crisis: Does the Stiglitz
Commission Report Go Far Enough?'
Concept paper prepared for DAWN
Development Debates.

Sen, G. and Durano, M. 2014. 'The
Remaking of Social Contracts: The
Promise of Human Rights' in Sen, G.
and Durano, M. (eds). *The Remaking
of Social Contracts: Feminist in a
Fierce New World.* London: Zed
Books.

Skjelbæk, I. and Smith, D. (eds). 2001.
*Gender, Peace and Conflict.* London:
Sage.

True, J. 2012. *The Political Economy of
Violence against Women.* Oxford and
New York: Oxford University Press.

True, J. 2016. 'Explaining the Global
Diffusion of the Women, Peace
and Security Agenda', *International
Political Science Review* 37 (3):
307–23.

Turshen, M. 2016. *Gender and the
Political Economy of Conflict in
Africa.* London and New York: Taylor
and Francis.

Von Holdt, K. 2013. 'South Africa: The
Transition to Violent Democracy',
*Review of African Political Economy*
40 (138): 589–604, https://doi.org/10.
1080/03056244.2013.854040

Von Holdt, K. 2014. 'On Violent
Democracy', *Sociological Review* 62
(2): 129–51.

Wieringa, S., Chhachhi, A. and Truong, T.
2006. *Engendering Human Security:
Feminist Perspectives.* New Delhi:
Woman Unlimited.

# 1 | THE CONSTRUCTION OF THE 'RESPONSIBLE WOMAN': STRUCTURAL VIOLENCE IN SRI LANKA'S POST-WAR DEVELOPMENT STRATEGY

*Vagisha Gunasekara and Vijay K. Nagaraj*

## Point of departure

Sri Lanka is on the cusp of a transition into a third republican era with constitutional reform and transitional justice processes currently under way. When we first started thinking about writing this chapter, in 2015, debates around these processes were in full swing. However, they failed to stimulate attention to the structured nature of gendered violence inherent in political economic arrangements threading through the pre-war, war and post-war periods. Ongoing contestations and struggles,[1] largely in the human rights arena, concerning war-related violence against women remain primarily fixated on certain types of harm, especially rape and sexual violence, while the gendered violence reproduced by political economic structures remains marginalised. At the same time, discourses on women and post-war economic development and repair, focusing as they do on particular entitlements, especially livelihoods, have often failed to consider how heteropatriarchy as a frame of abuse is in fact reproduced through these political economic arrangements and structures.

Despite new theories offering more nuanced understandings of the changes and continuities in political, economic, social and ideological structures in relation to armed conflict, there is a paucity of gender analysis in the literature. A handful of studies focus on gendered economic links that operate during war (Nordstrom, 2004), while others point out that we need to understand not only what happens to women within the political economies of war, but also why (Raven-Roberts, 2013). The point is that there is a need to link gender and political economy in ways that make feminist sense not only of the egregious forms of violence against women – at the apex of which apparently stand rape and sexual violence – but also of everyday violence, which includes sexual violence, experienced or reproduced through everyday political economic relations. During the war in Sri Lanka, and especially after its end, there has been a multiplicity of accounts of the violence the war and the conflict visited upon women and girls. But for the most part these accounts of violence have focused on a sexualised and ethnicised account of violence, especially rape (Satkunanathan, 2017; Jayawardena and Pinto-Jayawardena, 2017), and are part of highly globalised attention to rape and sexual violence in the context of war. Much of this attention to rape and sexual violence against women and girls is very much a result of feminist struggles, especially in the arena of international criminal law. Yet, as Ní Aoláin (2012) suggests, such feminist struggles have led to the framing of political objectives with criminal justice strategies focused on categorising victims and perpetrators. She also notes that this has led to prioritising 'certain issues (specifically, truth, justice, memorial practices and reparations)' but downgrading others, 'including social and economic equality, reproductive health and choices, cultural identity and the other criss-cross of interlocking identities in conflicted or repressive societies' (ibid.).

It is precisely at the point of this critique that we situate the present analysis. We understand structural violence as taking the form of 'expropriation of vital economic and non-material resources and the operation of systems of social stratification or categorisation that subvert people's chances for survival' (Anglin, 1998). In war-affected contexts such as Sri Lanka, people's struggles in negotiating their survival is positioned along many inimical social, economic and political fault lines. These fault lines operate not only on the level of gender, class, caste and ethnicity, but also in relation to capital and labour, the market and the state, and the centre and the periphery (Murray, 2001).

Placing gendered political economic relations at the centre rather than the war and the conflict itself enables us to place the latter two in perspective rather than accord them the overdetermining status they so often enjoy in contexts such as Sri Lanka. Grounded in the post-war context of Sri Lanka, this chapter essentially argues that the dynamics of mutual accommodation and constitution involving gender and violence can be mapped in terms of distinct and gendered relations of violence and specific modes of accumulation and dispossession, as well as certain modes of power and control. Such an approach or framework will in turn be useful, we hope, in understanding the mutually constitutive nature of gendered violence and political economic relations in the context of war and conflict.

## Violence in the political economy of conflict

We start off from the view that war and conflict are moments of eruption in 'an ongoing course of class, ideological and political formation in the context of accumulation processes' (Moore, 2015). This runs counter to the dominant understanding that war and conflict are ruptures in the otherwise 'normal' fabric of development (Nagaraj, 2015), which has been challenged by many. For example, Taghdisi Rad (2015) notes:

> Neoclassical economics views war and conflict as temporary, exogenous factors, whose intensity is measured by the number of battle-related deaths, and which, in turn, is 'too exceptional' to deserve a separate frame of economic analysis. It is assumed that conflict implies a postponement of 'normal' economic activities, an abnormal operation of institutions, and a halt to the process of capital accumulation; therefore, any concrete economic analysis of the situation is postponed for the 'post-conflict' phase. Such a view, which tends to equate the case of conflict and non-conflict countries, not only has an extremely limited explanatory power, but also gives little insight into the context of the dynamic relations between conflict and economy.

The treatment of war and conflict as a deviation from the 'normal' entails the association of 'post-conflict recovery' with achieving 'normal conditions of the economy'. This view – advocating the 'return to the normal' – fails to account for the violence that pervades 'normal' economic and political arrangements. It portrays violence as a phenomenon produced solely by war or conflict, thereby erasing the tracks of continuity of structural violence that predate the temporal boundaries of wartime. This view also produces a distorted image of the spatial arrangements of violence by often confining violence to spaces of combat. This depiction of war and conflict, which often forms the basis of post-war and post-conflict 'reconstruction', hence fails to account for how war and conflict conditions reproduce spatial, economic and subjective relations of violence. It is this view of war and conflict that frames Sri Lanka's trajectory in terms of the stark dualism of 'growth amid war'.

Contesting this dualist framing, Venugopal posits that the 'conflict in the north has in different ways been an enabling factor for the much contested economic reform process in the south' (Venugopal, 2003). The unfolding of the economic reforms in Sri Lanka coincides with the advent of the neoliberal framework integrating economic liberalisation, globalisation, free trade, democratisation and governance spearheaded by the World Bank and the International Monetary Fund (IMF).[2] The social dislocations emanating from the liberalisation process were institutionalised in the civil war.[3] Geographies of war were physically separated from locations of production. Spatially, this led to a geographical separation of the primary theatre of war in the north and east from the primary theatres of production, located in the west, the central hills and the south of the country.[4] In reality, the war cushioned some of the negative effects of reforms, partly because the security sector absorbed labour[5] due to a rapid expansion of employment opportunities.[6] Liberalisation of the economy, buffered by unprecedented levels of foreign aid, did not end ethnically biased rent-seeking from the state sector. Instead, it extended to new groups that profited from the environment of heightened tension and authoritarianism (Dunham and Jayasuriya, 2001). While liberalisation gave a much-needed boost to the export sector in the south, the northern agricultural production that depended on domestic consumption suffered from a sharp depression in prices. The uneven nature of regional development coupled with the unequal distribution of public-sector investment and the acceleration of demographically sensitive irrigation and settlement schemes intensified long-standing grievances among the Tamil people. A culmination of these factors led to increasing ethnicisation of economic competition in the shadow of an authoritarian and majoritarian state and fostered horizontal conflict along ethnic lines. Political partisanship within the trade union movement gradually transformed labour struggles in a way that shifted the focus from advocating structural reforms pertaining to the rights of labour to the primary concern of winning political power for the party with which they were aligned. Trade unions became an avenue for political parties to express their rivalries with each other, leaving the labour movement all but defanged.

Looking at the Sri Lankan civil war as a particular outburst embedded in the twin processes of state formation and development (or accumulation) and foregrounding political and economic relations by bringing to bear critical feminist political economic analysis to war and conflict help us further explore how these relations both condition and heighten women's vulnerability to violence. Feminist political economy is useful in unpacking the gendered nature of violence inherent in domestic and global political economic structures (True, 2012). Reviews of accumulation by dispossession by critical feminists invoke the contention that the globalisation of capital should be re-understood as a moment of primitive accumulation that is very significantly gendered (Mies, 1987; Federici, 2004; Hartsock, 2006; 2011; Keating et al., 2010; LeBaron and Roberts, 2010). Maria Mies (1987), for instance, identifies women, nature and people of impoverished countries as locations of extraction and dispossession. She argues that these groups make up the base upon which the processes of capitalist accumulation have historically been established, and their subordination and exploitation continue to be essential premises underlying the reproduction of the current model; therefore, it is crucial to understand the interactions, both historical and present, between the sexual, social and international divisions of labour.

But these divisions often represent hierarchies of both work and workers trapped in relations of violence. The starkest of these hierarchies are represented by the Hill Country Tamils (also known as *Malaiyaha* Tamils) – oppressed caste Tamils brought by the British from southern India beginning in the early nineteenth century to work on their coffee plantations, which later shifted to tea. Tea has long been a major export earner for Sri Lanka; once the highest, it is still second only to export earnings from textiles and garments, and it continues to account for more than half of all agricultural exports in terms of earnings.[7] Throughout the decades of war, the plantation sector remained an inner periphery generating valuable foreign exchange earnings that helped stabilise the economy.

However, the Hill Country Tamils, who suffered from bonded and slavery-like labour conditions and were left stateless and disenfranchised by a newly independent Sri Lankan state, have seen little of these benefits and are the worst off in terms of levels of economic and social development among Sri Lanka's four main ethnic groups. For decades after independence, the Hill Country tea plantations remained enclaves of company rule with a minimal presence of the state; indeed, even now there are limitations on the reach and power of public authorities. Hill Country Tamil women, who make up virtually the entire tea-plucking workforce, are at the very bottom of this hierarchy and suffer patriarchal and ethnicised violence not only as workers but also as women both from outside and within the community.

Violence is also inherent in the gendered public–private sphere division of labour, supported by gender ideologies that hold women primarily responsible for often invisible, unpaid or poorly remunerated work in the private sphere (Okin, 1991; Federici, 2004; True, 2012). This is central to processes of accumulation, since 'the productivity of the housewife is the precondition for the productivity of the (male) wage labourer' (Maria-Rosa Dalla Costa (Dalla Costa and Fortunati, 1977), cited in Mies, 1987). Such gendered structures and processes produce and reproduce violence by constraining women's public participation and their access to markets; this in turn creates household inequalities, trapping women in violent environments at home and at work (True, 2012). As True (ibid.) observes, some women in developed countries bypass the patriarchal, and potentially violent, situations in the domestic arena by delegating care work to poor women, especially migrant women from the global South.

This is mirrored in the global South itself when precarious care work is delegated to women from the peripheries. Although some of these caring occupations are in the 'public' labour market, they are akin to the unpaid care work women traditionally do in the home and are devalued as a result (Okin, 1991). In Sri Lanka, what is currently known as 'domestic work' – primarily to maintain households, to cook, and to care for the members of the household – is a gendered derivate of historical feudal structures. Domestic work is often carried out by poor women from the plantations or from other impoverished rural areas of the country; women from urban underserved settlements also take on cooking and cleaning in urban households. With more and more women from the Sri Lankan middle classes joining the formal labour force, Tamil women from the Hill Country or Sinhala women from rural areas have stepped into the role of the housewife. This 'housewifisation process', as Mies (1987) observed in the context of colonial plantations, 'was never a peaceful process' as it involved exploitation and physical, sexual and emotional violence perpetrated on the women by both men and women of the upper-class household.

Domestic work underlines the fact that oppression and domination are produced and reproduced not only in the legal and formal economies but also in those that are informal and illicit. As Raven-Roberts (2013) writes, illicit economies, both national and global, become intertwined with remnants of the formal economy, creating conditions through which people, mostly women, are trapped in an economy of survival. It is here that we highlight two sectors or spheres of work dominated by women but at two opposite ends of the spectrum of legitimacy – sex work on the one hand and, on the other, loan-based self-employment of women in war-affected communities in the north and east. Both are very much part of the political economy of war in Sri Lanka and that of post-war development. Although they are positioned at two extremes on the spectrum of legitimacy, they nevertheless share the feature of being trapped in distinct moral economies – in the case of the first as transgressive and dangerous, while in the case of the second as compliant and dutiful debtors.

During the war years in Sri Lanka, processes of economic globalisation stemming from neoliberalism transformed the nature of paid work itself. Current processes of accumulation by dispossession drive women's entry into paid work, and, through this, the creation of the feminised working class that contemporary capitalist flexible accumulation requires (Hartsock, 2006). Central to this is the renegotiation of the social contract and the redefining of social relations in favour of capital, which in turn also transforms processes of social reproduction and the whole set of social relations that shape them (ibid.). The country's free trade zones (FTZs), the focal point of the textile and garment industry, in which 70 per cent of the workforce is female, are a legacy both of the neoliberal turn in Sri Lanka's economic policy orientation, which came in 1977, and of the war years. FTZs became central to securing Sri Lanka's place in the global apparel value chain, but on the back of becoming a privileged enclave of capital exempt from normal tax and labour regimes. As Caitrin Lynch (2007) documents, '*gahenu-juki, pirimi-thuwakku*' ('*juki* (sewing) machines for women, guns for men') was a salient trope, or an ideological (and gendered) call to 'serve the nation', which comfortably accommodated the need to be part of global production chains in order to keep financing a civil war. This set the stage for yet another set of enclaves in which the social contract was underpinned by coercion and violence, especially of young women largely from the rural and peri-urban hinterlands who entered FTZs in large numbers seeking economic security for their families in an atmosphere of generalised precariousness and war. The large-scale emigration of women workers as domestic labourers to the oil-rich Middle East formed yet another labour enclave during the war years. As domestic production plummeted in the post-1977 liberalisation era, remittances became the highest foreign exchange earner for the country, offsetting close to 70 per cent of the trade deficit and helping to reduce the current account balance to manageable levels throughout the war years (Almeida, 2017). Women continued to migrate to countries in the Gulf region even after the war, although the numbers have decreased due to the sex-specific ban restricting women with children under the age of five.

The preceding analysis situates the Sri Lankan civil war, commonly viewed in the context of postcolonial state formation, within the equally violent and ongoing process of neoliberal development. Focusing on the latter, we outlined several 'enclaves' of production that were central to the political economy of the war. The role played by women occupying – and trapped in – these enclaves interrogates the dominant position of labelling women simply as victims of war. It is evident that women's labour made a substantial contribution to keeping households – and the national economy – afloat during the war years. Hence, this reiterates the view that women are participants and actors negotiating within a context of a militarised political economic system with supralocal if not global dimensions (Nordstrom, 2004). Our framing of women's work as a central feature of the political economy of war is in stark contrast to the currently popular narrative that women's contribution to the economy is 'insufficient'. Also significant are gendered analyses of political economies of war highlighting the historical and contemporary, local and global, political and economic relations that form, produce and reproduce violence, as well as the way in which wars magnify and reshape gender identities (see Raven-Roberts, 2013).

Deriving from the preceding analysis, our approach to gendered violence during and in the aftermath of Sri Lanka's war is to see the continuities in the gendered dimensions beyond the temporality of war and recognise them as being linked to patriarchy and the differential impacts of economic globalisation (True, 2012). Rather than accept the narrative that violence against women and girls in time of war is exceptional, we seek to redraw the tracks of continuity of structural violence inherent in political economic arrangements that predate the temporal boundaries of wartime and see such violence merely as different manifestations of sex/gender oppression and domination. With this framing, we also attempt to produce a counternarrative to the constant drone – 'not enough women in the labour force' – readily deployed by 'forward-thinking' middle-aged male politicians and other constituencies with neoliberal orientations (including those advocating 'women's right to work').

## Gendered accumulation by dispossession: the case of self-employed women in Passikudah, Sri Lanka

We attempt to demonstrate gendered violence in political economic arrangements that pervade times of war and peace by examining one gendered enclave in the current Sri Lankan political and economic landscape – self-employment of women, bearing the hallmark of 'post-war livelihoods'. The gendered enclaves are by no means limited to self-employment of women in war-affected areas, or to the other five enclaves briefly mentioned in the preceding section – FTZs, migrant workers, tea plantations, sex work and domestic work. For the purposes of this chapter, we focus on self-employment, which has a relatively stronger empirical basis at the time of writing. Self-employment of women in war-affected areas and around the island in general is *the* post-war development strategy of the state to uplift households from poverty and empower women. We argue that the push for self-employment, with its base in the world of finance capital, is a mode of accumulation by dispossession. Using qualitative empirical evidence collected intermittently throughout a period of three years from 2014 in Passikudah, a small coastal town on the eastern seaboard of Sri Lanka, we demonstrate the mutually constitutive nature of gendered violence and political economic arrangements and structures both during and after the war as they relate to the self-employment of women.

### Self-employment as a neoliberal policy

Self-employment through home-based livelihoods and micro-entrepreneurship is an important part of the post-war political economic vision, especially for women. Being an 'entrepreneur' is currently promoted as a survival strategy. This vision, however, is not entirely new. Alailima (2002) points out that the Sri Lankan state actively promoted self-employment programmes in the post-1977 period to assuage the effects of the liberalisation strategy in rural areas. Self-employment was part of a broader structural adjustment programme (SAP) package that aimed at creating employment opportunities in the modernised sectors of the economy, while removing the burden of employment creation from the state, a pre-1977 feature (Ruwanpura, 2000).

With the assumption that self-employment will lead to 'balanced growth', the state proceeded to implement sixteen integrated rural development programmes (IRDPs), a community-based development model advanced by the World Bank in many regions of the world at the time. The initial focus of IRDPs was the provision of infrastructure, which later shifted to supporting rural communities to undertake income-generating activities primarily through self-employment (Alailima, 2002).

SAPs conceptualised women as 'shock absorbers'; they were expected to serve as a buffer against the adverse effects of SAPs[8] through greater participation in economic activities and community management (Elson, 1989; Sparr, 1994; Lakshman, 1996; Rafeek and Samaratunga, 2000). Self-employment was gently forced on women and made attractive by offering financial assistance through various credit and other promotion schemes operated by state banks and various non-governmental organisations (NGOs). Women, too, resorted to various self-employment programmes, not least because handloom and other cottage industries that operated on a cooperative model closed as a result of economic reforms (Lakshman, 1996; Rafeek and Samaratunga, 2000). In the handloom cooperative set-up, women indeed completed certain tasks at home, on their own; however, they were part of a larger, collective production process where quality standards were checked and marketing and sales were well planned in collaboration with the state. The later model of self-employment that was pushed on women atomised them as producers and left them to their own devices with regard to quality control, marketing and sales. The only 'assistance' that was forcefully introduced was financial, mainly through microcredit. Despite a number of studies in the 1990s questioning the effectiveness of self-employment schemes as a poverty alleviation strategy in Sri Lanka (Lakshman, 1996; Senanayake, 2002) and a UNDP (1990) review finding these schemes to be ineffective, self-employment programmes coupled with microcredit initiatives remained resilient, relevant and common in development practice. This 'bottom-of-the-pyramid' development strategy continued and expanded in scope in the aftermath of the Indian Ocean tsunami of 2004 and in the arbitrarily determined post-war period after 2009. It was rebranded as a 'post-war development strategy', a way out of poverty for the war-affected, and in particular for women-headed households in the north and east of Sri Lanka. Home-based livelihoods and micro-enterprises are promoted by the state and by international and local NGOs as a means of strengthening livelihoods for vulnerable households. Microcredit and microfinance are a key modality through which self-employment schemes are supported, and, in the post-2009 period, the war-affected areas of Sri Lanka have witnessed a rapid financialisation of development, with the government and NGOs, as well as banks and other commercial institutions, actively promoting the idea.

## Displacement of primary production

Women in war-affected areas are often compelled to become entrepreneurs. There are several forces at play that trigger this compulsion. A slight digression is necessary to elaborate the nature of these forces and how they contribute to pushing women towards self-employment as the only livelihood strategy. Passikudah, the focus of this chapter, is characterised by the imposition of a capital-intensive resort economy on a landscape of precarious primary production in fishing and agriculture that is already infused with local inequities and burdened by a legacy of war and tsunami-related destruction. The resort economy has made its wage labour attractive to its labour force even as – or precisely because – it undermines other forms of primary production (e.g. fishing, agriculture, labour work in coconut plantations) as a secure livelihood. This is related as much to its privileging by the state and the lack of support for primary producers as it is to other environmental factors such as declining fish catches and consistent floods during the monsoon periods. The privilege assigned to tourism – and, in the case of Passikudah, high-end resort tourism – is a distinct post-war economic development strategy, stemming from the current economic philosophy of Sri Lanka. This philosophy, as Abbink aptly puts it, drives entire states and peoples to 'produce marketable commodities, develop trade, monetize everything, invest in material growth, build facilities, and acquire money and wealth' (Abbink, 2009).

The undermining of primary production is also inextricably connected to questions of access to the commons. The use of the beach by fishers, for example, rubs up against it being pristine and reserved for tourists. Some fishers continue to use the strip near the resorts because of problems with the official jetty being further away and smaller, but they are under constant pressure by the resorts to move. As we have written elsewhere (Gunasekara et al., 2016), in Passikudah today, the integration of primary producers into the local supply chain generally happens at the bottom, and the precarious nature of fishing means that fishers face disproportionate risks relative to other livelihoods that are also at the bottom of the value chain. This precariousness and its associated risks are pushing people towards wage labour in the tourism economy and other alternative forms of employment. For women in Passikudah, working in the tourism industry carries certain reputational risks, as resorts, hotels and guesthouses are seen in a negative light by the local community. They are viewed as spaces catering to human vices, especially those of male 'others', and this generates narratives of ethnic and cultural contagion (ibid.). The social anxieties arising from local Tamil women fraternising with Muslim businessmen, Sinhalese or foreigners pose barriers to women accessing the wage labour available to them in the tourism industry. In this context, self-employment has become the de facto livelihood for women, and also for some men, in Passikudah. Although this genre of work is now branded as 'entrepreneurship', very few self-employed women we met in Passikudah belonged to the quintessential category of 'go-getters'. Their business is a part-time activity for survival. Unlike the zest for growth and expansion that we associate with entrepreneurs, these women are not interested in graduating their micro-enterprise into a more profitable business. Their entire focus is on survival by ensuring subsistence and diversifying risk.

## Set up for failure

As discussed earlier, microcredit and microfinance are a key modality through which self-employment schemes are supported, and, in the post-2009 period, the war-affected areas of Sri Lanka have witnessed a rapid financialisation of development, with the government and NGOs, as well as banks and other commercial institutions, actively promoting the idea. Microcredit-based self-employment is portrayed as an economic space that is inherently empowering and builds confidence for those who pursue it. While disbursement of microcredit is quick and efficient, there is very little useful guidance on what to produce. Prospective entrepreneurs are given mediocre training on making items that are already in abundance in the market, such as soap, camphor balls or incense sticks, or they are trained to make handicrafts that have little to no market value. Without proper guidance on market needs or high-quality training, these women end up producing what they can, in their own capacity.

If one woman starts making candles, it is likely that all her neighbours will start doing the same. It is typical for self-employed women to move from producing one product to another within a span of six months. When we first met Rama,[9] she was making soap at home; seven months later, she moved to making *murukku* (a local fried snack) because she couldn't sell any of her soap bars. These women tend to encounter a lack of consumer demand for their goods, given that the customer base is their own impoverished neighbourhood. Several women entrepreneurs told us that venturing outside their village carries risks, as markets are a gendered terrain. Navigating and negotiating one's way through markets entail facing various forms of gendered violence and social control. For example, a woman peanut seller said that many men make sexual advances to her when she is in public spaces conducting business on a daily basis. At times the advances are aggressive, amounting to sexual assault.

Women also have to negotiate with their husbands or male partners to conduct business outside the home. Several women told us that they plan business activity outside their homes when their husband is not at home. Valli's daily mission is to sell her homemade sweets as quickly as possible and return home before her husband gets back from his work day. On occasions when she returns home late, disciplining by her husband comes in the form of blows and kicks. Many other women related to this reality, admitting that they take great precautions not to provoke their husbands in their attempts to make a living. Amidst the violence, humiliation and reputational damage incurred by such incidents, only a few women remain 'in the game' to make self-employment viable. It is hardly surprising that most self-employment ventures fail, trapping the women in vicious cycles of indebtedness that drive them further into poverty. These entrepreneurs are also insulated from broader market activity and lack the social capital and access to patronage networks necessary to tap into markets beyond their area of residence. And, as discussed above, local production in war-affected areas, as in most rural areas, is also constantly displaced by bigger economic players who view these geographic areas as untapped markets.

There is recent evidence that some have embraced self-employment and, drawing on a combination of microcredit, support from other sources and their own skills, have been able to take advantage of integrating with the local economy. A small minority of go-getter businesswomen have leveraged the state's support to build capacities for self-employment and to scale it up beyond subsistence. However, even in the handful of relatively successful cases, self-employment has worked primarily to enable diversification and spread risk rather than enabling capital accumulation to facilitate a transition out of precariousness (Gunasekara et al., 2016). The vast majority of de facto entrepreneurs are stuck in an endless battle to secure a steady income. They try their hand at various home-based enterprises because making ends meet by doing daily wage labour – the only work that is available to them in Passikudah – has become an uphill battle. These realities interrogate some of the underlying assumptions of entrepreneurship and the promise of prosperity vis-à-vis the self-employment of women.

The construction of the 'financially responsible woman' (Maclean, 2012) is much in evidence, as women are the favoured targets for micro-loans; NGOs, banks, financial institutions and the state have all implemented microfinance initiatives only for women. On a few occasions, we observed field officers on motorbikes on visits to the villages where they dispense loans and collect repayments.[10] Meetings regarding group loans followed a particular code or repertoire. A group of around ten or sometimes fifteen (mostly) women would gather together and sit in a circle, around the young, male loan officer. Sometimes, the meeting would begin with an oath uttered by the women in which they promised to use the money for the well-being of their families and make their repayments on time. Subsequently, the field officer would collect the week's loan repayments. He was pleased when all the instalments were paid in full. He would then dole out advice on what they should be producing next, recalling things that caught his eye during his travel to Colombo or other cities. This meeting usually ended with the officer dispensing new loans to his group and requesting the women to bring others who wanted to participate in loan schemes. We observe here the mode of control – financialisation, represented by the field officer of the finance company or the NGO. This repertoire enforces a particular construction of the financially responsible woman. It is intrinsically linked to the reproductive burden placed on the woman, which is also built into the oath they take. As Stephen Young observed in the case of India (2010), this performance also involves the male, financially savvy enforcer, the embodiment of financial responsibility and financial mobility.

When their home-based livelihood ventures fail and the women are unable to repay loans, however, labels of 'incompetence' and the inferiority of women's capabilities are readily brought up as causes of the failure (Gunasekara et al., 2016). The global trends of using micro-loans for consumption and 'loan-swapping' is much in evidence in Sri Lanka, and 'narratives of financial illiteracy' or lack of capacity among women hide 'the deeper structural dimension of financialisation of development and debt-driven self-employment and livelihood programmes, whose emergence is inextricably linked to the virtual end of remunerative, secure and long-term employment or primary production' (ibid.). The consequences of indebtedness are serious and even tragic. News items from war-affected areas linking suicides to indebtedness have become commonplace (Wijedasa, 2014; Guganeshan, 2015).

The proliferation of finance companies in war-affected areas in the post-2009 period has introduced new dimensions to this inherently violent arena of debt. Women who are late on payments often face intimidation and harassment from loan collectors from finance companies who commonly practise door-to-door marketing and loan collection (Gunasekara et al., 2016; 2015). Sexual favours in return for late repayments have become common practice. For this reason, in some areas the loan officers drop in to collect payments after hours. Aside from the physical and psychological dimensions of this type of violence, it also has a subjective dimension that is less explored. Women face reputational risks because intimidation and harassment take place on their own doorstep, in the community in which they live. This type of violence reached such chronic levels in the Eastern Province that, in 2014, the District Secretary of Batticaloa banned weekly house visits to collect loan instalments.

It is important that we juxtapose some of the repertoires embedded in the economic space of microcredit-based self-employment. In the performance of financial responsibility with the example of the male loan officer and the female borrowers, we observe a particular reinforcement of gender roles. The male loan officer embodies the promise of finance for the woman and her family, alongside an arsenal of mechanisms – both material and symbolic – to hold her accountable for the borrowed funds. The woman borrower is held responsible for setting up a viable self-employment venture, and ensuring and prioritising the well-being of her family in the prescribed roles of mother and wife. We observe in the same canvas the domestic violence that some of these women experience at the hands of their husbands when they have crossed the boundaries of accepted behaviour in their role of wife and mother, and violent encounters with the finance companies' hired goons in the event of a late or missed loan repayment. Taken together, these repertoires depict gendered dimensions of kinship that are privileged (both culturally and violently) in the construction of the financially responsible woman.

The construction of the financially responsible woman is a dynamic of neoliberal policies, cleverly scaffolding the rhetoric of individual responsibility in order to mask the increasing divestment of state services (e.g. safety net programmes, food stamps) and turn social reproduction entirely over to individual families, in this case to women, or sell state services on the market. This is a move to maximise the returns from the unpaid labour of social reproduction within the family and the limited expenditure on the social wage outside the home (Vogel, 2000). The construction of the financially responsible woman, in this case, becomes central to the processes of accumulation.

A win-win situation

The only consistent winners in the self-employment and microfinance game are the lenders, many of whom charge exorbitant interest rates that sometimes reach up to 200 to 250 per cent per annum. Even if most borrowers are aware of the interest rates, they resort to microfinance as it is the only option available to them. The convenience of micro-loans in terms of not requiring collateral or paperwork is not found in other secure credit schemes.

While petty moneylenders are labelled as 'loan sharks' for similar loan terms, microfinance providers pride themselves as being partners in development. In fact, one particular loan officer we met wore a name badge that said 'Dream achiever'. They crown themselves with a moral halo by finding new alliances in NGOs. As shown by Gunasekara, Philips and Nagaraj (2016), most microfinance arms of banks consider it a win-win situation to team up with NGOs. As articulated by a bank manager in the Eastern Province: 'This collaboration helps us canvass their humanitarian cause, and simultaneously do business with the communities. When they promote access to credit and microfinance as part of their programmes, I am able to open more accounts and offer loans to the people. So it is good for business.'[11] Hence, the combination of self-employment and microfinance has become a socially accepted mechanism for extracting wealth and resources from poor people, particularly women. It is an elegant post-war development strategy that carries the promise of poverty eradication, without any threat to existing political economic arrangements. It promises transformation of lives and communities without the messiness of class, caste or ethnic struggles; and it guarantees that the poor can be saved while making profits from them.

### Relations of violence: spatial, economic, subjective and sexual

Deriving from accounts of gendered violence in self-employment, we identify four interconnected yet distinct relations of violence against women workers in this area of the economy: spatial, economic, subjective and sexual.

We posit that the spatial organisation of women's work determines its visibility, thereby producing specific forms of vulnerability. Here, we observe two types of spatial organisation of women's work within the political economy of the war. First, during the war, the hubs of production became concentrated in geographic areas away from the north and east of Sri Lanka. As in other theatres of war, all economic life in Passikudah – mainly fishing and agriculture – had to contend with fighting between the Sri Lankan Army and the Liberation Tigers of the Tamil Eelam (LTTE), on land and at sea. No one escaped the surveillance regimes deployed by the Sri Lankan Army, the LTTE and other armed factions. Economic activity was high risk, mainly because it had to be organised around a complex and unpredictable regime of checkpoints, curfews, security zones and passes. Access to markets was inconsistent, resulting in significant losses for primary producers. In the wartime environment of fear, where men were vulnerable to abduction, murder and forced recruitment, women were better able to navigate through checkpoints to access markets (Bohle and Funfgeld, 2007; Fernando and Moonesinghe, 2012; Goodhand et al., 2000). But the attendant risks for women meant that this too was not always a reliable or secure channel. As a result, primary production – fishing or agriculture-based – became a subsistence or a survival economy, heavily dependent on external factors and the security situation.

Second, women's work became spatially organised in a way that enabled strict surveillance and control, two aspects that are deemed necessary for the process of production. For example, most women from Passikudah resorted to self-employment or domestic work, operating within the confines of homes, and laboured under the watchful eyes of their husbands and other male kin, or the '*mahaththayas*' and '*nonas*'[12] of middle- and upper-class, mostly ethnic Sinhala households. As shown in the case of Valli (illustrated in the preceding section), the modes of control and power embedded in these spaces make women vulnerable to verbal, physical and sexual abuse, and offer no redress mechanisms. It mutes the voice of the woman, as a worker and as a human being. We observe that this spatial organisation of women's work, while enabling forms of surveillance and control necessary for the production process, invisibilises the worker and disables intervention by a third party. Physically, too, households maintain strict codes of privacy. 'Out of sight, out of mind', the workers have limited mechanisms to hold perpetrators accountable for any type of violence.

Violent economic relations are deeply embedded in these modes of production in the value chains of self-employment. In the self-employment of women in Passikudah, financial returns are low, work arrangements are precarious and working conditions are hazardous and sometimes indecent. The work day of a domestic worker or a woman struggling to maintain her household through a micro-enterprise is more than twenty hours. Laws that mandate a minimum wage and employee benefits (i.e. Employee Provident Fund and Employee Trust Fund contributions) do not apply to de facto entrepreneurs. While a consistent wage seems a luxury for self-employed women, they are also often left out of state safety net programmes such as Samurdhi.[13] It seems that, as the visibility of the mode of accumulation decreases, the level of state intervention in providing basic security also decreases. Loans, or the world of finance, then become where such individuals access funds to fulfil basic needs. As discussed in detail in the preceding section, indebtedness is acute among self-employed women.

Considering women's work as part of the moral economy, we observe subjective or psycho-social relations of violence. 'Moral economy' might be defined as a kind of inquiry focusing on how economic activities of all kinds are influenced and structured by moral dispositions, values and norms, and how these in turn are reinforced, shaped, compromised or overridden by economic pressures. The moral order concerns norms (informal and formal), conventions, values, dispositions and commitments regarding what is just and what constitutes good behaviour in relation to others, and implies certain broader conceptions of the good and of well-being. The ways in which the moral economy plays out in society have violent subjective and psycho-social effects that leave permanent scars on women. For example, in the moral economy, meanings that economic relations and responsibilities have for women affect how they believe their work should be done and acknowledged. The oath-taking 'ritual', for instance, asserted different value labels for identities of women as mothers and women as producers. The pressure for women to generate income for the maintenance of their households invariably means that to some degree their roles as mothers are compromised. The ways in which this happens affect the moral texture of employment. Women's home-based livelihoods, in this regard, are encouraged as they contain the woman within the home, and therefore are thought of as activities that do not impinge on their roles as mothers. However, by confining women to domesticity through home-based livelihoods, the risk of domestic violence increases. And, as studies have shown, physical and psychological disciplining or control of women by their husbands adds to the burden of earning an income and taking care of the household that women have to endure, effectively creating a triple burden (Jayasekara and Najab, 2016). An emerging trend among self-employed, indebted women is that they spend hours of their day trying to hunt down other women in their group who have defaulted on their loan repayments. A few women we met spent at least two days a week tracking down defaulters, as non-repayment affects all the others in the loan group. During these two days, they do nothing but walk around their villages and adjoining areas. Poopathy told us that she is unable to borrow further unless others pay their instalments. This was a serious problem for her, as she used the funds from this particular group for household expenses. It significantly reduced the number of candles she produced in a week, hence her income was affected. It also distanced her from friends and other women in the community. Those who had defaulted on their repayments were her friends and family, and their inability to repay their loans affected the survival of Poopathy and others in the group. This had led to feuds between her and others who were once close to her. This narrative brings to the fore a moral economy of finance for de facto entrepreneurs, in which the values that drive this economic relation are slowly leading to a breakdown of social and kinship ties in the rural countryside of Sri Lanka.

Women's work outside their homes often leads to more generalised reactions and anxieties or a state of moral panic (Goode and
Ben-Yehuda, 2009; Krinsky, 2008), and moral panic enables greater
policing of women. Women working in these spaces therefore face serious reputational risks based on moral panic around sexual fraternisation.
While some women may overstep these boundaries despite malicious
gossip and character assassination, most stay bound by the rules of the
moral economy in order to maintain a reputation as a 'good', 'virtuous'
woman. Self-employed women have become targets of this moral panic
particularly because of transactional sex as a bargaining chip in negotiating access to working capital, inputs of production, credit and markets.
As mentioned earlier, some self-employed women in Passikudah were
trapped in highly exploitative sexual transactions in which they negotiated sex as a repayment for debt and the interest on loans.

## Financialisation: a mode of power and control

Our approach to unpicking gendered relations of violence (spatial,
economic, subjective, sexual) vis-à-vis a particular mode of accumulation and dispossession – self-employment – was an attempt to
illuminate certain broader economic, political and ideological forces
that are enmeshed in this complex web and that continuously reproduce violence. In the account above, we featured 'financialisation' and
'responsibilisation' as gendered 'modes of power and control' over
impoverished populations in the war-affected areas of Sri Lanka. The
context in which these modes of control currently exist is what we
know as 'neoliberal globalisation'.

Through the mode of control that we refer to as 'responsibilisation', women's work in the public sphere continues to carry the stamp
of undervalued, informal and unwaged work that she performs in the
private sphere. In the context of the United States, Susan Thistle
observes that:

> economists have long recognized ... that the development of new
> regions and the conversion of nonwage workers into wage workers can
> create great profits, leading corporations to set up factories overseas ...
> [W]e must realise that a similar lucrative process was happening within
> the United States itself ... [A]s the market reached into kitchens and
> bedrooms turning many household tasks into work for pay productivity
> rose greatly. (Thistle, 2006)

The 'responsible' woman, the ideological driving force of microcredit, labours in a context unregulated and free from labour laws, and, like housework within the home, this context is unending and functions throughout the twenty-four-hour day. The increased public visibility of working women has in turn created widespread anxiety about female sexuality and has contributed to increased violence against women. The increased incidence of rape and sexual assault, while associated with widespread commodification of sexuality, should also be read as an expression of deeper mechanisms of labour discipline and violence.

'Financialisation' is the pattern of how places and populations have been strategically repositioned in relation to the perceived opportunities or risks they present to global capital flows (Mitchell and Beckett, 2008). This 'financialisation' of space seeks to expand and accelerate the mobility of capital to move around the world easily. Underpinned by assumptions about fiscal illiteracy and incompetence in developing countries, 'financialisation' peddles the promise of moving out of poverty for households through microcredit and microfinance initiatives. Spending cuts are made to seem 'fiscally responsible', invisibilising and legitimising the drive to recruit cheaper (female) labour to public-sector hospitals and schools. It also produces flows of migrant workers from rural and impoverished parts of a country to undertake the care work of working women. These 'circulations' must be understood in 'dynamic relation to financial globalization' (Young, 2010). They coincide with the parallel flight of state and corporate capital due to market liberalisation and public spending cuts, and the production of financial flows in the form of remittances that workers send home to support their families (ibid.).

In this context, microfinance becomes less a political tool to support the rights of women in the event of restructuring state industrial policies (i.e. as in the case of SEWA in Gujarat, India). Rather, as Heloise Weber (2006) shows, microfinance, with its emphasis on entrepreneurship and self-reliance, was set up from the Emergency Social Funds of the World Bank to assist populations experiencing temporary hardship as a result of IMF-imposed liberalisation programmes in the 1980s. A Consultative Group to Assist the Poor (CGAP) was quickly mobilised by the World Bank as missionaries spreading the word of microfinance around the developing world. The idea of microfinance as a temporary injection to alleviate financial hardship carries the undertones of the investor's (Warren Buffett's) view that economic volatility brings opportunities for profit. So, microfinance and self-employment are encouraged, with the assumption that there is a world of 'endless opportunities' for the poor – and, in most cases, women. Accounts of self-employed and indebted women in Passikudah, however, problematise such assumptions and the world of hope introduced by such programmes.

Today, the microfinance industry is a multibillion-rupee enterprise, with many institutions recording more than 100 per cent in profits. In 2016, Sanasa Development Bank, a leading microfinance provider, recorded a net profit of Rs 1 billion for the first time in history (Lanka Business News, 2016). It marked a 48 per cent growth in profit in the 2015 fiscal year. As discussed earlier, the demand for loans is simply not due to the financial losses of families during the war, but results from the larger process of fiscal austerity that shifted the burden of household maintenance to women.

As discussed earlier, while women's limited mobility significantly impedes the success and the lifespan of their micro-enterprise, for microfinance companies, as Jonathan Morduch (1999) notes, this is a plus (as it decreases the likelihood of 'ex-post moral hazard', the fear that clients will 'take the money and run'). The dual attack of microfinance and self-employment reinforces limits on women's mobility through gendering entrepreneurial activities (i.e. running small shops, sewing clothes or rearing cattle, etc.) and by emphasising the need for women to be *Anagi*[14] (valuable), empowered 'good mothers' working towards the upliftment of their families. Financialisation, of which microfinance is but one product, promotes responsibilisation of various sorts that 'tend to reproduce gendered ideologies regarding the kinds of work, paid and unpaid, that women do, and the spatiality of this labour' (Young, 2010). This poses barriers to challenging broader structures of domination.

### Conclusion

The striking feature of the post-war development narrative of Sri Lanka is a coupling of two seemingly contradictory gender ideologies. One is the ideology of the woman as the mother who 'devotes her life to raise children, manage the family budget and ensure peace in the family' (Department of National Planning, 2010) that was adopted as official government policy. One of the first consequences was bringing in policies to restrict the number of women, especially married women, migrating abroad for work, which became a key policy goal in post-war Sri Lanka.[15] Where women's economic activity is promoted by the government it has tended to be in activities largely confined to sectors of the economy that are subsistence or self-employed and home-based or in precarious employment relations. This has continued well into the tenth year of 'post-war' development, with 'Enterprise Sri Lanka' (started in 2018) yet another loan scheme with its own sub-scheme geared towards 'the economic empowerment of women'. What comes with Enterprise Sri Lanka is another gender ideology that advances women as 'the engine of economic growth' (Minister of Finance, 2017). Enterprise Sri Lanka arrived at a time of continued unemployment, precarious work (as discussed above) and significant household debt problems. The Sri Lankan government's bright idea seems to be to introduce more loans and encourage people to be the 'natural' entrepreneurs they are (ibid.). Enterprise promotion, through self-employment, is put forward as *the* state policy (and is also readily promoted by non-governmental development organisations), not only as a way of achieving economic goals (i.e. graduating to an upper-middle-income country) but also as a pathway to reconciliation, through economic prosperity in war-affected communities. Our field work in Passikudah, as discussed above, has demonstrated how the state's hopefulness about this strategy sits uncomfortably with women's realities of survival and security.

In this chapter, we also point to a pitfall in contemporary discourses on justice and rights where rape and sexual violence against women are foregrounded in transitional justice and constitutional reform debates in Sri Lanka. What is less in focus in these discourses are the gender and sexual regimes embedded in political economic relations and the violence inherent in maintaining them. Our main contention is that underpinning the self-employment economies examined in this chapter are regimes of gender and sexual order and security that were – and are – maintained through coercion and violence. But considering the coercion and violence in isolation, for example as discrete acts of sexual violence or violence against women and girls, as the transitional justice agenda mostly does, fails, firstly, to address the structural conditions producing such violence. Secondly, such an approach invariably ends up relying almost exclusively on individualising responsibility and victimhood and actually risks fragmenting the possibility of collective political struggles to resist and transform such conditions.

These regimes of sexual order and security are by no means fixed or unidimensional in terms of the nature of their focus on the female body. Changing political economic contexts and dynamics, as well as the limits and possibilities of violence, mean that these regimes shift in focus and embody complex internal relations. In the post-war period, women in the north and east, who are the preferred targets of micro-finance lending and other debt-driven self-employment schemes, are forced into a socio-economic space where deeply gendered ideas of women being more reliable, responsible and compliant borrowers have tied them into home-based employment, leaving them vulnerable to multiple layers of structural violence.

The sexual orders and regimes also have clear spatial dimensions. A comparison with the other examples mentioned at the beginning of this chapter is useful in this respect. While the plantations and FTZs are physically demarcated zones of exception, domestic work and post-war loan-based self-employment are territorialised differently – individual women locked into specific privatised household/home-based relations with capital. Sex workers are zoned into an economy of criminalisation and, though ubiquitous, their visibility is fraught and always accompanied by the prospect of direct physical and sexual violence. It is also clear that these modes of accumulation by dispossession are in fact porous to each other. For example, many Hill Country Tamil women are forced to enter domestic work or factories in FTZs; sex work is by no means limited to sex workers alone, with workers in FTZs resorting to it; and domestic workers or women in debt may be 'forced' into transacting in sex. Hence, we observe sexualised exploitation as a relation that exists in various modes of accumulation and dispossession.

Inasmuch as this chapter sketches the political economy of violence against women, including its sexualised nature, in Sri Lanka in relation to the war, it is important to note that women are not merely victims of an inexorable pattern, and particularly significant would be relationships between women that defy or mark an exit from the standard hetero-patriarchal sexual contracts. The sexual orders and regimes explored above are not merely restricted to economic relations or spaces of production. In fact, the structural violence they embody underline that such relations and spaces of production are themselves firmly anchored in overlapping patriarchies. And they were sustained and reproduced during and after the war through violence that was physical as well as structural.

Women have been and continue to be exploited but also valorised as sustainers and reproducers of the family, race and nation, and such violence against them has always been and continues to be legitimised by a combination of legal regimes of impunity and moral regimes of responsibilisation. In the shadow of the focus on sexual violence against women and girls, particularly rape, in the context of transitional justice in relation to the war lie many unvoiced narratives of violence, including forms of sexual violence other than rape. This chapter is an attempt, limited as it is, to find ways to break this silence.

## Notes

1 It should be noted that processes such as the Consultative Task Force on Reconciliation Mechanisms and the Public Representation Committee made attempts to include socio-economic rights into broader discussions on constitutional reform. While economic and social rights were considered as urgent and important, neither process foregrounded these issues in relation to wartime atrocities.

2 The global development industry made economic liberalisation a key conditionality of concessionary loans under structural adjustment programmes (SAPs) offered to salvage declining economies of the global South. Sri Lanka's subscription to SAPs during this period led to a shift in foreign policy towards the US bloc, which in turn resulted in an unprecedented wave of foreign aid-sponsored public-sector investment projects. Contrary to the expectation that the degree of unrest and conflict would diminish as a result of reduced state intervention and a consequent increase in employment and economic opportunities, there was an intensification of political conflict during this period of transition that eventually culminated in a civil war in 1983.

3 After two decades of an economy driven by import-substitution policies, Sri Lanka entered a period of economic and political transition in the 1977–83

period with the election of the United National Party (UNP)-led government. Led by J. R. Jayawardene, the government halted import substitution and instituted an extensive programme of trade liberalisation, private-sector deregulation and discontinuance of many welfare provisions that were historically employed by the ruling elite to buy and maintain social peace (Dunham and Jayasuriya, 2001). While marked by a significant rupture in economic philosophy and arrangements, this period of transition not only inherited but also reproduced many of the political and economic legacies of the 1950s and 1960s. The transition from a plantation-export-based economy to a public-sector-based, import-substitution economy in the mid-1950s coincided with Sinhala–Tamil confrontation over uneven development and political power (Venugopal, 2003). The two decades of government regulation (1956–76) of private-sector enterprises, banking and external trade, and the nationalisation of key industries such as finance, ports and oil, led to a dependency on state patronage to access scarce employment opportunities and private-sector contracts and permits, and determined the location of public-sector industries, dry-zone irrigation and resettlement projects (Gunasinghe, 1984).

4 The free trade zones (FTZs) and tea plantations, both dependent on female

labour, and most tourist destinations located mainly in the west and the south were well insulated against the direct effects of the war.

5 The UNP government struggled at maintaining the initial pace of liberalisation. As economic growth slowed, the state became the 'employer of last resort' and security-sector expansion pushed Sinhala youth from rural peasantry and fisheries communities to enlist in the military (Venugopal, 2003: 32). The increased militarisation of the state under wartime conditions fuelled the authoritarian powers of the state to quell any serious political disturbances (ibid.). These conditions and the absence of transparency in many transactions created avenues for large-scale rent extraction in the war economy (Athukorala and Jayasuriya, 2012: 11). As a result, many privatisation measures were executed in ways that favoured businesses with links to the state and government officials who engaged in corrupt practices (i.e. commissions).

6 By 2001, this sector accounted for over 5 per cent of total employment and a much higher percentage of formal-sector employment for Sinhala men (Venugopal, 2003: 32).

7 See www.cbsl.gov.lk/pics_n_docs/latest_news/press_20150507ea.pdf (accessed 30 June 2018).

8 These effects included a reduction in public-sector expenditure, with the pruning of subsidies for agricultural production and the distribution of food, high inflation, retrenchment, etc.

9 All respondent names have been replaced with pseudonyms to protect their identities.

10 This is similar to what Stephen Young found in 2010 in Andhra Pradesh.

11 Interview with male, 4 March 2015, in Gunasekara et al. (2016).

12 The terms '*mahaththaya*' and '*nona*' (Sinhala) can be loosely translated as 'gentleman' and 'lady', but, in this context, they imply the power that the members of the households have over domestic workers.

13 Samurdhi is a state-sponsored social protection programme. '*Samurdhi*' (Sinhala) means 'prosperity'. The programme includes welfare, rural development and microfinance components that include food stamps, social insurance and financing to help overcome poverty. The focus of these programmes has been on 'empowering' the poor and providing a 'safety net' to overcome poverty.

14 'Anagi' is also the name of a women's saving account, offered by the Commercial Bank of Sri Lanka.

15 The near de jure prohibition on women with children under the age of five from migrating abroad for work (*Family Background Report 2013*, government circular no. MFE/RAD/1/3) was among a number of steps taken by the state to curtail women's right to paid work. This is reflected in the sharp decline in female labour migrants from the war years to the post-war period. In 1997, during the height of Sri Lanka's civil war, women accounted for 75 per cent of all migrant labour, making a substantial contribution to the country's foreign exchange earnings; however, by 2015, this figure had dropped to 35 per cent (Arambepola, 2018). Despite a change of government in 2015, the state continues to exercise a 'protectionist' policy towards women's work. The official rhetoric is that reducing the number of women sent abroad for work (with a simultaneous increase in males migrating for work) will scale down domestic issues that occur once women leave for work overseas (Sri Lanka Bureau of Foreign Employment, 2013). This view discounts the complexity of the reasons why women migrate for work: poverty, a lack of support and maintenance provided by the male members of the family, and, in some cases, domestic violence.

# References

Abbink, J. 2009. 'Suri Images: The Return of Exoticism and the Commodification of an Ethiopian "Tribe"', *Cahiers d'Études Africaines* 49 (196): 893–924.

Alailima, P. 2002. 'The Impact of Public Policy on the Poor in Sri Lanka: A Study of Policies Relating to Incomes, Assets and Living Standards and their Effects on the Poor, 1970–84'. PhD thesis, University of Bradford.

Almeida, K. 2017. 'Importance of Remittance to Sri Lanka and its Future in Digital World', *Daily Mirror*, 7 April, www.dailymirror.lk/article/Importance-of-remittance-to-Sri-Lanka-and-its-future-in-digital-world-126985.html

Anglin, M. K. 1998. 'Feminist Perspectives on Structural Violence', *Identities: Global Studies in Culture and Power* 5 (2): 145–51.

Arambepola, C. 2018. 'Is There an Alternative to the Family Background Report?', *Sunday Times*, 3 September, www.sundaytimes.lk/180930/business-times/is-there-an-alternative-to-the-family-background-report-313453.html

Athukorala, P. and Jayasuriya, S. 2012. 'Economic Policy Shifts in Sri Lanka: The Post-conflict Development Challenge'. Working Paper 2012/15. Canberra: Australian National University, https://acde.crawford.anu.edu.au/sites/default/files/publication/acde_crawford_anu_edu_au/2016-10/wp_econ_2012_15_athukorala_sisira.pdf

Bohle, H. G. and Funfgeld, H. 2007. 'The Political Ecology of Violence in Eastern Sri Lanka', *Development and Change* 45 (4): 665–87.

Dalla Costa, M. and Fortunati, L. 1977. *Brutto Ciao*. Rome: Edizioni delle Donne.

Department of National Planning. 2010. *Mahinda Chinthana, Vision for the Future: The Development Policy Framework of the Government of Sri Lanka*. Colombo: Department of National Planning.

Dunham, D. M. and Jayasuriya, S. 2001. 'Liberalisation and Political Decay: Sri Lanka's Journey from a Welfare State to a Brutalised Society'. The Hague: Institute of Social Studies.

Elson, D. 1989. 'The Impact of Structural Adjustment on Women: Concepts and Issues' in Onimode, B. (ed.), *The IMF, the World Bank and the African Debt. Vol. II: The Social and Political Impact*. London: Zed Books.

Federici, S. 2004. *Caliban and the Witch: Women, the Body and Primitive Accumulation*. New York: Autonomedia.

Fernando, P. and Moonesinghe, S. 2012. 'Livelihoods, Basic Services and Social Protection in Sri Lanka'. Working Paper 6. London: SLRC.

Goode, E. and Ben-Yehuda, N. 2009. *Moral Panics: The Social Construction of Deviance*. Oxford: Wiley-Blackwell.

Goodhand, J., Hulme, D. and Lewer, N. 2000. 'Social Capital and the Political Economy of Violence: A Case Study of Sri Lanka', *Disasters* 24 (4): 390–406.

Guganeshan, M. 2015. 'Rise of Financial Institutions and Northern Province Debt Trap', *Colombo Telegraph*, 31 July, www.colombotelegraph.com/index.php/rise-of-financial-institutions-northern-province-debt-trap/

Gunasekara, V., Najab, N. and Munas, M. 2015. *No Silver Bullet: An Assessment of the Effects of Financial Counseling on Decision-making Behavior of Housing Beneficiaries in Jaffna and*

*Kilinochchi*. Colombo: Centre for Poverty Analysis (CEPA).

Gunasekara, V., Philips, M. and Nagaraj, V. 2016. *Hospitality and Exclusion: A Study about Post-war Tourism in Passikudah*. London: Overseas Development Institute.

Gunasinghe, N. 1984. 'The Open Economy and its Impact on Ethnic Relations in Sri Lanka' in Committee for Regional Development, *Sri Lanka: The Ethnic Conflict: Myths, Realities and Perspectives*. New Delhi: Navrang.

Hartsock, N. 2006. 'Globalization and Primitive Accumulation: The Contributions of David Harvey's Dialectical Marxism' in *David Harvey: A Critical Reader*. Oxford: Blackwell.

Hartsock, N. 2011. 'A New Moment of Primitive Accumulation'. Inaugural Inkrit Conference.

Jayasekara, P. and Najab, N. 2016. *The Political Economy of Violence: Women's Economic Relations in Post-war Sri Lanka*. London: Overseas Development Institute.

Jayawardena, K. and Pinto-Jayawardena, K. 2017. *Search for Justice: The Sri Lanka Papers*. New Delhi: Zubaan.

Keating, C., Rasmussen, C. and Rishi, P. 2010. 'The Rationality of Empowerment: Microcredit, Accumulation by Dispossession, and the Gendered Economy', *Signs: Journal of Women in Culture and Society* 36 (1): 153–76.

Krinsky, C. 2008. 'Introduction: Moral Panic Concepts' in *The Ashgate Research Companion to Moral Concepts*. Abingdon: Ashgate Publishing.

Lakshman, W. D. 1996. 'Socio-economic Impact of Structural Adjustment Policies in Sri Lanka'. Discussion Paper 6. Perth: Edith Cowan University, Centre for Development Studies.

Lanka Business News. 2016. 'Sanasa Bank PBT Tops Rs. 1 bn with Impressive Growth', *Lanka Business News*, 25 April, www.dailynews.lk/2016/04/25/business/79647

LeBaron, G. and Roberts, A. 2010. 'Towards a Feminist Political Economy of Capitalism and Carcerality', Signs: *Journal of Women in Culture and Society* 36 (1): 19–44.

Lynch, C. 2007. *Juki Girls, Good Girls: Gender and Cultural Politics in Sri Lanka's Global Garment Industry*. Ithaca and London: Cornell University Press.

Maclean, K. 2012. 'Banking on Women's Labour: Responsibility, Risk and Control in Village Banking in Bolivia', *Journal of International Development* 24 (1): 100–11.

Mies, M. 1987. *Patriarchy and Accumulation on a World Scale*. London: Zed Books.

Minister of Finance. 2017. 'Budget Speech'. Sri Jayawardenapura Kotte: Parliament of Sri Lanka.

Mitchell, K. and Beckett, K. 2008. 'Securing the Global City: Crime, Consulting, Risk, and Ratings in the Production of Urban Space', *Indiana Journal of Global Legal Studies* 15 (1): 75–100.

Moore, D. 2015. 'Conflict and After: Primitive Accumulation, Hegemonic Formation and Democratic Deepening', *Stability: International Journal of Security and Development* 4 (1): 1–21.

Morduch, J. 1999. 'The Microfinance Promise', *Journal of Economic Literature* 37: 1569–614.

Murray, C. 2001. *Livelihoods Research: Some Conceptual and Methodological Issues*. Manchester: CPRC.

Nagaraj, V. K. 2015. 'War, Conflict and Development: Towards Reimagining Dominant Approaches', *Economic and Political Weekly*, 28 February.

Ní Aoláin, F. 2012. 'Advancing Feminist Positioning in the Field of Criminal Justice', *International Journal of Transitional Justice* 6: 205–28.

Nordstrom, C. 2004. *Shadow Wars: Violence, Power and International Profiteering in the Twenty-first Century*. Berkeley: University of California Press.

Okin, S. M. 1991. *Justice, Gender and the Family*. New York: Basic Books.

Rafeek, M. I. M. and Samaratunga, P. A. 2000. *An Analysis of Competitiveness of the Rice Sector in Sri Lanka*. Peradeniya: Socio Economic and Planning Center, Department of Agriculture.

Raven-Roberts, A. 2013. 'Women and the Political Economy of War' in Cohn, C. (ed.), *Women and Wars: Contested Histories Uncertain Futures*. Cambridge: Polity Press.

Ruwanpura, K. 2000. *Structural Adjustment, Gender and Employment: The Sri Lankan Experience*. Geneva: International Labour Organization.

Satkunanathan, A. 2017. 'Sri Lanka: The Impact of Militarization on Women' in Ní Aoláin, F., Cahn, N., Haynes, D. F. and Valji, N. (eds), *The Oxford Handbook of Gender and Conflict*. Oxford: Oxford University Press.

Senanayake, S. M. P. 2002. 'An Overview of the Micro Finance Sector in Sri Lanka', *Savings and Development* 26 (2): 197–222.

Sparr, P. 1994. *Mortgaging Women's Lives: Feminist Critiques of Structural Adjustment*. London: Zed Books.

Sri Lanka Bureau of Foreign Employment. 2013. 'Circular on the Family Background Report'. Colombo: Government of Sri Lanka.

Taghdisi Rad, S. 2015. 'Political Economy of Aid in Conflict: An Analysis of Pre- and Post-Intifada Donor Behaviour in the Occupied Palestinian Territories', *Stability: International Journal of Security and Development* 4 (1): 1–18.

Thistle, S. 2006. *From Marriage to the Market: The Transformation of Women's Lives and Work*. Berkeley: University of California Press.

True, J. 2012. *The Political Economy of Violence against Women*. Oxford and New York: Oxford University Press.

United Nations Development Programme (UNDP). 1990. 'Employment and Poverty Alleviation Project', 3 volumes. Colombo: mimeo.

Venugopal, R. 2003. 'The Global Dimensions of Conflict in Sri Lanka'. Paper presented at the conference on 'Globalisation and Self-Determination Movements', Pomona College, 21–22 January.

Vogel, L. 2000. *Marxism and the Oppression of Women: Toward a Unitary Theory*. Chicago: Haymarket Books.

Weber, H. 2006. 'The Global Political Economy of Microfinance and Poverty Reduction: Locating "Livelihoods" in Political Analysis' in Fernando, J. (ed.), *Microfinance: Perils and Prospects*. London and New York: Routledge, Taylor and Francis.

Wijedasa, N. 2014. 'North in Debt Trap', *The Sunday Times*, 7 December, www.sundaytimes.lk/141207/news/north-in-a-debt-trap-131679.html

Young, S. 2010. 'The "Moral Hazards" of Microfinance: Restructuring Rural Credit in India', *Antipode* 42 (1): 201–23.

## 2 | ENDING VIOLENCE AGAINST WOMEN IN PAPUA NEW GUINEA'S HIGHLANDS REGION: THE ROLE OF THE STATE, LOCAL CIVIL SOCIETY AND EXTRACTIVE INDUSTRIES

*Elizabeth Cox*[1]

### Introduction

This chapter explores the political economy of violence against women in Hela and Jiwaka, two newly established and conflict-affected provinces in the Highlands Region of Papua New Guinea (PNG). It examines the role of the state, civil society and extractive industry in addressing PNG's post-independence legacies of patriarchy, violent conflict and violence against women in PNG's Highlands Region. In these 'new provinces', the state is tasked with building public infrastructure, effective civil service and service delivery – virtually from scratch. The chapter maps conflict and violence against women in both provinces and asserts that abrogation of state responsibility, the absence of civil society and failure to broker peace or enforce laws to protect women and girls are the face of extractive-led development, behind which multidimensional violent relations are at play.

The drafters of PNG's constitution drew on human rights norms and standards as well as lessons learned from resource-rich, extractive industry-driven African and Latin American economies. They urged caution and restraint in exploiting PNG's known vast natural resource wealth, to prevent environmental destruction, alienation of customary owned lands and neglect of a promising agricultural sector. They predicted that unregulated extractive industries would leave future generations dispossessed and prone to conflict (Papua New Guinea Constitutional Planning Committee, 1974). However, since PNG's independence in 1975, a succession of male-dominated national and local governments have forged an extractives-dependent economy that has exacerbated the urban–rural divide and high-level corruption and have prioritised 'awe and envy' capital city infrastructure development and hosting expensive showcase international events while a large proportion of the rural population languishes in hardship from 'drying funds for much needed goods and services' (Sawang, 2017).

Extractive industry revenues have led to reckless state spending and have failed to translate into more equitable and inclusive development. Despite several 'boom decades',[2] a high proportion of remote, rural Highlands citizens still live without roads, electricity or a safe water supply. PNG's rates of maternal and infant mortality, illiteracy, corruption and crimes of violence against women (VAW) are ranked among the highest in the world. The remote Highlands provinces hosting extractive industries remain severely underdeveloped, conflict-prone and among the most dangerous places in the world to be female. State resolve to accelerate natural resource exploitation remains unshaken by ongoing fiscal management crises, deadly surges of new forms of armed conflict between tribes and land-owning groups and recent natural disasters devastating remote and under-serviced villages within a huge radius around PNG's 'best-performing' key extractive industry sites.

The UN Committee on the Elimination of Discrimination against Women (UNCEDAW) and the UN Special Rapporteur on Violence against Women (UNSRVAW) have urged the PNG government to accelerate implementation of laws focusing on gender-based violence and to deal with a resurgence of armed conflict and many extreme forms of VAW, which are particularly prevalent in Highlands provinces. For almost three decades, Australian aid and external advisers have led efforts to strengthen PNG's law and justice systems, including funding VAW-dedicated facilities in the police and health systems and piloting a national strategy to prevent and respond to gender-based violence. Aid to local non-government organisations (NGOs) that address conflict and VAW is indirect and channelled through international NGOs and a select few local NGOs that have considerable corporate sponsorship.

The emergence, growth and capacity of civil society organisations (CSOs) is highly uneven across PNG's provinces. Few provinces have progressive women's rights organisations sufficiently networked, informed and resourced to translate global standards for women's rights and recent VAW laws and policies into local education, advocacy and demand for state accountability. Few progressive local organisations have access to direct funding and the autonomy, agency and voice needed to advocate and influence the state or powerful corporations.

*Patriarchy, conflict and gendered violence – enduring and resurgent*

PNG is comprised of a National Capital District (the capital and seat of government), twenty largely rural provinces and a former province (now the post-conflict Autonomous Region of Bougainville or AROB); the latter was disrupted by a mining-related civil war, has taken decades to recover, and is currently preparing for a referendum on independence from the PNG state (see Box 2.1).[3] Jiwaka and Hela are PNG's two 'new provinces', established in 2012. They add to the five existing provinces that constitute the populous inland Highlands Region, where a significant number of PNG's largest resource projects are currently operating and planned (see Figures 2.1 and 2.2 below).

The seven provinces of PNG's Highlands Region are home to 40 per cent of the PNG's total population of over 8 million. The mountainous interior was 'explored' by 'gold hunters' from the early twentieth century, but Australian colonial administration was only established in the Highlands Region after 1950. The colonial administration outlawed tribal fighting and Christian missionaries contributed to 'pacification', but the introduction of coffee, and subsequently extractive industries, created new bases of male rivalry and competition. Shortly after independence (1975), men in the Highlands Region were manufacturing homemade guns, then purchasing factory-made small arms. Neither violent conflict nor crimes of violence could be countered by a weak police force and justice system. By the early 1990s, Australian aid was supporting programmes to strengthen the police, occasionally through heavy-handed responses to Highlands conflict and crime. Deployment of specialised mobile police squads to trouble spots in the Highlands often resulted in state actors razing villages, killing livestock and raping women. Several human rights cases reached the highest courts and the use of mobile squads was, for a time, curtailed.

The state has long been aware of community-based caches of lethal homemade and high-powered weapons that are smuggled into and across the Highlands Region (Alpers, 2004; 2005). Successive governments have ignored urgent recommendations for state action to disarm ordinary citizens, criminal youth and Highlands warriors. But guns and tribal blocs have become important in political campaigns and elections. Guns are also stockpiled by tribes and communities as a form of security, because citizens lack confidence in state policing, law and justice systems. Tribal loyalties are strong, internalised, and serve

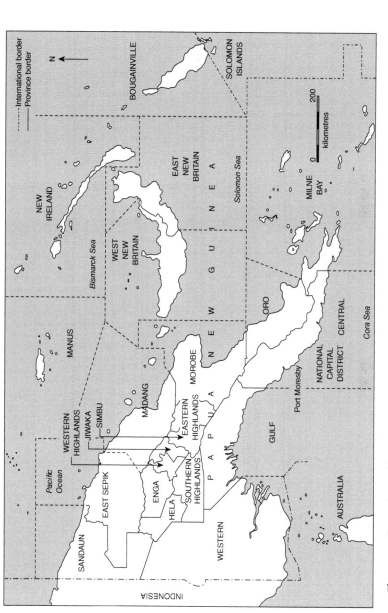

**Figure 2.1** The provinces of Papua New Guinea

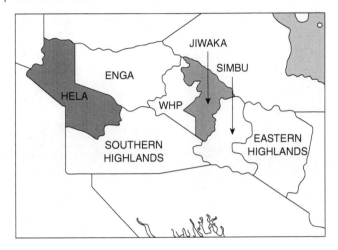

**Figure 2.2** The seven provinces of the Highlands Region of PNG

to mobilise men in a range of local conflicts that continue to undermine peace, justice, democracy and development across contemporary Highlands societies. Within these conflicts, women are increasingly targeted, raped and killed in ways that were not traditionally permitted (Chandler, 2014).[4]

Most land in PNG (97 per cent) remains customary-owned. Most conflicts are mediated in a traditional manner and petty civil and criminal offences are adjudicated in custom-based village courts. Patriarchy is not codified in law and is at odds with fundamental constitutional provisions on equal rights and participation, yet it remains the most powerful norm in the operation of contemporary political and economic institutions, including extractive industry negotiations and benefit-sharing agreements with traditional landowners. Post-independence Highlands societies and their structures and processes of governance and development have accommodated, with impunity, patriarchy and enduring tribal conflict, the proliferation of guns and the escalating normalisation of violence perpetrated against women.

*Late colonialism, a weak state and normalised patriarchy and violence*

PNG's coastal and island regions experienced almost a century of heavy-handed colonial administration, enforced pacification and significant Christian conversions. Over time, they internalised new norms and values and adopted new political, administrative and judicial systems. As a result, violent tribal conflict and traditional customs that dehumanise or harm women and girls were progressively reduced.

In the 1930s, fifty years after the colonisation of PNG's coastal and island regions, gold prospectors and colonial explorers led the first expeditions into the mountainous interior, now known as the Highlands Region. There they encountered large, patriarchal and agricultural societies with complex cultures built on cycles of war, peace, compensation and exchange. Australian colonial rule reached the Highlands Region two decades later, after the Second World War.[5]

In the heavily populated Highlands Region, colonially enforced pacification and efforts to end violent coercion and control over women were short-lived. For two decades before independence in 1975, Highlands men, who persisted with tribal fighting, were regularly arrested and imprisoned. Law-breakers were dealt with in 'native courts' presided over by Australian colonial officers, often ill-equipped to understand, intervene or adjudicate appropriately in cases of complex traditional cycles of violent conflict and gender-based violence. Highlands men brought before colonial courts developed strategies to avoid prison sentences or at least minimise the impact of imprisonment on customary political and economic activities and obligations that were integrally linked to the ownership of land, the control of women and transactions of valuable traditional currency (Reay, 2014).

Anthropological studies among the tribes of the (new) Hela and Jiwaka provinces commenced in the late 1940s and provide an important snapshot of traditional gender relations. They reported marriages characterised by high levels of violent male control over women's fertility and productive labour. Powerful Highlands men were traditionally permitted many wives and flirtations. Fathers and brothers arranged the marriages of pubescent girls to men who might already have many wives and be elderly, if they offered a high bride price and strategic economic and political ties for the young bride's male relatives. Defiant, resistant and non-conforming women and girls were subject to violent punishment by the husband's family and stigmatisation and banishment from their own family and community (Harvey-Kelley, 1997; Reay, 2014; Wardlow, 2006). Women accused of adultery, imagined or actual, were punished with brutal beatings, marital rape and gang rape. Female suicide was not uncommon (Reay, 1959; 1966; 2014; Read, 1965; Strathern, 1972; Josephides, 1975).

Delivering justice to females in colonial 'native courts' proved too complex and fraught for young and inexperienced male colonial magistrates (Read, 1965; Harvey-Kelley, 1997; Reay, 2014) and the rudimentary colonial social welfare system introduced in coastal areas barely touched the Highlands. Violent conflict, coercive control of women, child marriages and polygamy have persisted post-independence, enabled by the progressive transition into a cash economy that commenced with colonisation.

Highlands combatants manufacture guns and purchase military-style assault weapons (Alpers, 2004; 2005; ICRC, 2017b). Internal displacement due to conflict is widespread and can last for decades. Internally displaced persons (IDPs) who are forced to seek refuge on the land of 'friendly' neighbouring tribes depend on their hosts' resources to survive and incur debt. Indebtedness heightens IDP women's vulnerability to violence by opportunistic, sexual predators in the host community. When displaced, men focus on raising cash to purchase (illegal) arms for revenge attacks, to reclaim their land and livelihood resources and to redeem their masculinity. Self-styled warlords emerge among displaced men, demand taxes from their tribespeople to buy arms, obligate male 'tribesmen' (and boys) to join in revenge fights, and pressure women and girls to raise funds and engage in the illegal trade in ammunition (Be'Soer, 2012).[6]

Highlands tribal conflicts result in massive loss of property and economic resources and direct and indirect loss of lives. Petty incidents involving contested allocations of extractive industry rents and benefits and disputed election results ignite ancient feuds and enmities. Traditional conflict resolution can take up to ten years when peacemaking rests on demands for inflated, cash-based compensation payments. Thousands of productive members of Highlands farming communities may be internally displaced, their coffee plantations and small businesses destroyed and their access to large tracts of productive land denied. Women's agricultural production is vital to subsistence, food security and local trade, but inter-tribal conflict can transform their gardens to no-go zones and virtual wastelands for decades. The economic and social impacts are huge and the high levels of trauma largely overlooked.

Some local women leaders and their organisations have documented the gendered impacts and social and economic costs of conflict for at least a decade. They highlight women's reduced mobility, agricultural productivity and financial autonomy, and their increased vulnerability to crimes of sexual violence.[7] High prevalence and long periods of internal displacement resulting from Highlands inter-communal conflict have only recently been acknowledged. Expanding extractive industries pose additional challenges to ending conflict and violence against women in the Highlands. The trickledown of cash to local men increases access to the trade in illegal guns, exacerbates conflict, and heightens the terrorisation and victimisation of women.

## Extractive industries, men's conflict and women's marginalisation

In 2018, thirty-three companies were operating extractive industry (EI) projects in PNG, many of them large scale and located in remote and underdeveloped parts of the country. 'Fly-in fly out' (FIFO) operations are staffed by large, highly mobile, predominantly male expatriate and national employees. High-security EI enclaves are surrounded by displaced landowning communities anticipating significant rents and royalties, and mushrooming makeshift settlements of opportunistic, inter-provincial EI migrants: informal traders, alluvial miners, miners of tailings, pimps and sex workers.

Global contractors providing security for EI plants and companies heavily subsidise the operations of the regular local police (transport, accommodation, meals, uniforms, vehicles and fuel) but they are often overwhelmed by the heightened local conflicts that emerge as armed local tribes contest land ownership and compete for benefits, and they are often 'out-gunned' by the high-powered weaponry used by protesters in the surrounding community (Alpers, 2004; 2005; Main, 2017). As the state becomes more dependent on the flow of extractive industry revenues, it frequently invokes state of emergency powers to prevent disruption of EI operations. Special mobile police units and military personnel are regularly deployed to protect EI plants and quell resurgent protest and conflict, but their impact is limited and shortlived, and the root causes of violence remain unresolved. Some of the larger EI projects in the Highlands currently operate under continuous states of emergency, and with a heavy military presence.

Extractive-led development perpetuates the marginalisation and containment of women. State mechanisms and processes dealing with extractive industries regard men (only) as customary landowners, justifying the exclusion of women from direct receipt of royalty and equity benefits. State and EI corporates have normalised women's place as, at best, the last and least paid in unjust, male-controlled, intra-clan distribution systems of cash-based royalties. World Bank-funded 'Women in Mining' (WIM) programmes were proposed in response to concerns raised by women in EI-impacted communities. Two decades of WIM efforts channelled through private-sector and state entities have failed to support the formation of independent local women's organisations. Rather, EI companies tend to artificially 'construct' women's organisations that are led by their local female employees or favoured local leaders.

WIM programmes are essentially welfare-oriented and based on outdated notions of family and gender-based power dynamics (Wardlow, 2014; Macintyre, 2011). They typically deliver outmoded, conservative training to pacify and domesticate local women, rather than provide information, education and understanding of their fast-changing society and economy. They do not strengthen women's voice and agency to effectively identify, articulate and advocate their priorities, needs and concerns – including their exclusion from benefit sharing and their desire to end violent conflict in public and private domains. Australia's gender equality aid window is currently funding several partnership initiatives that involve mining companies, their corporate social responsibility (CSR) arms and international NGOs and are aimed at greater inclusion of women in decision making around EI benefit sharing and ways to address violence against women and girls. These *post facto* efforts may be too little, too late, and are unlikely to succeed without long-term support for the emergence, growth and sustainability of strong women's rights organisations and a supportive local civil society. Formation of human capital in the fast-changing context of extractives will take decades, and the best catalysts are the most dynamic local leaders, supported and linked to networks for solidarity and knowledge sharing with local women's organisations and those human rights defenders that have made the most progress in ending conflict and VAW. Embedded support for the bottom-up empowerment of local women leaders and activists and their organisations and networks cannot be found in any of the districts that currently host large-scale extractive industries.

## Hela's triple trauma: extractives, armed conflict and violence against women

In 2012, Hela Province was carved out of PNG's oil-rich Southern Highlands, where infrastructural development was accelerated by several decades of public works support from a special engineering unit of the Australian Defence Force. Over the past twenty-five years, Hela's people (formerly Southern Highlanders) have hosted several large-scale, high-tech oil and gas projects, sustained in remote enclaves, far away from public scrutiny. Various corporate community relations strategies and state security interventions have kept their often turbulent operations out of the public eye. Local people have witnessed successive deployments of police and military special forces to put down landowner unrest and protest; these have been treated as 'tribal fights' that threatened the security and continuity of the oil and gas plants that provide very significant state revenues and power PNG's largest gold mine in neighbouring Enga Province. National elections in Southern Highlands Province were violent in 1992 and 1997 and failed in 2002. In 2006, a state of emergency was declared, and the army was deployed to restore order and oversee the 2007 elections. Large numbers of locals have migrated to the capital city. The 2012 elections were mired in unrest, and, following the 2017 elections, instability has persisted in the provincial capital of Mendi town, once more hostage to hordes of armed, disgruntled voters.

The persistence of conflict and the proliferation of guns have been seriously understated in the extractive industries' CSR and community development reporting (Burton and Onguglo, 2018). Corporate community development (CCD) programmes around the oilfields of Southern Highlands involved EI corporate partnerships in the 'top-down creation' of local women's organisations and an NGO. These initiatives purported to give women greater access to benefits but did not support their empowerment or give them agency or voice. A senior female representative of PNG's Department of Petroleum and Energy noted the negative gendered impacts of the Southern Highlands largest oil projects (Yuyuge, 2003). By the late 1990s, state service delivery had significantly declined across the EI-impacted areas of Southern Highlands and the lead developer, Oil Search, assumed corporate responsibility for the delivery of almost all basic health services.

The establishment of Hela Province in 2012, covering three districts that were formerly in the Southern Highlands Province, was the outcome of thirty-six years of local male leaders' advocacy, justified by a specific indigenous religious and prophetic world view and aspirations for unity and identity (Zurenuoc and Herbert, 2017). First steps towards the political transition into a new province coincided with and were reinvigorated by negotiations to start up the Papua New Guinea Liquified Natural Gas (PNG LNG) project on Hela's customary-owned land. ExxonMobil, Oil Search and Santos,[8] joint venture partners of the PNG LNG project, promised huge and 'transformative' economic benefits for the state, the province (employment) and landowners at the source of the gas (royalties and rents). In early 2018, Exxon announced its plans to almost double the facility's export capacity to 16 million tonnes per year, together with its joint venture partners. Meanwhile, they are accelerating efforts to start producing from nearby gas reserves by 2023 or 2024 to supply rapidly growing demand for LNG in Asia fuelled by a lack of new projects in other parts of the world.

Hela Province is home to several ethnic groups, but the Huli people predominate. First contact reports (circa 1934) and early anthropological accounts of Huli society described poor soils, food insecurity, 'unsettled and conflictual nature' (Allen and Frankel, 1991) and endemic warfare. The Huli, Duna and other major ethnic groups share common ancestry and mythology. Their prophesies include 'a strong sense of decline and deterioration of the earth and cultural decay into anarchy and immorality' (ibid.). Ethnic cooperation and commitment to ancient beliefs and cultural links, customs and ceremonies have been disrupted by the decisions of Huli tribes over the past twenty-five years to give land over to gold and gas projects.[9]

The township of Tari is the provincial 'capital' and administrative centre of new Hela Province. In the 1980s it was a lively district centre and home to a promising and entrepreneurial women's association. However, the unity, successful enterprise and aspirations of organised Tari women were violently undermined during a brief, disruptive and overwhelming gold rush in the late 1980s. The initial chaos and lawlessness of alluvial mining was displaced by highly contested and ultimately aborted efforts of mining giant Conzinc Riotinto of Australia (CRA), together with joint venture partners, to start up the Mount Kare gold mine. The low-cost Tari women's tea house/guest house turned into a frontier transit house for male alluvial gold miners from all over PNG. The leaders and members of the enterprising Tari Women's Association were divided when factions fought over potential EI benefits and pressured women to align with 'their brothers' in rival landowning tribes.

In 2009, Rex Tillerson, then CEO of ExxonMobil, led negotiations for a joint venture partnership to exploit Hela's vast natural gas reserves for export to China and Japan. Construction of the PNG LNG project commenced rapidly once agreement was reached between the PNG state, a formative provincial government, barely existing local governments and self-identified (now heavily contested) customary male landowners. The state and the lead operator (Exxon) promised that PNG LNG would transform the national economy, boosting GDP through export revenues, local employment and spin-off contracts, and providing royalties, social and economic infrastructure and services to the landowners. The US$19 billion project imported a large, foreign, skilled workforce (80 per cent) and constructed an impressive gas-processing plant and 700 kilometres of overland and underwater pipeline in record time. During this 'construction phase', national staff (20 per cent) held mostly short-term unskilled and security roles. The state reiterated the project's transformative potential and prepared a new national development vision and strategy centred on PNG LNG's anticipated revenues. Wages for workers, compensation for land use and relocation were paid promptly in this construction phase and would have boosted Huli men's acquisition of high-powered, military-style weapons, smuggled across PNG's borders with Indonesia and Australia and, allegedly, also supplied through local politicians, businessmen and rogue police.

Gun proliferation has created a heightened state of anarchy and lawlessness in Hela's underdeveloped administrative centre, Tari town. Local police are overwhelmed and 'outgunned' and frequently call for state reinforcements – both military and police. In late 2016, Tari town descended into crisis with defiant public display of weapons in the hands of local young men. Repeated drive-by shootings that forced the closure of shops and banks, the airstrip, hospital and schools prompted local businesses and public servants to consider leaving Tari for good. The state responded with the deployment of 150 soldiers and 150 police from special mobile units. A gun amnesty, which was mostly about protecting and preventing costly disruption of the PNG LNG operations and the imminent (2017) elections, cost K11 million (approximately US$3.4 million) over two months and was largely unsuccessful. Elected leaders, who monopolise local businesses including hire cars and guest houses, benefited most from recurrent state deployments of special security forces. The failure to ensure strong foundations for state law and justice in the new Hela Province has resulted in more people buying arms to safeguard their lives and property.[10]

PNG LNG exports commenced ahead of schedule in mid-2014. However, due diligence was not done, and the state failed to identify authentic landowners or facilitate mandatory incorporated landowner groups (ILGs). By 2018, PNG LNG was reaching full production, but land ownership was heavily contested and the state could not confirm who should receive royalties and equities and what form of cash benefit distribution would prevent the escalation of conflict (Filer, 2016; Main, 2017).[11] The total amount of outstanding royalties currently owed to Hela landowners has reportedly reached billions, but the state is not delivering and local resource owners are increasingly angry and frustrated.

Hela is the most resource-rich province of PNG, but among the poorest performing in social and economic development. PNG's 2005 Small Arms Survey reported that all Huli men have a gun; these are mostly homemade but included 2,500 high-powered weapons (Alpers, 2004; 2005). A decade later, with the PNG LNG project in full production, no one really knows how many high-powered guns are in the possession of Huli men. By 2017, local armed youth were committing unprecedented random armed attacks on rural communities, terrorising and displacing remote populations. In 2018, the state's administrative presence and banking services were reduced to skeleton operations, guarded by military personnel. Women reported high levels of terror and violence, sniper attacks, executions and decreased access to justice and medical support when subjected to violence.

Prior to the start of the PNG LNG project, Oxfam conducted participatory research on violent conflict and gender-based violence against women in Tari, the provincial capital of Hela Province. The report confirmed low levels of education in Hela society (30 per cent literacy for women, 41 per cent for men), limited transport, communication and basic goods and services, high levels of deadly armed conflict among men and crimes of extreme violence committed with impunity by men against women. The village court system was dysfunctional, district court services were absent, the police and human and financial resources were inadequate, and the prison was neglected and not operating. Judges, state ministers and donor representatives visiting Tari town needed armed state security escorts. Mobile police forces were frequently deployed to protect existing EI projects. Hospital data confirmed that physical trauma was the most common cause of hospitalisation and death in Tari and many survivors urgently required post-traumatic counselling. Men's traumatic injuries were sustained in violent dispute resolution and ongoing tribal conflicts, while women's traumatic injuries resulted from husbands, fathers, brothers and co-wives committing grievous bodily harm, including stabbing and severing of limbs (Kopi, 2011). A second report commissioned by Oxfam and several faith-based agencies covered impacts and threats to human security during the PNG LNG construction phase. The report highlighted the need for more time and space for the state and civil society to work together to build peace in their new province and to strengthen human development and improve the status of women well before the onslaught of EI impacts further sidelined them (McIlraith, 2012).

Oxfam's findings on Tari's high levels of violence and poor state health services prompted the international humanitarian NGO Médecins Sans Frontières (MSF) to establish a presence in the local hospital. Government medical staff lacked resources for emergency surgical care, major and minor surgery, so MSF established these facilities and a thirty-bed inpatient facility. Up to a quarter of the eighty to a hundred surgeries conducted monthly were for injuries caused by physical trauma – typically bodies chopped with axes and digits and limbs severed by machetes, perpetrated by men against men in local conflicts and men against women in family and spousal violence. MSF built more evidence of the terrible impact of armed tribal conflict and physical and sexual violence against women and girls and confirmed that Hela men's fury is a significant contributing factor to the high incidence of new forms of warfare and horrific crimes of violence committed by men against their female family members.

In 2009, MSF established a specialist family support centre[12] in Tari hospital to provide psychological and medical first aid, HIV prophylaxis and emergency contraception to women and girl survivors. Many thousands of cases of family and sexual violence are treated each year in Tari family support centre, but, following hospital care, there are no safe houses or support services available to women survivors. The ongoing lack of security for MSF personnel at Tari hospital often resulted in threatened hospital closure, and, after eight years of dedicated services, MSF exited Hela Province in 2015 (MSF, 2011; 2016).

Over the past six years, the International Committee of the Red Cross (ICRC) has documented and responded to the escalation of tribal fighting in Hela, flying in and out, mostly on post-conflict, humanitarian missions to support IDPs. ICRC regards the surge in tribal conflicts as more like small-scale warfare, where increasingly armed combatants target civilian non-combatants, women and children and destroy houses, food gardens, cash crops, livestock and household possessions, as well as churches and health and education services. ICRC informs local communities on international humanitarian law in order to discourage increasing attacks on non-combatant persons and property and the killing of women and children.

There are few local NGOs active in Hela. The Tari Women's Association, which was very active in the 1980s, is now largely defunct. Young Ambassadors for Peace (YAP), established for the Southern Highlands Province in 2003, is associated with a local church and has worked with Oxfam and now ICRC in Tari. The male-led YAP aims to bring about a cultural shift among the tribes of Hela through peace building and capacity development for early intervention and mediation to prevent small disputes escalating into tribal conflict. In 2008, prior to the inception of PNG LNG, YAP was instrumental in the signing of a peace agreement between thirty-two warring clans in Tari. By 2017, YAP leaders reported feeling overwhelmed by the normalisation of conflict and guns, the lack of state accountability to broker peace, and the lack of resources to conduct their own local programmes (ICRC, 2017a).

The international NGOs – MSF, ICRC and Oxfam – have not supported the formation and growth of local women's organisations. PNG LNG operators have built new infrastructure in Tari under tax credit schemes, but other planned townships have failed to materialise. Workers' barracks have been looted and new women's resource centres have been burned down in landowner protests.[13] Hela's women live off the land in remote villages, sit in the rough dirt marketplaces to trade for small cash incomes and suffer greatly from violence perpetrated by increasingly discontent men as the rudimentary services available to them decline.

Men's violence against women in Hela Province ranks among the worst in PNG, comparable to the world's worst conflict-affected regions. Between 2015 and 2017 there were many violent tribal conflicts and many deaths in Hela. Tari town and Hela Province are now generally considered too dangerous for international NGOs or volunteers to reside and operate there. After MSF exited Hela in 2015, Oil Search Foundation (OSF), the CSR arm of joint venture partner Oil Search,[14] assumed management of Tari hospital and later the delivery of rural health services. In the process, some of the best-trained local gender-based violence trauma counselling staff were lost and took up employment with a children's library – another OSF community development initiative in Tari.

Hela's women have been politically and economically excluded from local EI project planning and benefit sharing. They must now cope with multiple layers and escalating levels of trauma – deadly, armed conflict and extreme, often fatal violence against women and girls. This nightmare situation became hellish in February 2018 when a powerful 7.5 magnitude earthquake struck the most remote, rugged and least developed parts of the PNG Highlands. With its epicentre at Exxon's key gas plants, the quakes triggered landslides that buried villages and destroyed infrastructure. An estimated 150 people were killed, hundreds were injured and thousands were traumatised – dispossessed and displaced (Davidson, 2018). People already displaced by tribal fighting were displaced once more when homes in their host villages were destroyed. Aftershocks were ongoing for three months and 270,000 people were left in need of urgent assistance, including 125,000 children (UN News, 2018a). Armed conflict and the targeting of women were resurgent in this period, overwhelming UN and humanitarian plans to create safe spaces for women to recover (UN News, 2018b). Oil Search quickly restored its oil and gas operations, and OSF mobilised its resources – especially infrastructure and transport – to lead a large-scale humanitarian response.

In 2017, when gun violence surged in Hela, random attacks on remote villages were led by youthful males with high-powered weapons, looking for any excuse to execute innocent civilians.[15] Local police estimated that a third of the population was displaced by this terrorism. Courageous local women leaders united to lead a cross-country campaign during the sixteen days of 'Activism against Violence against Women'. They worked day and night, documented in photographs and film, and wrote a press release that they hoped would alert the state and the wider world to their plight. But they were sponsored by Exxon, and the press release was edited and its publication delayed. The anticipated impact was not realised and Hela women were deeply disappointed. Nothing changed.

In 2018, after the earthquake hit Hela, youthful armed violence escalated again. Humanitarian relief action that required people – especially women – to congregate made them more vulnerable to roving armed gangs and snipers. Churches, schools and health facilities were shut down. Most aid programmes were suspended, and only humanitarian relief activities proceeded. Hela women desperately sought a light at the end of the tunnel. Their associates brought their situation to the attention of the Australian government, Australian NGOs and Oil Search. They put forward a proposal to establish a phased community-to-community solidarity and learning exchange with Voice for Change and the Highlands Women Human Rights Defenders Movement as their willing hosts and mentors. The total budget for an intensive, twelve-month programme was less than half the cost of one external consultant. After a brief exchange of letters and an expression of interest in this locally led 'out of the box' strategy, again nothing happened. And again, Hela women were disappointed. Nothing changed.

### Where there are no extractives: Highlands women build equality, development and peace

PNG's Highlands Highway climbs up and across PNG, from the industrial city and port of Lae through the Eastern Highlands Province, Simbu Province, Jiwaka Province and the Western Highlands Province. Built in the 1960s to facilitate the acceleration of colonial administration and agriculture, it now links the seven provinces of the Highlands Region. The highway is a vital supply route for the extractive industries in Enga, Southern Highlands and Hela, but is considered too dangerous for the movement of EI personnel, who are flown in and out on chartered flights. Mount Hagen in Western Highlands is PNG's third largest town, and a hub for transiting local and EI employees, truck drivers and EI migrants, mostly from other Highlands provinces. Mount Hagen city is notorious for its high levels of crime and violence, drug and sex trafficking and illegal trade in marijuana, gold and guns. In this chaotic context, local women negotiate myriad forms of violence in public transport, public markets and on the streets. Established church-based programmes and local CSOs and international NGOs struggle to coordinate their efforts to counter violent conflict and violence against women.

To the west are the three most remote of the seven Highlands provinces (Enga, Southern Highlands and Hela), all heavily impacted by large-scale gold, oil or gas projects that the state and investors frequently refer to as 'world class' and the 'dynamic drivers' of PNG's economy. Since the late 1980s, barely a decade after PNG's independence, these provinces have seen a resurgence in tribal conflict led by youthful warriors armed with increasingly high-powered weapons. The triggers, motivation and consequences of these conflicts are vastly different to traditional warfare (Banks et al., 2018; Burton and Onguglo, 2018; Wiessner, 2006; Wiessner and Pupu, 2012). Traditional rules of engagement have changed as a generation of culturally dislocated youth 'own' the fights and acquire fearful status as 'hired guns', 'heroes' and 'warlords' – owners of the fight, snipers and executioners.

To the east are three Highlands provinces (Eastern Highlands, Simbu and Jiwaka) where there are no extractive industries, and where, since the early 1990s, homegrown, women-led NGOs have made significant progress in countering patriarchy, armed conflict and multidimensional discrimination and violence against women. Over the last decade, local women's organisations in these three provinces have partnered with international NGOs and have grown in capacity, outreach and coordination within and across the Highlands provinces. The bravest women activists and leaders are united by the Highlands Women Human Rights Defenders Movement, which extends across the three provinces, strengthening local and provincial safety nets for women. Their demands for rapid police responses and improved access to justice are increasingly being heard. They have successfully engaged local men in advocacy and actions in support of women's human rights and day-to-day safety and security. The gendered impacts of conflict are addressed in all conflict mediation, a critical early intervention in which women are now actively participating, standing alongside their male counterparts.

Highlands provinces that do not have extractive industries (with the exception of Western Highlands) are currently performing better than many coastal provinces, as they work strategically, systematically and in unity to end conflict and violence against women. They are confronting historical continuities of patriarchy and tribal conflict and the contemporary proliferation of high-powered weapons and marijuana production, consumption and trade. This is clearly evidenced in Jiwaka Province, which was established simultaneously with Hela Province and is the newest of the Highlands' extractives-free provinces. Jiwaka is located centrally in the Highlands Region and straddles the Highlands Highway. It was created to give the Waghi people greater political representation and improved access to state administration, goods and services. The creation of Jiwaka was also intended to increase development opportunities for the majority remote, rural and agricultural communities.

Jiwaka's coffee industry, established pre-independence, developed as a male domain, entrenching a gendered cash crop–food crop divide in Highlands agriculture. It was intended to accelerate smallholders' entry to the cash economy, but customary 'big men' soon became local 'coffee barons', consolidating smallholdings and seeding capitalism in Highlands society (Donaldson and Good, 1998; MacWilliam, 2013).

Jiwaka's women lead in the province's dynamic and continuously diversifying food production and trade. This is the backbone of Jiwaka's local economy, family livelihoods and inter-provincial trade along the Highlands Highway, up into the remote mining enclaves and down into PNG's two largest cities. Jiwaka's greatest productive resources are customary-owned fertile land, industrious and proficient female farmers and road access to inter-provincial markets. But this economic productivity is regarded as informal, and rarely counted.

Large-scale EI projects operating in neighbouring provinces since the late 1980s have had a range of indirect negative impacts on the districts that now make up Jiwaka Province. These impacts occur through the employment of some local men, who become absent husbands and fathers, often neglecting their wives and children. Jiwakan men (and men from other provinces) working in extractive industries have money and are highly mobile. When they come home on regular leave, they frequently indulge their male friends and relatives in drunken binges that disturb families and communities and waste money. They also contribute to the inflation of bride-price payments that are often linked to child brides and polygamy. The transitory highway truck drivers buy sex and young brides, adding significantly to the Highlands' high rates of HIV transmission (McCallum, 2012; Voice for Change, 2015).

In spite of these external impacts, being an extractives-free province is a blessing for Jiwaka, as its leaders, civil servants and citizens set about envisioning and building their new province. Jiwaka has the opportunity to develop its human capital and to learn about its constitution, human rights, domestic law and state development policies. Civil society is emerging and uniting to support human development and complement the work of the formative provincial government in building Jiwaka's infrastructure and machinery of provincial and local governance. Jiwaka's civil society includes faith-based organisations (FBOs) that have been active for many years in health (including HIV and AIDS), adult education and some women and youth organisations. In Jiwaka's 'extractives-free' context, women citizens – many of them survivors of conflict and family and interpersonal violence – are organising and emerging as leaders, enabling the people of their province to work towards a collective vision for a future free of conflict and violence against women.

Jiwaka's local NGO, Voice for Change (VFC), is a secular, home-grown women's rights organisation, founded in 2003 by a Jiwakan woman agriculturalist. Experienced in gender in agricultural policy, programmes and markets across the Highlands Region, she knew how violent conflict disrupts and displaces communities, preventing agricultural extension workers from routinely reaching and delivering vital technical and marketing support to women. In the course of their work, both female agricultural extension workers and female farmers or long-distance traders, who must frequently travel through Jiwaka's remote rural areas, were constantly at risk of violent sexual assault. Women's incomes supported their families and sustained cultural obligations, including bride-price payments and compensation payments for restorative justice and peacemaking. But women in local markets endured dangerous and insecure conditions and multiple layers of exploitation and harassment. Men used their disposable cash, mostly from coffee, for local travel, leisure and pleasure. VFC's founder also knew well that in Highlands society women's productive agricultural labour and trade were not recognised or counted and that government agencies and services must become more gender aware and responsive so that women can directly participate in and benefit from development and change. Further, continuing violent conflict and violence against women in the private and public domains would prevent the new province from prospering.

VFC gradually grew into a strong women's rights organisation. Early programmes offered technical advice on food crop production, on trade, and on informal savings clubs that enabled women to manage and control their incomes. Many members were found to be survivors of systemic physical and psychological violence committed by their husbands, including neglect, resulting from polygamy and absenteeism. Shared experience as 'survivors' of conflict, violence and polygamy galvanised members' determination to save their incomes in order to access justice in village courts. Village court magistrates demand a sitting fee, and if women seek a divorce, they are usually ordered to repay their bride price.

Many VFC members had experienced long years of internal displacement resulting from ongoing tribal conflicts. They had survived harassment, rape and forced marriages while living as IDPs on other tribes' land and resources. They struggled to control their own incomes or save, because husbands and male relatives frequently commandeered their cash to purchase arms and ammunition for revenge attacks or to finance male-led peace ceremonies, extravagant bride-price payments, compensation payments and political campaigns. By 2008, VFC's leaders were building new knowledge regarding the impact of Highlands tribal conflict on women and the local economy. They organised, strategised and advocated to end local wars and discrimination and violence against women and girls and consciously adopted the post-Beijing rallying call of the global feminist movement – gender equality, development and peace – because it captured what Jiwakan women wanted most (Be'Soer, 2012).

By 2012, when the new province of Jiwaka was declared, VFC was already scaling up its provincial programme. VFC analysed Jiwaka's cycles of conflict, the build-up of guns, the exclusion, alienation and anger of male youth and the resulting multiple forms of violence committed against women and girls. When mapping the forms of violence reported by Jiwakan women, they included the multiple negative impacts of local men commuting in and out of the EI enclaves – their high mobility, long absences and frequent polygamous relationships – as well as the effects of cash-rich landowners and EI employees.

During the past six years, while the establishment of Jiwaka's administrative, legal and judicial systems was still ongoing, VFC built a cadre of women (and men) conflict mediators and trauma counsellors fanning out into its rural and remote districts. Increasingly, women participate in early intervention to prevent minor disputes escalating to full-scale armed tribal fighting. Jiwakan women, with increasing support from their communities, are advocating capped bride-price and customary compensation payments so that women do not become trapped in violent marriages and so that post-conflict peace and normalcy can be restored rapidly, the duration of internal displacement can be greatly reduced, and agricultural production and trade can prosper. Gradually, these are becoming the new norms and standards and some communities are committing to by-laws to prevent conflict and violence against women.

VFC has managed to work in ways that unite community-based organisations (CBOs), FBOs and a range of pre-existing small, local NGOs – a significant achievement in the face of ongoing resource scarcity to fund emerging local civil society. VFC has demonstrated a capacity to raise and manage modest grant funding, and to build strategic partnerships with local NGOs, CBOs and FBOs as well as with state actors in the law and justice, community development and health sectors. VFC trains village court magistrates, peace mediators and elected local government leaders, and is progressively breaking down gender barriers to increase women's political participation. VFC assists communities in developing their own by-laws that are aligned with human rights standards, the PNG constitution and domestic laws to protect women and girls from violence

Modest funds channelled through partner international NGOs and a reliable network of technical and moral supporters have enabled VFC to develop Jiwaka's provincial strategy to prevent and respond to gender-based violence. Effective implementation now requires the provincial government to recognise the vital contribution and role of local civil society, and to make adequate budget allocations. The formalisation of strategic government–CSO partnerships and priority commitments to eliminating disruptive cycles of armed tribal fighting and persistent violence against women are needed to build on the foundation that VFC has gifted this new province.

There are no extractive industries in Jiwaka Province, and, despite its 'newness' and its struggle, it is not among the provinces selected to benefit from the large Australian Aid-funded programme to strengthen law and justice systems. Being an extractive-free new province is a blessing because it provides a space for enlightened women leaders to rise up and to forge links with national and regional feminist networks and partnerships with international NGOs that enable them to access funding for transformative development and change. Jiwaka's progress in ending armed conflict and violence against women is built on local leadership and homegrown strategies and knowledge. Jiwaka's provincial strategy to prevent and respond to gender-based violence was developed locally, through an NGO-led process, without FIFO and highly paid experts or high cost aid inputs. A UN grant of US$300,000 over three years (2013–15) enabled VFC to start scaling up. Dutch aid channelled through an Australian NGO sustained that funding level for a further three years. For US$100,000 per year – the equivalent of one international consultant's annual salary – Jiwaka's VFC has developed a programme and training campus that builds the awareness and capacity of thousands of its citizens – female and male, young and old, urban and rural, religious and secular, government, faith-based and civil society workers. Together they are shaping a shared vision for Jiwaka to be a prosperous new province free of violent conflict and violence against women.

There is no comparable emergence of women-led civil society committed to ending violent conflict and eliminating violence against women in any of the three Highlands societies with extractive industries. By comparison, CSR and CCD interventions led by EI CSR and aid-funded FIFO consultants are costly and unsustainable. They are encumbered and inhibited by corporate and individual safety and security concerns and their operations are regularly suspended. They lack a deep human rights framework and the Highlands style of feminist leadership found in successful programmes in the extractive-free provinces of the Highlands.

### The extractive industry's CSR organisations: de facto state, surrogate civil society

The majority of PNG's women experience interpersonal and sexual violence and are subjected to many forms of violence in the public domain. But ending VAW is not regarded as a priority in national or local planning, policy or budgeting. Current laws to end violence against women are the outcome of long-term advocacy and action led by local non-government women's rights organisations, not the result of political will and state budgetary support.[16] Over the past two decades, programmes to strengthen state enforcement of PNG's hard-won VAW laws and policies were largely donor-dependent, as state resources continue to be directed to securing ongoing exploration, operation and expansion of mining, gas and petroleum projects and rapid modernisation of the capital city. Through expanding tax credit schemes and emerging public–private partnerships, extractive industries contribute directly to expanding modern infrastructure to serve local elites and international workforces, boosting the image of PNG as a prosperous young nation. In recent years they have partnered with donors, other private-sector partners and Femili PNG, a new and rapidly rising NGO, to promote high-profile initiatives to end VAW in PNG's cities. Meanwhile, armed conflict and the brutal control of women are normalised in the 'source provinces'.

The state ignores increasing evidence that violence against women and girls is worse in communities impacted by armed conflict and that both violent conflict and violence against women are exacerbated by extractive industries. Recent studies of CCD activities implemented in mining-impact areas in PNG found that they focus on 'law and order, women's activities, local health services, livelihood programs and support for business development' (Banks et al., 2018). CCD inputs are mostly technical, material and infrastructural. Some are bigger than large donor programmes but are more socially and culturally conservative, 'defensive' and 'depoliticising' (ibid.). CCD initiatives are in constant tension with the more organic and unruly changes ('immanent development') occurring as communities access new economic opportunities and cash flows. Some CCD has the potential to provide long-term support, but 'successful sustainable activities are rare'. Extractive industries' CCD is generally not informed by lessons learned or good practice documented and shared in the mainstream development sector. Such programmes are not subjected to standard monitoring or evaluation obligations and companies have limited ability (or will) to shape the longer-term trajectory of community social and economic change around their projects (ibid.: 208–23).

Burton and Onguglo (2018) analyse state and EI companies' respective responsibilities to PNG communities against the commitments made in the 'disconnected development worlds' of the global mining industry's sustainability agenda, the global development agenda and PNG's national sustainable development planning agenda. Eighty-two per cent of the thirty-three mining companies currently operating in PNG do not report on sustainability indicators.

Only two companies report on indicators regarding their relations with and impacts on indigenous populations, including grievances that landowners may have over mine operations. EI company reports revealed 'a history of obfuscation and denial by companies', including concealment of police and defence force operations in mining neighbourhoods to flush out 'warlords' and deal with outstanding and volatile resettlement issues and protests. For example, there was initial denial then a long delay in responding to multiple incidents of rape and gang rape perpetrated by security staff employed by Canadian company Barrick, which operates Porgera gold mine in the Highlands province of Enga (ibid.: 274–7).

Extractive industry gestures of corporate responsibility – even those claiming to promote gender equality and empower women – are mostly cynical and token (Macintyre, 2011; Wardlow, 2006). Women suffering economic exclusion and high levels of violence in private and public domains are 'gifted' prefabricated resource centres and sewing and cooking classes – this token 'Women in Mining' (WIM) formula has no relevance to women's real-life struggles. World Bank and aid-funded WIM programmes do not provide objective information or reflection on the critical social, political and economic issues and changing gender norms in EI-impacted communities. For example, they do not empower women in impacted communities to challenge the flow of royalties to powerful local men, who claim landowner rights but frequently corruptly abscond without distributing benefits to their clan members or family – or the trickle-down to lower-status men who spend their money on guns or more wives with little regard for the rights and needs of impacted women and children.

Oil Search Limited is the most prominent joint venture partner of ExxonMobil in Hela's gas project. OSF, its CSR arm, aims 'to set the standard for private sector contribution to sustainable development' and has taken the role of EI CSR in local and national development to a whole new level. OSF's 2016 performance summary reported success in lobbying the state for a zero goods and services tax rating for oil and gas exports and the retention and expansion of a controversial EI companies' tax credit scheme used to finance (mainly) infrastructure projects across PNG's provinces. OSF lists a total social-economic contribution of US$284 million, including US$32.2 million on infrastructure projects it manages on behalf of the state, under the infrastructure tax credit scheme. These include road infrastructure, hospital and school redevelopments in the Hela and Southern Highlands provinces, housing for police in the Southern Highlands, Hela provincial hospital upgrades and family support centre operations. OSF has assumed responsibility for running the Hela hospital since MSF's departure, and with military support since the recent earthquakes. OSF took credit for supporting specialised treatment for 1,000 survivors of family and sexual violence in 2016 (Oil Search Foundation, 2017). OSF works closely with Australian bilateral funding initiatives and contracts selected national NGOs to fly in and out of Hela, conducting training to strengthen local state and civil society representatives and urging them to collaborate to develop Hela's provincial strategy to end violence against women. But these inputs are intermittent and drawn out over years because they are driven by consultants who cannot travel during times of civil upheaval or natural disasters.

Through an expanding tax credit scheme, Oil Search is becoming an increasingly influential national actor, constructing key political and economic infrastructure in the capital city, most recently a new office for the prime minister and a massive new venue and roads to impress Asia-Pacific Economic Cooperation (APEC) attendees. Critics of tax credit schemes refer to lost tax revenues and infrastructure poorly aligned with government plans and policies, often built to serve a political elite and bypassing proper fiscal planning and procedures. EI CSR is increasingly delivering as de facto local government in remote EI-impacted areas, but, unlike the state, these industries are not accountable to constitutional or international treaty obligations, nor are they mandated or equipped to prioritise ending tribal conflict and violence against women.

The state continues to neglect the huge law and order and social development challenges in Hela (and in other EI-dominated Highlands provinces) and only intervenes occasionally to declare states of emergency if oil and gas projects are threatened or elections are imminent. Meanwhile, Oil Search is expanding its role in maintaining the infrastructure and operations of health, education and community services in Hela Province. Oil Search greatly enhanced its reputation when it swiftly assumed a lead role in Hela's 2018 earthquake relief operations, providing the relief supplies and transport needed to reach thousands of people in remote communities. OSF is producing a documentary on its new role in humanitarian relief and has been accorded kudos from the state, awards from the international community and appreciation from desperate, traumatised and confused communities. There is some speculation that the state might opt to use some form of public–private partnership strategy to transfer even more of its obligations and duties to OSF – for example, for long-term earthquake recovery, and possibly even to design and deliver an equitable strategy for overcoming the huge backlog of years of outstanding royalty payments currently owed to Huli landowners (Filer, 2016).

Aid-funded and corporate interventions in social development are remote, irregular and reliant on FIFO international consultants or corporate-sponsored NGOs. In this context, there is limited political will, space and resources to support the emergence and growth of local civil society. Unless the historical continuities of patriarchy and male violence are intentionally addressed and a rights-based approach is adopted, there will be no opportunities for women to lead local organisations and community mobilisation for justice and peace.

Hela women observe that 'the vast oil and gas deposits that flow under our ground, are extracted and exported to profit the EI corporates, while the blood of Hela's people flows above ground'.[17] Oil Search is promoting its image as a benevolent corporate citizen and important partner for development. But where its corporate profits are sourced, violent conflict and gender relations deepen and oppress and punish women, girls and children caught up in new forms of armed warfare and armed male protest. Experienced women leaders and activists in Hela, working independently of Exxon sponsorship or OSF grants, are critical of the lack of sustained funding from EI CSR to support the formation of local women's rights organisations in Hela. They call for seed funding specifically to enable autonomous women's organisations that develop their own agenda. They want to link with and learn from the experience of women-led movements to end violent conflict and violence against women in Highlands provinces that are extractives-free and where considerable progress has been made. But the low budget strategies they propose fall on deaf ears.

### Conclusion

Hela Province cannot achieve peace, equality and sustainable development while its armed conflict and extreme violence against women are ignored by the state. Extractive industries' CCD and CSR can 'patch up' the collateral damage in EI-impacted communities but they will not halt their highly profitable operations to ensure peace and inclusive, locally led social development. Their humanitarian or health services cannot substitute for accountability of the state and citizens to end armed conflict and violence against women. They run a high risk of covering for a corrupt government's dereliction of duties. Extractive industries may continue to partner large-scale aid programmes, please a corrupt state and boost the profitability of thousands of Australian companies now doing business in PNG, but they will condemn women in Hela to spiralling terror, death and destruction, leaving the province as a gaping black hole of anarchy and violence over which plans are drawn for ever larger gas, gold and oil projects.

---

**Box 2.1 Lessons from the Bougainville experience**

*Michelle Kopi*

The Bougainville copper mine, PNG's first large mine, has one of the largest copper reserves in the world. First developed by the Australian colonial administration in the late 1960s and later operated by Bougainville Copper Limited (BCL), the mine provided up to 45 per cent of PNG's national export revenue. The PNG government held a 19 per cent share. Despite this large flow of national revenue there was local dissatisfaction with the way in which benefits from the mine were distributed and the destruction it was causing. Whole villages were relocated, while loss of land, environmental degradation and the influx of outsiders caused other problems. The local population became bystanders, powerless on their own land (Regan, 2017). The effects on women were far worse. In Bougainville, one of PNG's few predominantly matrilineal indigenous cultures, where women are the rights-holders to land, male relatives acting as proxies in public negotiations largely shifted the power dynamics within the existing social structure and undermined the traditional authority of women (O'Callaghan, 2002).

Frustration built up over the years as local grievances were not addressed and demands not met. This eventually resulted

*(continued)*

*(continued)*

in landowners taking action against the mine, forcing its closure in May 1989, cutting a vital source of state revenue. Police mobile units and later the PNG Defence Force, functioning as the corporation's personal security force, were deployed with direct orders from BCL to use whatever force was necessary to reopen the mine (PNG Mine Watch, 2017). They used harsh bullying tactics, igniting and feeding long-standing secessionist sentiments that date back to 1975. This brought about broader support from the islanders, who took up arms in defence, and it ultimately led to a decade-long civil war (Tierney et al., 2016). The conflict escalated to become the largest armed conflict in the Pacific since the Second World War.

This resulted in an estimated 20,000 largely civilian deaths, widespread human rights abuses, destruction of property and people's livelihoods and the displacement of more than a third of the local population. Young men used excessive and uncontrollable violence as the whole island descended into anarchy (Akanon, 2013). A culture of impunity fuelled violence against women perpetrated by state and non-state actors. Reports range from the sexual assault of individuals to gang rapes in care centres, women were murdered after being raped, women committed suicide after being raped, and people were intimidated and sexually assaulted over weeks (Tierney et al., 2016).

In the midst of the pain and hardship, women remained resilient and showed great courage. Women organised themselves and used their traditional role to broker peace between warring factions. A ceasefire was eventually reached in 1999 followed by the signing of the Bougainville Peace Agreement in 2001, establishing Bougainville as an autonomous region. Many years of war deepened a pan-Bougainville identity and strengthened the call for secession. As part of the peace negotiation, it was agreed that Bougainville would hold a referendum to decide its political future before 2020. This is scheduled to take place in June 2019.

### The future of mining in Bougainville

In 2015, the Autonomous Bougainville Government (ABG) passed the Bougainville Mining Act, effectively giving ownership rights of minerals to customary landowners. This means that no mine will be able to operate in Bougainville without a social licence. There are now talks to reopen the Panguna mine with varying opinions on the matter. For many, it is about the economic self-sufficiency of a people wanting their political and economic independence. However, the women of Bougainville are adamant that land cannot be compared to money (Wilson, 2011). In June 2017, Panguna women protesters blockaded the copper mine to prevent the signing of a memorandum of understanding by the ABG and BCL. Their message was simple and non-negotiable: 'No to BCL, no to mining.' Women claimed that they had never been consulted on the reopening of the mine and would not allow it to happen (Masiu, 2017).

These disagreements have led to a moratorium being placed over the mine indefinitely and the decline of BCL's application for an extension of its exploration licence. BCL has since taken the matter to court with the hope that it will find a way back to Panguna. Ironically – and to complicate matters – ABG has a commercial interest in the mine, with a 36.4 per cent shareholding in BCL. Nevertheless, regardless of what happens, what is clear is that the future of mining in Bougainville is now in the hands of Bougainvilleans.

**What are some lessons?**

Bougainville presents a unique and valuable opportunity for PNG to reflect on what went wrong and how a similar human and environmental catastrophe can be avoided at all costs. Yet, looking back, how much have we truly learned from the Bougainville experience?

*Public interest versus private interests*

The extractive industry continues to be the main revenue earner for PNG; in 2017 it accounted for 86 per cent of the country's export earnings.[18] The Bougainville experience shows that a high dependency on the Panguna mine compromised the position of the state, allowing BCL to influence its decisions. In a lawsuit against the mine alleging war crimes, genocide and crimes

*(continued)*

*(continued)*

against humanity, the former prime minister of PNG, Sir Michael Somare, signed an affidavit stating that, due to the financial influence of the company in the country, 'the company controlled the Government' (PNG Mine Watch, 2017). What we are witnessing is global corporate interests growing in strength, dictating policy, and undermining the state. The state's financial and commercial interests in extractives question its ability to remain impartial in its role as industry regulator to protect the interests of its people. Indeed, in the eyes of the Bougainvilleans who shut down the Panguna mine, the problem lay with the 'white mafia' that controlled the PNG economy (Akanon, 2013). State power was seen as having been captured by foreigners and subject to external influence (Rolfe, 2010).

In light of this growing risk and the many problems associated with extractives, one would think the government would consider resource extraction as a last option and not the first. Yet the exploitation of resources in the name of economic growth is being pursued more than ever before. We have forgotten what our forefathers in their wisdom inscribed in the constitution – to practise restraint and to put people first.

### Gendering the discourse of extractivism

The Bougainville experience highlights the masculine nature of extractive industries, politics and war. For far too long, decisions on the resource sector in PNG have continued to be made without due consultation and consideration of the detrimental impacts on the lives and well-being of women. They are the least to benefit from these decisions and yet are the ones most affected.

Even now, almost two decades after the Bougainville crisis, women are still bearing the effects of the war. Gender-based violence and other social problems are said to be far worse now than before the war (Tierney et al., 2016). Unresolved mental health issues and trauma from the experience of war continue to impact the home and community in the form of substance abuse, excessive alcohol abuse, domestic violence, sexual assault, depression and a lack of engagement in society (ibid.). These long-term effects have not yet been properly dealt with, and, as a result, many women in this situation continue to carry the pain and relive the terror of the war in their everyday lives.

Women are now calling on the ABG to be transparent in mining affairs, and have called on their leaders to consider the voice of women in all decisions that are made (Masiu, 2017). Recognising the important role of women, the ABG has made deliberate efforts to increase women's voice and participation at all levels. And while it will take time for women to fully and meaningfully participate in these spaces, what is important for now is that they are there.

The experience that women went through as a result of the mine and the decade-long conflict in Bougainville offers a sober lesson on the perils of extractivism. Driven by the global demand for resources, corporate profit seeking and state addiction to resource rents, the Panguna mine created conditions of inequality as well as dispossession and environmental destruction that ultimately led to violence, military repression and war, which impacted on women the most.

## Notes

1  Key informants for this chapter were Alice Arigo (policewoman) of Hela Province and Lilly Be'Soer (feminist activist and founder of Voice for Change) of Jiwaka Province, both long-term frontline human rights defenders committed to ending violent conflict and violence against women in their new provinces.

2  Over the four decades since independence, PNG has experienced a series of 'resource booms' when new projects and high commodity prices have dramatically increased GDP. The first boom resulted from oil and gas and projects in the Southern Highlands during the 1990s, but was short-lived as high-level corruption and financial mismanagement saw state and provincial government coffers emptied by corrupt leaders and their cronies. Following painful economic recovery, high gold and copper prices and expanding gas fields supported a second boom in 2002–12. Despite GDP increases, yet again extractive industry revenues failed to translate to equitable and inclusive development (Howes et al., 2014; Howes and Fox, 2016).

3  The Autonomous Region of Bougainville (AROB), formerly the North Solomon Province, was host to PNG's first major post-independence mining operation, initiated by the outgoing Australian administration and intended to provide substantial national revenue for the budget of the newly independent state of PNG in 1975. Social and cultural dislocation, pollution and inadequate benefits to the local community were some of a range of triggers for an

armed landowner uprising that led to a decade-long civil war with the PNG state. Bougainville is the only place in the world where host community violence has resulted in the long-term closure of a large-scale mine.

4  A. Arigo, personal communication, 2017.

5  During the Second World War, the New Guinea island was a key site of the Pacific war and ultimately for the surrender of the Japanese army.

6  L. Be'Soer, personal communication, 2017.

7  L. Be'Soer, personal communication, 2017; A. Arigo, personal communication, 2018.

8  The partners in the PNG LNG project were ExxonMobil (33.2 per cent and operator), Oil Search (29.0 per cent), Santos (13.5 per cent), National Petroleum Company of PNG (PNG Government) (16.8 per cent), JX Nippon Oil and Gas Exploration Company (4.7 per cent) and Mineral Resources Development Company (2.8 per cent).

9  Duna, the second-largest ethnic group of Hela, allege that the Huli have forsaken both the regional ritual projects which they once strongly promoted and the ties that made such cooperative performances possible. Instead of being concerned to preserve the fertile substance of the earth's core, Duna see the Huli (in Hela Province) and the Ipili (in Porgera) as pillaging it. They regard the gold, oil and gas being extracted at Porgera, Mount Kare, Nogoli, Moran, Kutubu and Gobe as examples of this fertile substance, and insist that the Huli are wantonly consuming fertile substance that should be conserved to sustain them and the world.

10  A. Arigo, personal communication, 2017.

11  Filer (2016) unpacks the intractable problem of landowner identification through a historical analysis of the current problems of unpaid landowner benefits in the HIDES and PNG LNG projects. Essentially, the state is locked into a pragmatic 'patrol box method' made possible through amendments to colonial laws. The system assumes that selected landowner representatives will have a stake in maintaining stability around EI sites, but there is no guarantee of onward equitable distribution to a larger group of landowners, particularly by gender and age.

12  Family support centres (FSC) are 'one-stop-shop' facilities established at hospitals to receive and treat victims/ survivors of gender-based violence against women. The first FSCs were established with the support of NGOs, and then by the Australian Department of Foreign Affairs and Trade with the PNG Family and Sexual Violence Committee. Their protocols and services were further refined by MSF and captured in national guidelines. The establishment of FSCs at all major hospitals is now national policy, and hospital boards are mandated to allocate an annual budget for their establishment and operations. There are now FSCs across PNG, most financed by Australian aid.

13  Information provided by the leaders and members of Hela Women Never Give Up, during conversations with the author over four evenings of the sixteen days of 'Activism against Violence against Women' (25 November–10 December 2017).

14  Oil Search Limited is the largest oil and gas exploration and development company incorporated in Papua New Guinea, and it operates all of the country's oilfields.

15  A. Arigo, personal communication, 2018.

16  Five years after independence, PNG's peak body for women voiced

outrage over high levels of normalised domestic violence and rising rates of sexual violence committed with virtual impunity. They worked directly with the Law Reform Commission to conduct nationwide research, popular campaigns and direct advocacy to parliament for specific legislation to protect women and

girls from violence. An insensitive and intransigent state took thirty years to endorse recommended law reforms.

17  A. Arigo, personal communication, 2018.

18  See https://eiti.org/papua-new-guinea#extractive-industries-contribution

## References

Akanon, C. 2013. 'Papua New Guinea and Bougainville Conflict: Women in Peace and Reconciliation', www.uaf.edu/.../Papua-New-Guinea-Bougainville-Conflict-Akanoa-C.-3-21-13.pdf (accessed 7 April 2018).

Allen, B. and Frankel, S. 1991. 'Across the Tari Furoro' in Schieffeline, E. and Crittenden, R. (eds), *Like People You See in a Dream: First Contact with Six Papuan Societies*. Stanford: Stanford University Press.

Alpers, P. 2004. 'Gun Violence, Crime and Politics in the Southern Highlands Community: Interviews and a Guide to Military-style Small Arms in Papua New Guinea'. Background Paper for Special Report 5. Geneva: Small Arms Survey, http://apo.org.au/files/Resource/alpers_sas_png_background_paper.pdf (accessed December 2017).

Alpers, P. 2005. *Gun-running in Papua New Guinea: From Arrows to Assault Weapons in the Southern Highlands*. Special Report 5. Geneva: Small Arms Survey, www.smallarmssurvey.org/fileadmin/docs/C-Special-reports/SAS-SR05-Papua-New-Guinea.pdf (accessed December 2017).

Banks, G., Kuir-Ayius, D., Kombako, D. and Sagir, B. F. 2018. 'Dissecting Corporate Community Development in the Large-scale Melanesian Mining Sector' in Filer, C. and Le Meur, P.-Y. (eds), *Large-scale Mines and Local-level Politics: Between New Caledonia and Papua New Guinea*. Canberra: ANU Press, https://press.anu.edu.au/publications/series/asia-pacific-environment-monographs/large-scale-mines-and-local-level-politics (accessed 1 May 2019).

Be'Soer, L. 2012. 'Leveraging Women's Rural Leadership and Agency'. Fifty-sixth Session of United Nations Commission on the Status of Women, New York, 27 February–9 March, www.un.org/womenwatch/daw/csw/csw56/panels/panel2-Lilly-Be-Soer.pdf (accessed 3 December 2017).

Burton, J. and Onguglo, J. 2018. 'Disconnected Development Worlds: Responsibility towards Local Communities in Papua New' in Filer, C. and Le Meur, P.-Y. (eds), *Large-scale Mines and Local-level Politics: Between New Caledonia and Papua New Guinea*. Canberra: ANU Press, https://press.anu.edu.au/publications/series/asia-pacific-environment-monographs/large-scale-mines-and-local-level-politics (accessed 1 May 2019).

Chandler, J. 2014. 'Violence against Women in PNG: How Men Are Getting Away with Murder', Lowy Institute, August, www.lowyinstitute.org/publications/violence-against-women-png-how-men-are-getting-away-murder (accessed 1 May 2019).

Davidson, H. 2018. 'Papua New
Guinea Earthquake: Death Toll
Rises as Disease Threat Grows',
*The Guardian*, 15 March, www.
theguardian.com/world/2018/mar/15/
papua-new-guinea-earthquake-
death-toll-rises-disease-threat-grows

Donaldson, M. and Good, K. 1998.
*Articulated Agricultural
Development: Traditional and
Capitalist Agricultures – Papua New
Guinea*. Aldershot: Gower.

Filer, C. 2016. 'The Intractable Problem
of Landowner Identification in the
PNG LNG Project: An Historical
Perspective'. State, Society and
Governance in Melanesia SSGM)
seminar, 12 September, https://
devpolicy.crawford.anu.edu.
au/sites/default/files/events/
attachments/2016-09/smli_seminar_
sept_2016.pdf (accessed 10 January
2017).

Harvey-Kelley, L. 1997. *Toropo: Tenth
Wife*. Port Melbourne: Heinemann

Howes, S. and Fox, R. 2016. 'PNG's
Resource Boom: A Fiscal
Retrospective', Development Policy
Centre, http://devpolicy.org/
Events/2016/PNG-Update/1a_Howes_
Fox.pdf (accessed 6 November 2017).

Howes, S., Mako, A. A., Swan, A., Walton,
G., Webster, T. and Wiltshire, C. 2014.
*A Lost Decade? Service Delivery and
Reforms in Papua New Guinea 2002–
2012*. Canberra: National Research
Institute and the Development Policy
Centre.

ICRC. 2017a. 'Spears to Semi-automatics:
The Human Cost of Tribal Conflict
in Papua New Guinea', International
Committee of the Red Cross (ICRC),
www.youtube.com/watch?v=wo4uf-
fXsUk (accessed December 2017).

ICRC. 2017b. 'The Old Ways Are Gone:
Papua New Guinea's Tribal Wars
Become More Destructive',
International Committee of the Red
Cross (ICRC), https://medium.com/@
ICRC/the-old-ways-are-gone-papua-
new-guineas-tribal-wars-become-
more-destructive-ade38205196f
(accessed December 2017).

Josephides, L. 1975. *The Production of
Inequality: Gender and Exchange
among the Kewa*. New York and
London: Tavistock.

Kopi, M. 2011. *Violence and Insecurity
in the Southern Highlands of Papua
New Guinea*. Auckland: Oxfam, www.
oxfam.org.nz/sites/default/files/
reports/Tari-report-final_2011.pdf
(accessed 6 September 2017).

Macintyre, M. 2011. 'Modernity, Gender
and Mining: Experiences from
Papua New Guinea' in Lahiri-Dutt,
K. (ed.), *Gendering the Field:
Towards Sustainable Livelihoods
for Mining Communities*. Canberra:
ANU Press.

MacWilliam, S. 2013. *Securing Village
Life: Development in Late Colonial
Papua New Guinea*. Canberra: ANU
Press, http://press-files.anu.edu.
au/downloads/press/p223381/pdf/
book.pdf?referer=402 (accessed 7
October 2017).

Main, M. 2017. 'Papua New Guinea
Gets a Dose of Resource Curse as
ExxonMobil's Natural Gas Project
Foments Unrest', Australian
Broadcasting Corporation,
10 March, www.abc.net.au/
news/2017-03-10/png-gets-a-dose-
of-resource-curse-from-exxonmobils-
lng-project/8343090?WT.
mc_id=newsmail&WT.tsrc=Newsmail
(accessed 5 December 2017).

Masiu, R. 2017. 'No Mining and No BCL,
Women Say', *Post Courier*, 4 June.

McCallum, I. 2012. *Tingim Laip Social
Mapping Report: Highlands
Highway*. Madang: Tingim Laip,
https://issuu.com/loumcc/docs/tl_
social_mapping_highlands_highway
(accessed October 2017).

McIlraith, J. 2012. *The Community Good: Examining the Influence of the PNG LNG Project in the Hela Region of Papua New Guinea.* Dunedin: National Centre for Peace and Conflict Studies, University of Otago, www.oxfam.org.nz/report/the-community-good-examining-the-influence-of-the-png-lng-project-in-the-hela-region-of-papua-new-guinea (accessed 5 September 2017).

MSF. 2011. *Hidden and Neglected: The Medical and Emotional Needs of Survivors of Family and Sexual Violence in PNG.* Port Moresby: Médecins Sans Frontières (MSF), www.doctorswithoutborders.org/publications/reports/2011/06-15-Papua-New-Guinea-Sexual-Domestic-Violence%20report.pdf (accessed 5 September 2017).

MSF. 2016. *Return to Abuser: Gaps in Services and a Failure to Protect Survivors of Family and Sexual Violence in Papua New Guinea.* Amsterdam: Médecins Sans Frontières (MSF), www.msf.org.au/sites/default/files/attachments/msf-pngreport-def-lrsingle.pdf (accessed 5 September 2017).

O'Callaghan, M. 2002. 'The Origins of the Conflict' in Garasu, L. and Carl, A. (eds), *Accord. Weaving Consensus: The Papua New Guinea–Bougainville Peace Process.* London: Conciliation Resources and Bougainville Inter-Church Women's Forum.

Oil Search Foundation. 2017. 'Performance Summary', Oil Search, www.oilsearch.com/sr-report-2016 (accessed 1 February 2018).

Papua New Guinea Constitutional Planning Committee. 1974. 'Constitutional Planning Committee Report 1974', www.paclii.org/pg/CPCReport/Cap2.htm (accessed 7 November 2017).

PNG Mine Watch. 2017. 'Mothers Unite Against Re-opening Bougainville Panguna Mine', https://ramumine.wordpress.com/tag/mekamui/ (accessed 27 November 2017).

Read, K. E. 1965. *The High Valley.* New York: Charles Scribner's Sons.

Reay, M. 1959. *The Kuma: Freedom and Conformity in the New Guinea Highlands.* Carlton: Melbourne University Press.

Reay, M. 1966. 'Women in Transitional Society' in Fiske, E. K. (ed.), *New Guinea on the Threshold: Aspects of Social, Political, and Economic Development.* Canberra: ANU Press.

Reay, M. O. 2014. *Wives and Wanderers in a New Guinea Highlands Society: Women's Lives in the Waghi Valley.* Canberra: ANU Press, http://press-files.anu.edu.au/downloads/press/p303901/pdf/book.pdf?referer=468

Regan, A. 2017 'Bougainville: Origins of the Conflict, and Debating the Future of Large-Scale Mining' in Filer, C. and Le Meur, P.-Y. (eds), *Large-scale Mines and Local-level Politics: Between New Caledonia and Papua New Guinea.* Canberra: ANU Press.

Rolfe, J. 2010. 'The Melting Pot: Ethnicity, Identity, and Separatism in Bougainville, Papua New Guinea' in Wirsing, R. G. and Ahrari, E. M. (eds), *Fixing Fracture Nations: The Challenge of Ethnic Separatism in the Asia-Pacific.* New York: Palgrave Macmillan.

Sawang, K. 2017. 'Who Actually Pays for PNG LNG Royalties?', *The Papua New Guinea Women*, 15 January, https://ramumine.wordpress.com/2017/01/16/who-actually-pays-for-the-png-lng-royalty-and-project-development-levy-benefits/ (accessed December 2017).

Strathern, M. 1972. *Women in Between: Female Roles in a Male World – Mount Hagen, New Guinea.* London: Seminar Press.

Tierney D. et al. 2016. 'The Mental Health and Psychosocial Impact of the Bougainville Crisis: A Synthesis of Available Information', *International Journal of Mental Health Systems* 10, https://ijmhs.biomedcentral.com/track/pdf/10.1186/s13033-016-0054-x (accessed 15 April 2018).

UN News. 2018a. 'UNICEF Scales Up Psychosocial Support for Papua New Guinea's Children after Devastating Quakes', 28 March, https://news.un.org/en/story/2018/03/1006151 (accessed 1 May 2019).

UN News. 2018b. 'Papua New Guinea: A Month after Deadly Quake, UN on the Ground Delivering Life-saving Aid', 26 March, https://news.un.org/en/story/2018/03/1005921 (accessed 13 May 2019).

Voice for Change. 2015. 'Violence against Women and Girls in Jiwaka Province, Papua New Guinea'. Voice for Change Community Survey Report, https://iwda.org.au/assets/files/20160203-Voice-for-Change-WEB_FinalSmall.pdf (accessed 5 November 2017).

Wardlow, H. 2006. *Wayward Women: Sexuality and Agency in a New Guinea Society.* Berkeley: University of California Press.

Wardlow, H. 2014. 'Paradoxical Intimacies: The Christian Creation of the Huli Domestic Sphere' in Choi, H. and Jolly, M. (eds), *Divine Domesticities: Christian Paradoxes in Asia and the Pacific.* Canberra: ANU Press.

Wiessner, P. 2006. 'From Spears to M-16s: Testing the Imbalance of Power Hypothesis among the Enga', *Journal of Anthropological Research* 62 (2): 165–91.

Wiessner, P. and Pupu, N. 2012. 'Toward Peace: Foreign Arms and Indigenous Institutions in a Papua New Guinea Society', *Science* 337 (6102): 1651–4, http://doi.org/10.1126/science.1221685 (accessed November 2017).

Wilson, C. 2011. 'Papua New Guinea: Women Call the Shots on Mega Copper Mine', Inter Press Service, 16 October, www.ipsnews.net/2011/10/papua-new-guinea-women-call-the-shots-on-mega-copper-mine/ (accessed 22 April 2018).

Yuyuge, E. 2003. 'Women Forgotten in the Race for Benefits in the Petroleum Sector'. Paper presented to the 'Women in Mining Conference: Voices for Change', Madang, PNG, 3–6 August.

Zurenuoc, M. and Herbert, F. 2017. 'The Creation of Two New Provinces in Papua New Guinea: A Story of False Starts and Near Fatal Collisions'. SSGM Discussion Paper 2017/2. Canberra: State, Society and Governance in Melanesia (SSGM), Australian National University.

# 3 | RURAL WOMEN IN COLOMBIA: FROM VICTIMS TO ACTORS

*Cecilia López Montaño and María-Claudia Holstine*

## Introduction

The Colombian conflict is frequently described as complex, long-lasting, and therefore difficult to define. Even now, as the post-conflict phase advances, between successes and failures, analysts still have dissimilar interpretations of its causes and dimension, as well as of the costs of the war and the benefits of peace. However, there is no dissent concerning the situation of women, for Colombia seems to follow the book: their experience is strikingly similar to that of women in other wars. Negative gender bias about female war victims, their contribution, the costs they bear, their new roles, and certainly their necessary but often ignored involvement in both war and peace are part of the universal inequality that prevails between women and men around the world.

Stewart (2010) reviews the numerous ways in which women engage in and are affected by armed conflicts, facts that often go unnoticed by analysts who limit their focus to the sexual abuse that women are subjected to. The economic, social and political conditions in which women live are usually set aside under the covert hypothesis that they play a minimal role in their societies.

Of the many documents written by national and international experts about this nation's war, few approach the intrinsic causes behind gender-based violence against Colombian women, and then only within the traditional definition of sexual violence – rape, sexual slavery, forced prostitution, etc. In fact, gender-based violence against women (GBVAW) is rarely considered in its widest conception, as such analyses tend to overlook economic, social, political and cultural aspects related to the situation of women in war.

Setting aside the fact that traditional women's studies focus on women first, this research takes those variables as its departing point.

Simply by widening the spectrum of analysis to include a political economy approach redefines the costs that these women have paid and their contribution to peace building. Only by doing this can GBVAW be fully understood and women's actions during the conflict truly valued. This is the main goal of this research: to look at women in conflict from a different angle.

Colombian women played a very important and unrecognised role during the war. They were not just victims – as exclusively considered; they were also civilians, combatants, and even perpetrators. However, most of all, they were crucial actors within the conflict. This role is probably unknown in other armed conflicts around the world, since the prevailing similarity among wars is the historical underestimation of women's situation.

## Colombia's conflict in a nutshell

Amidst worldwide coverage after signing the Final Accord with the FARC,[1] Colombia began its long walk towards peace with few truly understanding the war's context, its roots, its actors, or how deeply its facets hurt Colombians, and especially how it impacted women. Interestingly, they are not alone, for the 'Colombian Society has not established consensus on the nature and origins of the armed conflict' (González, 2004: 11). What seems to be indisputable is that the conflict was long, very complex, ever changing, and with so many actors involved that it is difficult to grasp.

Colombians still struggle through 'the intricacies of a sixty-year-old internal conflict where drug trafficking and terrorism act as one, where a significant change in values of the population goes hand-in-hand with government corruption, with countless national and international actors involved, and with considerable economic and political interests at play ... issues never seen all at once in the history of any other country' (Cueter, 2015: 24). These are all key reasons for appreciating the hard road ahead for peace in Colombia, a road on which women should play a definite role towards the future sustainability of peace. However, women barely participated in the negotiations, despite representing more than 50 per cent of the victims. Today, female leaders are absent from the front line of post-conflict action or only marginally included in follow-up and evaluation of the accord's[2] implementation. This is a product of systematic disregard for their importance during the conflict, their key role in the transition from war to post-conflict, and their potential contribution to peace.

This research confronts an important contradiction. On the one hand, it states that women are not mere victims but essential actors; on the other, that the actions undertaken to support the new-found peace counters this by excluding them from this important process. The key question here is: where is this gap coming from? To answer it, one must begin by understanding the past.

### When did it all begin?

Perhaps one of the most controversial issues surrounding the conflict is its beginning. This is a central factor, for only through precise timing can the reasons behind the war be identified and truly resolved (Call, 2012). To understand this country, one must start by recognising the violent nature of its past. For instance, numerous civil wars between Liberal and Conservative[3] political elites characterised the nineteenth century. The transition to the twentieth century saw the War of a Thousand Days (1899–1903), when the 'economic malaise and dissension within the Conservative camp emboldened Liberals to launch another uprising last[ing] three years' (US Library of Congress, 2013: 34). Today, most believe that Colombia's most recently negotiated and ended war lasted fifty years, while a few uphold that it has been a sixty-year conflict. Neither view is correct: the latter links the war's beginning to FARC's founding in 1964 as a revolutionary communist group, and the former associates it with the end of *La Violencia* (1948–58).

The truth is that the seed for the emergence of guerrillas in Colombia grew as a result of ferocious attacks against Liberals perpetrated by the *Chulavitas*, the Ospina Conservative government's secret military police, which initiated *La Violencia*. As a response, simple Liberal peasants armed themselves to protect their communities and lands, but they were not guerrillas per se. Guzmán et al. (1962: 405) describes this period as 'a time of bipartisan cruelty where violence became a social process; where political elites ... eliminated those who disagreed with their views'. That war ended as modern wars end today, by signing the *Frente Nacional*, the peace agreement between those involved, yet few recognise this as a peace treaty. The *Frente Nacional* (1958–74) bluntly enforced a power-sharing arrangement between the Conservative and

Liberal parties for sixteen years, excluding any other ideology from the political arena.

Cueter (2015: 19) believes that, at the time, 'the actions of Conservative and Liberal elites, supported by the Catholic Church, turned violence into a social process that abandoned traditional moral values ... just to remain in power ... [P]olitics became a weapon of war to justify mass murders as the Military Forces of the nation executed the orders coming from the highest ranks of the Colombian Government.'

In a period that was strongly influenced by the American Cold War, communism was marginalised all around the world, at any cost. Colombia was no different. Despite President Alberto Lleras Camargo (1958–62) appointing Liberal peasant armed groups as rural military police during the first *Frente Nacional* government, under the subsequent Conservative rule of Guillermo León Valencia (1962–66), a ruthless attack by 16,000 Colombian and American soldiers devastated Marquetalia, where the entire combatant leftist group resided: a total of fifty men and two women (Verdad Abierta, 2013). The five survivors fled to return months later, fully armed, and with as many as seventy-five men to announce the formation of the FARC. The year was 1964 (Figure 3.1).

When looking into the violent past of this tortured nation, one thing becomes clear. Political exclusion has been – and continues to be – at the epicentre of Colombia's conflicts. It all boils down to the efforts of the party in power to exclude any other. Therefore, suggesting that the Colombian war has been ongoing for either fifty or sixty years is incorrect, as: (1) 'political exclusion and governmental persecution of an ideology does not mean the country is at war' (Cueter, 2015: 190); and (2) those dates fall within the timeframe of *Frente Nacional*, a peace process that lasted sixteen years. Political exclusion is not commonly used to explain why peace has been more the exception than the rule in Colombia. Given this, it would be a mistake to undermine other historical facts that show the malleable nature of the nation's conflict, and the vastly different factors fuelling it.

Soon after announcing their formation, the new FARC disappeared: there are no known or registered acts of war from 1968 until the beginning of the 1980s. The reason for their believed demise was lack of funding from communist countries that supported revolutionary forces. Yet, in 1982, the FARC came back stronger than before,

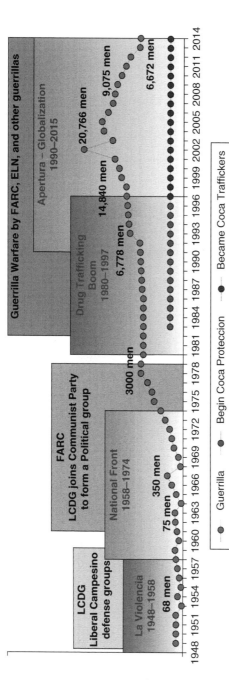

**Figure 3.1** The FARC's presence in rural Colombia

*Source:* Cueter (2015).

with 3,000 men in its ranks ready to fight the Colombian military. Its actions were no longer just ideological but also propelled by the duty to guard the business of its financier – drug trafficking – and its valuable routes out of Colombia. From this moment on, protecting coca routes became the reason behind the ideological survival and newfound strength of the FARC. A different conflict was born – one that was no longer only political, but rather financially motivated, and that lasted thirty-five years. This conflict is better known around the world and there is general consensus on when it began and why (Cueter, 2015). During this period, the government's economic decisions also paved the way for the comeback of paramilitaries, another well-known violent force.

When identifying the different stages of Colombia's conflicts, it becomes clear that the most coherent explanation for why it is so difficult to agree on when the war began relates to the guerrilla groups, the one constant actor throughout different historical moments of the nation's violent past. Very few see the changing nature and characteristics behind their actions, and, even less so, the changes within the group, which went from Liberal armed peasants, to governmental rural military police, and finally to a revolutionary group financed by drug trafficking.

Analyses by other experts add to the confusion: some believe that disparity within Colombian society is a determinant of the conflict. 'Inequality is a widely-cited cause … from economists and academics in international institutions to the average Colombian' (Colombia Reports, 2015a). Furthermore, because rural areas are the war's battleground, land has also been identified as being at the root of the long-lasting conflict.

Stewart (2002: 9) believes that 'land is of huge importance where agriculture accounts for most output and employment, but gets less important as development proceeds', further emphasising that access to land is imperative for the welfare and sustainability of individuals and their social group, and, most importantly, that such disparity can contribute to prolonging a war. Although her theory seems to apply to Colombia, long before the start of the conflict, in 1901–17, the Gini coefficient for land ownership was exceptionally high, and it remained at similar levels until 1984 (Graph 3.1), which contests that belief. On the other hand, one cannot refute the fact that rural land is always part of debates in the country. However, a few myths about why land is

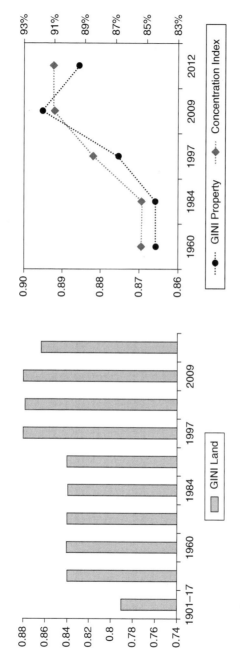

**Graph 3.1** Land ownership in Colombia, 1901–2012

*Source:* Cueter (2015).

not central to the conflict must be debunked. To begin with, inequality and land concentration in the hands of very few are characteristics that have always been intrinsic to Colombia, and therefore are not the cause of the conflict. This is a bold statement by any standard, but one that can be understood if one grasps the behaviour behind the actions of key factions at the core of this war.

> The answer is in differentiating *land ownership* from *territorial control*. The lack of State presence gave guerrillas unrestricted access over *baldios*, lands belonging to the State. Guerrilla and paramilitary groups exerted *territorial control* over vast extensions of [privately owned] land; their reason was not land appropriation but safe passage for cocaine shipments. Constant military pressure forced both groups to shift coca routes often to evade raids. *Land ownership* was detrimental to their goal of moving swiftly and safely between areas. Their need for *territorial control* is what truly ignited the ongoing conflict. (Cueter, 2015: 192)

So many facets and different actors make it difficult to understand where women fit in this Colombian conflict. For that reason, the way in which the war affected women is better understood if analysed by looking at the actions of the different armed groups and how state decisions fuelled their violence and methods. In most studies combatant groups directly fighting the war are referred to as *actors*; this analysis identifies those armed groups as *perpetrators* or *victimisers*.

### Who is fighting whom?

To truly understand GBVAW in Colombia it is important to differentiate clearly the groups at war and what specific circumstances motivated their violent actions against women. A very simplistic and generalised approach would establish only one enemy in this conflict – guerrillas, all of them[4] – and the good guys as the Colombian military forces. However, this is another misconception that hides the real reasons behind the pain of many. Crandall (1999: 223) correctly claims that 'even those who make a career out of tracking events in this Andean country are often unable to clearly differentiate between the currently active belligerent groups, let alone their goals, funding sources, and degree of popular support'. This is perhaps why one of the most difficult issues to grasp is not merely the role of all the perpetrators involved, but especially how each group swiftly shifted from friend to enemy and back again, depending on the geographical location or the social status of the person asked. Yet they all share one characteristic: the number of victims they left behind.

A key unrecognised perpetrator is the Colombian military. From *La Violencia* and its *Chulavitas* to the second stage of this war, when the enemy was the drug route-protecting guerrillas, victims recount examples of the military forces committing heinous crimes against the rural population without reason or explanation.

However, the most ruthless group emerged when sectors of the elites, including multinational corporations, financed paramilitary forces to protect their lands and activities from the guerrillas' tax or to avoid kidnapping. The hidden truth is that paramilitary groups are even older than the oldest guerrillas in the world. Throughout history, these private guns for hire have adopted different names and have acted in different territories, yet the people they protect and their cruel methods for controlling the population have changed very little. Clearly establishing that the guerrillas were not the only enemy in this war is key to fully understanding violence against women in the Colombian conflict, as women endured cruelty and different forms of brutality at the hands of at least two other armed forces.

Given the unspoken differences and relationships between these three armed groups, in this chapter we split them into two specific categories of GBVAW perpetrators. The military forces and the paramilitary shared their support for the establishment, but, most importantly, patriarchal values were prominent in their actions. In contrast, the guerrillas – who opposed the government – promoted a more gender equalitarian discourse, which was not always supported by their actions, which were still patriarchal.

### Patriarchal men, faceless women

There is nothing novel in the statement that, in patriarchal social structures, men are providers and women caregivers. But the concept takes on a new dimension when it comes to rural Colombia. Two elements unrelated to the conflict are inherent in ordinary life there. The first is the unusual level of intrafamilial violence that became a norm for most *campesinas*.[5] The second is the government – its laws, its social and economic policies, and its institutions' narrow understanding of patriarchal values.

The extremely common intrafamilial violence that has always existed in rural homes is systematic, effected in private, behind closed doors. From a very young age, rural women are subject to some form of physical abuse from fathers, brothers, husbands or other men known to them (INML, 2015). In their minds, the abuse they receive is normal, a lesser kind of violence, but it nonetheless creates angst and there is no space in which to deal with the physical or mental consequences. On its own, this is already quite serious; however, when governmental policies enter these scenarios, the lives of rural women become even more invisible and their pain non-existent.

Up until 1988, rural women could not own land. Despite policies and laws to facilitate women's production, in reality institutions rarely – if ever – help women's economic activities in rural areas. For example, loans were – and still are – for men and not for women, and technical assistance ignored the possibility that women could also require it or could be interested in receiving it. In other words, rural institutions are still as patriarchal as rural men. Additionally, public social policies also emphasise the role of women as weak and defenceless caregivers who cannot fend for themselves without their men, reinforcing men's role as needed protectors rather than providers. As a result, very few rural women perform agricultural duties, but they are over-represented in informal services (DNP, 2015b). For these reasons, 'Colombian rural women are the poorest of the poor in the country' (López Montaño, 2011). This context explains why women entered the war as vulnerable, easy targets for perpetrators of violence. However, in Colombia, rural women are not weak, and they were not targeted simply for being women or casual bystanders.

*Rural women: the epicentre of a war?*

Perhaps one of the better-known, and most bewildering, tragedies in Colombia is the immense number of internally displaced people as a result of the war. With over 7 million affected, Colombia's internally displaced population is the second largest in the world (NRC, 2015). The Registro Único de Víctimas (RUV, 2017) shows that women make up 51.3 per cent of the total displaced population, a small majority compared with men, but not enough to speak of a systematic persecution of *campesinas*, nor to consider displacement a GBVAW crime.

Some analysts argue that these figures stem from the number of men killed by one or other of the victimiser groups, yet the difference between genders – only 1.4 percentage points – does not support this belief, indicating that other factors are behind the displacement figures. In fact, age disaggregation of the displaced population provides categorical evidence that entire families, as a group, left everything behind to flee violent areas affected by war (Graph 3.2).

When searching for an explanation, threats appear to be a key victimising factor linked to familial displacement (Graph 3.3). Although men and women were threatened evenly, the huge number of reported displacement cases compared with the rather small number of reported threats means that the former is not a viable cause of the latter (CGR, 2015).

This pattern is repeated when we look at land dispossession figures as a reason for displacement (Graph 3.4). In this comparison, the extremely low number of land dispossession reports versus the high displacement figures unequivocally confirms that land was not at the root of the conflict. The 4,705 cases reported highlight one of Colombia's oldest problems: informal access to land and a well-documented lack of land titles in rural areas. Therefore, once again, how can it be a conflict for land when land ownership cannot be proven, or when land is clearly in the hands of wealthy landowners with deeds, whether legally or illegally acquired?

The same phenomenon can be found in all the other victimising factors,[6] unambiguously proving that men and women suffered equally, with four exceptions: there were more male victims of

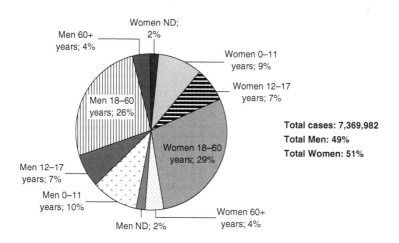

**Graph 3.2** Forced displacement, 1985–March 2017

*Source*: RUV (2017).

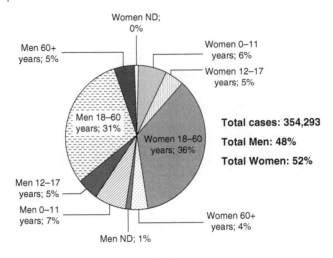

**Graph 3.3** Threats, 1985–March 2017

*Source*: RUV (2017).

improvised explosive device (IED) injuries, torture, and forced recruitment, whereas sexual violence in all its forms was primarily and explicitly perpetrated against women (Graph 3.5).

The official data collected on victimising acts during the conflict limits gender-based violence to reported sexual violence cases only.

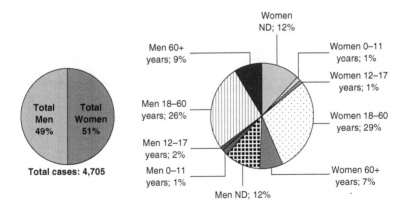

**Graph 3.4** Land dispossession, 1985–March 2017

*Source*: RUV (2017).

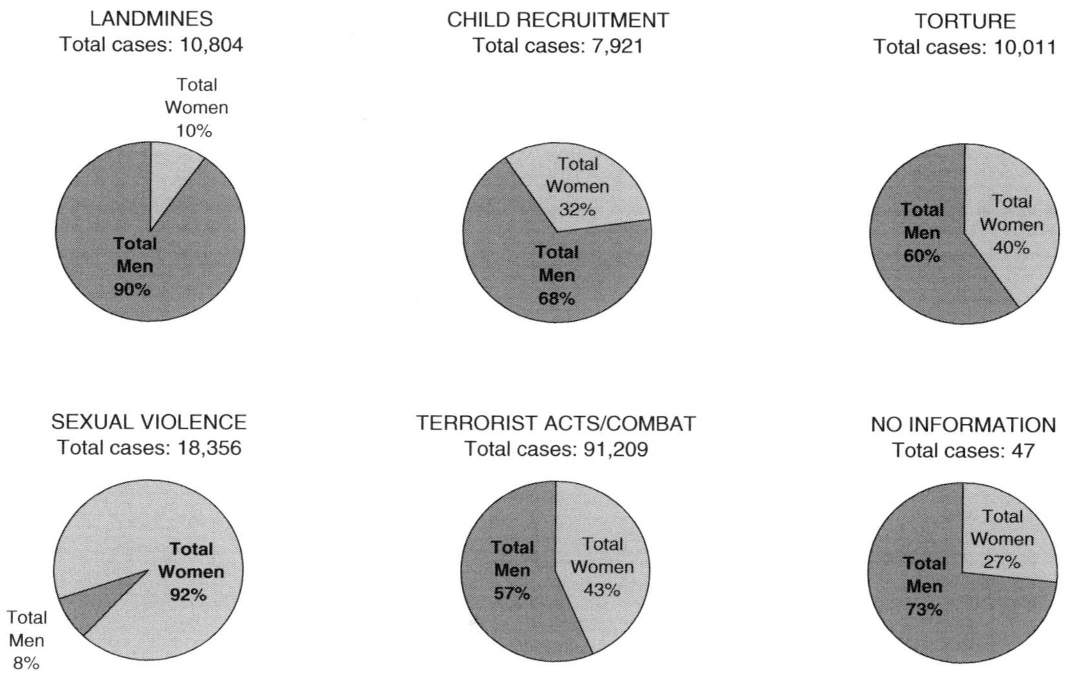

**LANDMINES**
Total cases: 10,804

Total Women 10%

Total Men 90%

**CHILD RECRUITMENT**
Total cases: 7,921

Total Women 32%

Total Men 68%

**TORTURE**
Total cases: 10,011

Total Women 40%

Total Men 60%

**SEXUAL VIOLENCE**
Total cases: 18,356

Total Women 92%

Total Men 8%

**TERRORIST ACTS/COMBAT**
Total cases: 91,209

Total Women 43%

Total Men 57%

**NO INFORMATION**
Total cases: 47

Total Women 27%

Total Men 73%

**Graph 3.5** Other victimising acts, 1985–March 2017

*Source:* RUV (2017).

These figures were used in this research exclusively for the purpose of understanding whether GBVAW explained women's displacement. Notwithstanding this limitation, it should surprise no one that, in a war with too many armed groups with strong patriarchal views, rural women accounted for 92 per cent of the 18,356 sexual crimes recorded (Graph 3.6); of these, only 1 per cent were girls of eleven years and under and 2 per cent were aged twelve to seventeen.[7] More often than not, *campesinas* who are victims of sexual violence do not report the crime, nor do they undergo medical or psychological treatment to overcome the gruelling experience (Corte Constitucional, 2015). Nonetheless, the overall figures for victimising acts clearly show that threats rather than sexual violence against women are a statistically more significant reason for displacement.

How is this possible? Colombia's history shows that sexual violence against *campesinas* is intrinsic to the rural culture and not just a result of war. That is why, in many cases, not only are *campesinas* blamed for the abuse (if reported), but the perpetrator expects them to continue fulfilling their sexual duties. In fact, this cultural bias and the idea that a woman's body is an object that belongs to men are so widespread that international organisations repeat them as a given.[8]

However, this is a very loose generalisation that not only lumps all victimisers into one group, clearly obscuring the extent of the horrific acts of violence against rural women, but also – and especially – overtly conceals the reason why and the way in which women shifted from

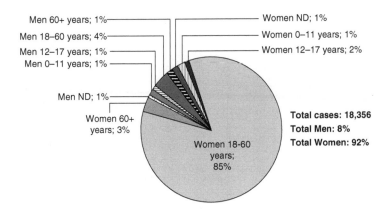

**Graph 3.6** Sexual violence, 1985–March 2017

*Source*: RUV (2017).

victims to actors in this war instead of being destroyed by the sexual transgressions they endured.

According to the Prosecutor General, 45.8 per cent of sexual violence attacks were by paramilitary offenders, with 19.4 per cent committed by public forces and 8.5 per cent by the guerrillas (Colombia Reports, 2015b). The staggering differences in sexual violence cases perpetrated by each armed group indicate distinct motives and modi operandi. Paramilitary forces used diverse forms of sexual violence against women. Chief among them were rape as a form of pleasure for the perpetrator, to punish those who disobeyed the regressive rules they imposed, or to make an example of those who dared stick their neck out to lead other women. These are all despicable crimes that cannot be ignored, but they must be set aside temporarily in order to disentangle the purpose behind the practice.

The illegal paramilitaries were traditionally financed by wealthy landowners, the extreme right, and some multinational corporations. Their codes were based on archaic values regarding the roles of men and women in society. Rather than seeing men as providers and women as caregivers, paramilitaries redefined those roles as protectors and the protected. With that idea in mind, commanders realised early on that women were a very effective weapon that served multiple purposes. Basically, for paramilitaries, sexual violence was a method, and women the means to enforce it.

Unlike in other conflicts, when it came to weakening the opposition, *campesinas* turned out to be the most efficient weapon available to paramilitaries to destroy their enemy – patriarchal men – such a powerful weapon that it killed two birds with one stone, for it also 'quickly forced entire communities out of the wanted land' (Acosta, 2015: 217). This is another seemingly bold statement, yet one that can be easily explained. Although rural men are perpetrators at home, their role as protectors is a vital characteristic of their masculinity. Their inability to stop acts of GBVAW against their women in front of the entire community destroyed their male ego. In essence, the respected protectors cowered, becoming weak and worthless. Legal and illegal armed forces clearly identified women as the Achilles heel of rural men. As such, to take control of entire areas of the country, all they had to do was publicly expose men's inability to protect their women. And Colombian rural women thereby became undefeatable weapons of war, the only weapon capable of emasculating men.

The equal representation of men and women in displacement figures is proof of the effectiveness of this strategy.

There was another type – and degree – of GBVAW crime perpetrated by paramilitaries. In towns they considered their own, commanders openly divided women between mothers and prostitutes. The former were raped in order to procreate, and the latter were sterilised, raped, and then forced into prostitution to satisfy lower-ranking troops. However, the paramilitaries' viciousness and cruelty transformed their chauvinism to pure misogyny when it came to the enemy. The women of their adversaries were not only gang-raped but 'subjected to physical mutilation, disfigurement, dismemberment' (Corte Constitucional, 2015), and, in many cases, their slow, painful deaths were witnessed by their loved ones.

Paramilitaries were not alone in this practice. Reports about the Colombian military forces using sexual violence against civilians keep surfacing; in most cases, this violence was perpetrated against women who were deemed to be complicit with guerrilla groups. Colombia's forensic authority confirms that, in over 50 per cent of the 219 rape cases officially reported between 2008 and 2010, the victims indicated that the offender was either a police officer or an army soldier (INML, 2015). Surprisingly, not all soldiers were Colombian; fifty-three girls also reported sexual abuse by US military personnel (Otis, 2015). Independent of the degree of violence, sexual attacks by soldiers are more harmful and damaging to women because these men represent the highest authority – men who once vowed to protect civilians with their own life. Their sexual abuse increases women's vulnerability and fear, as the violence is soon equated with having no one left to protect or defend them. However, such crimes are rarely reported due to the powerful influences trying to keep them concealed.

When looking into the actions of guerrilla forces against civilian women, the findings are unexpected. The reports on sexual violence attributed to the guerrillas document isolated cases and do not follow specific patterns or reasons. Guerrillas did not 'use *sexual violence* to impose social and *territorial control* over everyday activities of women' (CNMH, 2013). Nonetheless, the seemingly lesser actions do not mean that the FARC was blameless when it came to GBVAW crimes.

Most studies looking at guerrillas' sexual violence point to women in their ranks as the victims of abuse, a fact that raises very interesting questions. What protected civilian women from sexual violence from the FARC? Perhaps the answer is to be found in the 40 per cent female combatants living with males in a supposedly more gender-equal troop, the only one that incorporated women. The answer may be twofold. On the one hand, sexual freedom helped maintain discipline within the ranks; on the other, given that *guerrilleras* were charged with community relationships, to participate in, condone or ignore sexual violence against civilian women would jeopardise that role. Can this mean that having women be part of a combatant group in a war softens the traditional sexual abuse endured by civilian women? Perhaps.

Notwithstanding that GBVAW was deeply ingrained in Colombia's rural society before the start of the conflict, what changed with the war was that the phenomenon moved from being a private family matter to being in the public sphere; this was a successful technique to instil fear and reassert power over entire towns. Yet, the violence against *campesinas* or their condition as victims should not take precedence over the important role they played in introducing long-lasting change for all Colombian women.

### The games men play

Gates et al. (2012: 1720) believe that 'conflict has clear detrimental effects on poverty, hunger, primary education, reduction of child mortality, and on access to potable water'. However, Colombia disproves this claim. Unlike in other wars, this nation's behaviour is paradoxical because its economy experienced continuous economic growth (Graph 3.7), except for one year (Banco de la República, 2016).[9]

Social advances were also significant, even in the rural sector, where poverty decreased from 61.7 per cent in 2002 to 38 per cent in 2016 (DANE, 2017b). Yet this reduction was not enough: too many continue to be very poor, and the growth experienced cannot hide the fact that the various facets of this confrontation did affect development in the country.

Despite the above, to place all the blame for the rural sector's failings only and exclusively on the war is simplistic. The truth is that two economic governmental decisions added to the effects of the war and were equally at fault for the devastation endured by rural Colombia. Their greatest economic impact widened the rural–urban gap, which speaks directly to how much faster urban centres developed and grew, not having to battle the war threatening rural Colombians. More

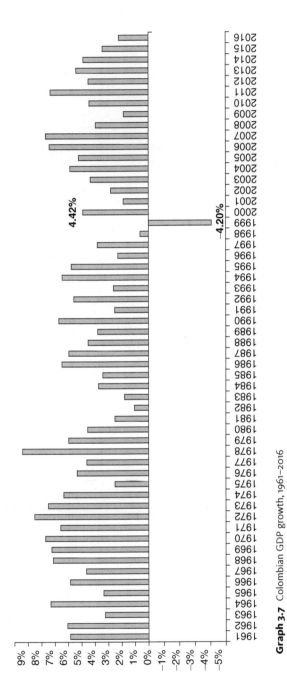

**Graph 3.7** Colombian GDP growth, 1961–2016

*Source:* World Bank (2016); DANE (2017a).

importantly, these decisions were key contributors to the worst period of GBVAW Colombia has ever seen.

## Agribusiness weakened rural men's masculinity

Cueter (2015) explains that 'globalization touches the heart of the conflict [as] the 1990 *Apertura*, the country's globalization initiative, was a process that forced Colombia out of its self-contained economy into the open market' (Graph 3.8).

Following the Washington Consensus, President Gaviria (1990–94) completely ignored the productive base of the country when implementing a rather speedy and unplanned *Apertura*. He grossly underestimated small *campesino* production, which failed to compete with low-priced food imports invading national markets. Until then, this sector had supplied 60 per cent of Colombian national demand for vegetables and fruit (DNP, 2015a: 14). The result was devastating. During the first years of the *Apertura*, small producers lost 1 million hectares while large-scale agriculture spread over the land the peasants had lost.

There is a clear connection between the *Apertura* and the growth of paramilitary forces. To understand this symbiosis, it must be noted that, while irreparably wounding small producers, the *Apertura* also encouraged large landowners to enter into agribusinesses. These landowners quickly realised that 'the trick of the trade was in defeating [agribusiness's] extensive nature by increasing the original size of their farms' – and who better to help them with the task at hand if not their well-known old associates (Cueter, 2015: 94). This new endeavour changed the 'existing relationship between landowners and paramilitaries[, which] evolved from protection to expansion' (ibid.).

Their method of choice to force *campesinos* off their land was effective and fast: strike hard at *campesinos*' masculinity and ego by showing them how incapable they were when it came to protecting their women from sexual violence, and by publicly exposing such weakness. Therefore, the worst and most violent forms of GBVAW stemming from the paramilitaries turned women into the most effective weapon of war against men. The final confirmation of its effectiveness can be found in a comparison of displacement figures: equal numbers of men and women fled, while agribusiness production flourished (Graph 3.9).

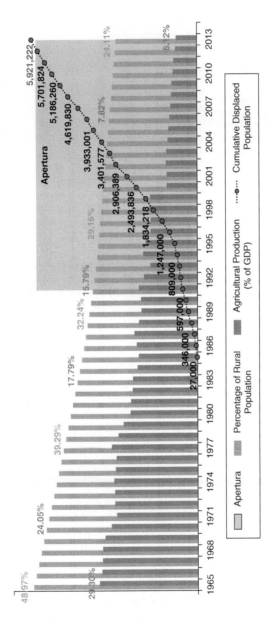

**Graph 3.8** Globalisation joins the conflict, 1965–2013

*Source:* Cueter (2015: 94).

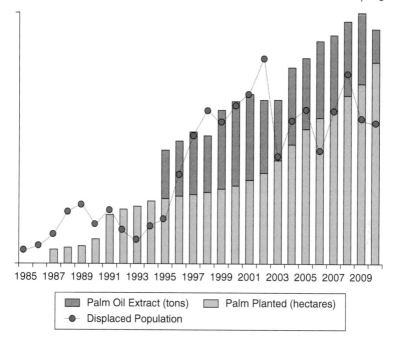

1985 1987 1989 1991 1993 1995 1997 1999 2001 2003 2005 2007 2009

■ Palm Oil Extract (tons)    ▢ Palm Planted (hectares)
-●- Displaced Population

**Graph 3.9** Palm oil and displaced population, 1985–2009

*Source*: Cueter (2015: 97).

Decentralisation fortified machismo rule

Decentralisation is not new to Colombia: it has been adopted since the 1970s. Following globalisation's promotion of smaller central government in favour of more equitable societies, the *Apertura* transferred all public resources assigned to health, education and public services to regional administrations.

Mantilla (2012: 55) believes that 'decentralisation plays a very important role when it comes to the escalation of the conflict'. The reason is now clear. As of 1991, the election of mayors and governors by popular vote transferred political power to the regions. Paramilitary groups knew well the areas without state control and had the support of the local and regional elites, which facilitated the imposition of their own candidates who could then take over decentralised funds. Having political and fiscal control over many towns in their areas of interest led to a second form of GBVAW, one that harshly enforced old patriarchal values, restricting how women dressed, the length of their hair, and especially their sexual conduct. The decision to sterilise a woman to serve the troops or to make her the mother of their children by force rested solely on the whim of the paramilitary chief.

Even though this new form of GBVAW did not turn women into a weapon of war, it used them to maintain cohesion among the troops and to clearly redefine the line between *my women* and *my enemies' women*. By controlling all women, paramilitaries swiftly regressed entire communities to archaic patriarchal and religious values.

The suffering and violence rural women endured during the war is well known. They braved unimaginable and horrific attacks and abuse. In the eyes of the world, they were undeniable victims of GBVAW; yet despite this classification, a new *campesina* emerged in Colombia.

### From victim to actor

Throughout the history of conflicts around the world, women have been identified as victims. The loss of husbands, children and even material possessions is reason enough to label them as such. In 1995, as a result of the Beijing Declaration and Platform for Action, GBVAW as a weapon of war became visible. The declaration was well-meaning and important, but, unfortunately, it continued to portray women as casualties of war, a term indicating 'temporality in the victim's condition ... with a hidden message that conveys that innocent citizens are victims "by chance, accidental[ly], without much thought or premeditation"' (Cueter, 2015: 81). Nothing is further from the truth – at least not in Colombia, where the actions against women during the war were neither accidental nor fortuitous, and definitely not unintentional.

One of the problems of limiting the condition of women during conflict to that of victims is the implication that women – and the abuses against them – are nothing more than casualties of war; yet the crimes against them are not simply 'unfortunate collateral damage of war'.[10] The undertones of the term 'victim' imply weakness and defencelessness, and characterise women as having diminished capacity. The inference hides their strength, their drive to survive, and, most of all, how perpetrators deliberately used them to achieve political, economic and territorial control. This is the perfect war to show that different ways of interacting with women do not always produce change in their favour, but can rather ratify traditional patriarchal beliefs, a 'structure that gives some men power over other men, and all men power over women' (Game and Pringle, 1984).

Still, Colombian *campesinas* are not just victims; they are first and foremost actors. This honours all women affected in one way or another by the war, but it especially gives women the recognition and respect they deserve. For that reason, we now set aside our focus on the perpetrators' actions to highlight the courage of the different types of rural women who endured their brutality.

### Women in arms

A very common stereotype is that, during war, 'all men are in militias, all women are victims' (Enloe, 2004: 99).[11] This is not the case in Colombia, as the existence of female combatants in guerrilla groups has been documented since the 1970s, and women entered the Colombian military forces in 1976 (ENC, 2015). By worldwide standards, Colombian women arrived late to combat, yet their roles as members of different armed groups – managing dissimilar gender narratives – are revealing; in the end, even the most forward-thinking reverted to traditional patriarchal behaviours and patterns.

Although there were many guerrilla groups following leftist ideologies, the FARC was the most open to women, who entered their ranks in two ways: either by force, when girls were kidnapped to be indoctrinated; or by women buying into the FARC's very egalitarian rhetoric that promoted equal rights and tasks for combatants, both men and women. It is easy to understand why some *campesinas* bought so quickly into the egalitarian sales pitch, as rural women endured verbal and even physical aggression within their family. To finally be on an equal footing with men was probably very appealing, not just to stop the abuse in their lives, but because it also entailed a new-found freedom to decide, to fight for a cause, and to improve their opportunities. Interestingly, even those girls who coercively entered the group found some fulfilment in guerrilla ranks (Herrera and Porch, 2008). By contrast, paramilitary groups were reluctant to incorporate women in their forces, believing that femininity is at odds with military life (Otero, 2006). The Colombian military had a gender-oriented discourse very similar to that of the guerrillas; yet, in practice, their actions were closer to those of the paramilitary groups.

Despite the enormous differences in the reasons and tactics of these three armed forces when incorporating females into their ranks, a common characteristic is that women in arms were charged with care[12] and communications duties. Aside from cooking, cleaning and taking care of the ill, these women also managed the relationship with civilians, for they were perceived to be harmless, gentle, compassionate and friendly, which in turn facilitated recruiting efforts.

Of course, there are dissimilarities that are worth mentioning. For instance, paramilitary forces completely rejected the idea of women in combat, a very patriarchal position that was reinforced by their scepticism about women's ability to fight fearlessly. Therefore, they encouraged those interested in joining their ranks to 'choose another job [for] this is war ... War isn't a fun job' (CNMH, 2012: 53). Only a handful of paramilitary women became commanders, and were only charged with controlling other women (Acosta, 2015).

In 2012, the Colombian military finally authorised women to take part in active combat (Vergel, 2012: 236). To date, high-ranking officials still maintain that women should have 'a special kind of treatment. Fortunately, vanity will always be present. We don't want them to look like men' (Vélez, 2013). It may all boil down to protecting female soldiers from the sexual violence that other women are subjected to – a very noble thought, though not very gender-equal, and definitely one that members of the military did not uphold when it came to civilian women in rural areas.

The most forward-thinking group was the FARC. They believed that a gender equality-based enrolment policy 'increases the quantity and quality of the recruitment pool' (Herrera and Porch, 2008: 613). Ability rather than gender was the main criterion to assign tasks among the troop (Otero, 2006), and they assigned care duties equally between genders. Women also participated in active combat. However, the gender-equal discourse ended where sexual behaviour began. *Guerrilleras* enjoyed some sort of sexual freedom as they could choose their partners, as long as they still complied with their duty to provide other *guerrilleros* with sex to stop desertion. In other words, *guerrilleras* were the most stable 'supply of sexual partners to ... a corps of forlorn, largely celibate male [soldiers]' (Herrera and Porch, 2008: 613).

By society's standards, the duties imposed on *guerrilleras* are evidence of sexual violence against them and identify them as victims of sexual slavery, rape, forced abortion and sterilisation. However, based on interviews, the abuse was not necessarily seen as such by the female soldiers involved. The first indication of this comes from Londoño and Nieto (2006), who surveyed men and women on the reasons behind their enlistment. Of those who joined to escape intrafamilial conflict,

46 per cent were women and 26 per cent men; of those citing economic betterment, 48 per cent were women and 26 per cent men; 56 per cent of women felt resentment towards another armed group but only 7 per cent of men did. Interestingly, of those who joined for political reasons, 28 per cent were women and 26 per cent men.[13] These figures counter the idea – promoted in demobilisation campaigns – that girls were *always* torn away from a safe family home and forcibly coerced to become soldiers. Their voices explain that the guerrilla movement allowed many of them to escape economic and social vulnerability, and that, at one point or another, most *guerrilleras* made a very conscious decision to enter the FARC's ranks. This reconfirms that not all female recruitment was under duress.

Civil society's use of the term 'forced' before 'conscription' denies women's freedom to follow a path that is traditionally masculine, or their autonomy to choose how to deal with challenges threatening their career. Now a senator, Victoria Sandino, FARC's most visible woman, clarifies misconceptions regarding rape, sexual slavery, abortion and sterilisation within the ranks. 'When birth control fails and pregnancy happens, *guerrilleras* face a decision between ... continuing their chosen career or abandoning it to become mothers' (Castrillón, 2016). Her words rebuff stereotypes about women's inability to freely choose

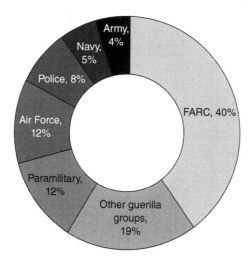

**Figure 3.2** Women in armed groups

*Source*: Vergel (2012); Ministerio de Defensa Nacional (2010).

sexual partners, whether to be mothers, or even their right to place career over having a family. More importantly, civilian women have different standards from combatant women. The latter's decision to be warriors entails making choices that move them further away from the traditional female roles and lives of the former. Neither is equipped to judge the other.

The differences in the percentages of women combatants within the armed forces (Figure 3.2) is a reflection of each group's perception of women, its explicit policies, and implicit norms regarding female participation. What is indisputable is that, in the end, all groups reverted to traditional patriarchal values, trying to control what women can or cannot do, especially when it comes to their bodies, regardless of how progressive their gender equality rhetoric is. For instance, although the FARC women carried guns to actively participate in battle, and care duties were distributed equally between genders, the only ones with mandatory sexual duties were female, following a directive tantamount to rape. Similarly, the guerrilla and paramilitary abortion and sterilisation practices were not just cruel but an unquestionable violation of women's rights over their bodies. This method was harsher than birth control, and not always applied evenly, since commanders in both groups were allowed the birth of their own children. Although these practices did not take place within the military forces, the sexual atrocities military personnel perpetrated against civilian women were just as cruel, or even more so.

Independent of how legal or illegal forces treated their women, the way in which society perceives 'women in arms' speaks volumes about their lives once they become civilians again. A notable case is that of the FARC women, since many people find it unimaginable that some *guerrilleras* chose that life and willingly participated in combat. This bias has meant that most women in illegal groups have been denied the financial and social benefits received by male combatants during previous demobilisations. Inexplicably, only those who truly participated in combat were counted as members of the group. All those charged with care, logistics or communication duties were deemed *collaborators* – by force, of course – and therefore not part of the group demobilising. And despite this classification, Colombian society labels all these women victims, completely diminishing the fact that they 'overcame feminine stereotypes and breached unsurmountable frontiers previously forbidden for [them]' (Wills, 2005: 63) by choosing to take part in the war as soldiers. Women in arms are perhaps the best example of the way in which women moved from being victims to actors in the Colombian conflict, but they are not the only ones who did so.

## The quiet rise of civilian campesinas

While women in arms were fighting for their career choice to be respected, civilian rural women took a different path, one on which their voices became their weapon. Their struggle against patriarchal values began long before the war's ferociousness, and their leadership could not be stopped by the paramilitary violence they endured. Their quiet advances evolved as speedily as the war marched through three different stages. RUV (2017) shows that rural women account for roughly half the registered casualties in the war, yet always portraying them as powerless victims ignores their rise as silent heroes.

During the 1960s, in the midst of the *Frente Nacional* peace agreement, *campesino* mobilisations contested land ownership rights and redistribution. Rural women struggled to be included in these groups to defend their care activities, but they were underestimated and openly ignored as political subjects (Defensoría del Pueblo, 2014: 21).

Although rural women are less financially autonomous, given their dependency on men, they are not powerless – and they are definitely not weak, as they proved during the 1980s. Amidst the intensity of the war to protect coca routes, these women began playing vital roles in their own movements, which seemed to align with the struggles of rural men claiming political and economic rights. At the time, the possibility of female ownership of land in a country where property titles were accorded only to men further drove female advocacy. The government recognised the need to formulate strategies specifically geared towards *campesinas* (DNP, 1984). After four years of their unstoppable pressure, Agrarian Law 30 of 1988 – reaffirmed in 1994 – mandated men to add their women's names as equal owners in their rural property titles (Congreso de la República, 1988). Rural men did not react well and tried to discourage women's participation in peasant associations (Defensoría del Pueblo, 2014: 33), but the negative atmosphere did not dissuade the *campesinas*.

Rural women's activism visibly amplified during the 1990s. Soon after the *Apertura* led to the return of paramilitarism, the war turned against civilian *campesinas* for the first time. The paramilitaries' tactic was to cruelly use women as a method of controlling men and communities, yet the escalating viciousness only served to fortify female voices. Protecting their loved ones and their communities increased their exposure as they chastised the state for leaving them to fend for themselves. The cruelty of paramilitary crimes strengthened their will to demand concrete action from their government. Its delayed response and the violence caused by the military forces sent to protect them awakened women to the power that political status offers. As a result, Afro-Colombian rural women became the first female group ever invited to participate in drafting the constitution in 1991 (Defensoría del Pueblo, 2014).

Unfortunately, their noticeable steps forward slowed down when paramilitaries silenced their voices by strategically targeting their movements and forcing their decline (Defensoría del Pueblo, 2014: 35). To single out perpetrators of violence as the only culprits for the demise of *campesina* movements, however, would not honour the lives of the women who died fighting for their rights, families and communities. Their tragedies also taint the government, and a heartless urban society consistently dismissing their suffering because, to them, the horrors of the war were just a television show.

Rural women did not give up. In fact, they quickly reorganised and led resistance groups to stop paramilitary land expropriation. Nothing deterred them from their goal, not even the danger of being identified as FARC sympathisers, whether true or false, which guaranteed violent torture and death at the hands of the paramilitaries. On the contrary, despite being the targets of the worst cases of GBVAW and despite being abandoned by public institutions, *campesinas* still found the strength 'to report violence against themselves and their families' (Defensoría del Pueblo, 2014: 36). Their courage moved the Constitutional Court – twenty years too late – to censure the state for its unconstitutional approach when aiding victims of the war.

Their achievements continued. The enactment of Law 731 of 2002 granted rural women access to public goods and agrarian benefits and opened up a real space for their political participation (Congreso de la República, 2002). However, their most important accomplishment was the enactment of Law 1448 of 2011, which finally acknowledged Colombia's long-lasting war and its victims (Congreso de la República, 2011). Unfortunately, this law fails to recognise the crucial role of *campesinas* as the force behind vital state mandates transforming the lives of all Colombian women. To deny that rural women became genuine agents of change during Colombia's toughest historical moments is a terrible injustice. An analysis of the cruel GBVAW they endured during the conflict clearly demonstrates how, instead of succumbing to tragedy, they found strength in their pain to change important dynamics, quickly moving away from the stereotype of victims – an important shift still unacknowledged by those with the power to change their future. Rural women must be saluted today as essential actors in the war.

### Women: the way for a rural war to enter the cities

It is well known and accepted that rural areas were the battleground of this long-lasting conflict. The detachment from the war of urban Colombia reflects the fact that it never felt the war's ferocious impact or consequences. However, although gunfights, bombs and mass murders remained in rural Colombia, the conflict did come to the cities, quietly, undetectably, and through a very unexpected channel: women.

### From *campesinas* to displaced urban workers

A known characteristic of displacement is that people tend to flee to urban centres first. It was no different in Colombia, where over 7 million rural men, women and children suddenly and consistently arrived in towns and cities that were unprepared to receive them. This was not an easy transition for those rural families who abruptly found themselves empty-handed, in the middle of fast-moving cities, so different from their homes. The government's initial emergency response was relatively quick, but finding long-term solutions to integrate them into urban life or to help them return to their land are still slow. The massive arrival of *campesino* families into urban centres was a wake-up call for urban Colombia for it made the war real. However, the struggles of displacement remained foreign to them.

The way in which rural women and men tackled this challenge speaks once more to women's innate flexibility to adapt to harsh environments and new situations. Men struggled because their expertise was useless in urban centres; women rose to the occasion quickly, taking advantage of the high demand for their field of knowledge – care services. Surprisingly, these women confronted a new wave of GBVAW when frustrated and unemployed displaced rural men saw their *campesinas* empowered, gaining economic autonomy, and swiftly taking on the role of providers, leaving them behind. Statistics show that domestic violence among displaced people is higher than among those still living in rural areas (Ibáñez et al., 2011). Then again, these new scenarios brought out the best in women instead of diminishing them. They quickly stepped into leadership roles at home and within their new community. Today, households led by displaced women in cities comprise roughly 39 to 46 per cent (DNP, 2013), almost twice as many as the 27.8 per cent in rural areas (DANE, 2015). Furthermore, despite the increasing dependency ratio, these women still found time to lead or participate in female organisations that forced the government to include their informal neighbourhoods in the network of public services (CNRR, 2011).

## Coca and beauty: unlikely allies

Drug trafficking in Colombia is always analysed and perceived as a self-contained problem, parallel to the war, associated exclusively with illicit crops and coca routes managed by guerrillas as the sole culprits for the conflict. For most, drug dealers' actions were limited to urban distribution centres and participation in the world market. That is a misconception. The connection between drugs and war runs deep, and the impact was not just economic or urban. Drug trafficking changed an entire society, especially its women.

Drug dealers led lavish lives, where money was king, and everybody had a price. In a very class-conscious society, they were at the bottom at first, but they quickly found that money was the way to climb the inaccessible ladder into the highest spheres of society. Faster than one could expect, 'drug dealers entangled themselves only with powerful elites in the country – the wealthy and the politicians, often one and the same – simply by dangling money in front of their eyes. These new mergers triggered a sequence that rapidly tore down traditional moral and ethical values across the nation; and just like that, a *drug culture* was born in Colombia' (Cueter, 2015: 105).

There are many aspects to the drug culture, yet its most devastating effects were felt by women. Drug dealers surrounded themselves with beautiful young women whose only job was to please and serve them. In return, the women lived surrounded by riches, as long as they were flawless, and not just in terms of their behaviour. 'The perfect female form adopted by *narcos* replicated the looks of the 1970s American prostitutes – blond, very voluptuous, and highly sexualized' (Yagoub, 2014). This was not precisely a characteristic of Colombian females, yet it was one that encouraged *narcos* to pay plastic surgeons to turn their women into that prototype. Unnoticed, but rather quickly, 'the perception of beauty shifted when Colombian women ... began to associate physical enhancement with a better life. Even more damaging was that as beauty changed in Colombia, so did the way in which men viewed and treated women' (Cueter, 2015: 112).

> The darkest side of *narco-beauty* gave rise to an inexplicable form of *human-trafficking-by-consent* when ... girls and young women from rural villages, or even lower-class neighbourhoods, [were] taken by force or in agreement with parents to be 'pimped' to perfection; or when they themselves took the initiative to go to the big city to 'make it big,' ... to eventually have their economic issues resolved by a rich man. (Cueter, 2015: 112)

In essence, 'the drug culture's legacy intended to lose *the woman* by making women more invisible, to induce men to see objects with curves first, to replace education with beauty ... The *narco-lifestyle* tried to swiftly squash and reverse gender equity advances previously achieved' (Cueter, 2015: 113). In a country where intrafamilial violence continues to grow, the narco-lifestyle perception of women helps explain the rise of GBVAW across the nation. Since few see *narcos* as key victimisers in the war, not many realise how their role in changing the perception of what is acceptable for a woman to look like to be considered pretty or desirable is one of the ugliest and most aggressive forms of GBVAW.

Fortunately, many did not fall for the new standard of beauty and defied the narco-lifestyle influence. As in any war, there were casualties, and many young women were lost to that foreign ideal prototype, but even more fight today to uphold that women are first and foremost human beings with rights independent of how they look or behave, where they live, and how poor or wealthy they are. Most of all, women continue to stand up to old patriarchal values that still prevail, not just on their own behalf, but for *campesinas* young and old. Colombian women, both urban and rural, are part of this greater resistance, and, for that reason, they are crucial actors in this ending war.

## Rural women: Colombia's strength

Consensus around the world is clear: the devastation left by any war is excruciating. There is also agreement on who the casualties of war are: men usually become the majority of those who die, too many children are left orphaned and scared, and women suffer greatly the loss of their loved ones while enduring profound violence. However, this study takes issue with limiting the analysis of GBVAW tinted by the lens of traditional bias, for it ignores key roles played by women, more definitive and complex than just being victims struggling to survive.

*Campesinas* are a great example to show how, despite much suffering, they stood up and effected real change across the nation. To recognise them, the Colombian conflict cannot – and should not – be compared with other wars. Aside from the shifting nature of the conflict at the hands of the same group of perpetrators who swiftly changed goals while maintaining methods and cruelty through time, what really differentiates this war is the strength of its women. The war fought in rural Colombia fits no category or theory; its multiple, complex scenarios demand an open mind to realise the relationship between political economy and GBVAW.

Two mainstream approaches tackle this new relationship. The first forces an understanding of the 'contextually specific social, cultural, political and economic determinants that inform the conflict and give meaning to violence' (Meger, 2016). The second 'attends to the local and global contexts in which violence against women occurs' (True, 2010: 4). The unusual characteristics of the Colombian war, and the idiosyncrasies of those involved, are central to the core of the political economy–GBVAW relationship. Any thorough analysis must take all these elements and both approaches into account.

True's (2012) framework is immediately contrary to the realities of Colombian rural women when it states that 'there is a relationship between women's access to productive resources such as land, property, income, employment, technology, credit, and education, and their likelihood of experiencing gender-based violence'. As previously stated, in Colombia most *campesinas* do not own any land, nor do they have access to grants, loans or technical assistance received by men. Therefore, the living circumstances of *campesinas* quickly tear down True's basic premise, whereby their situation makes them more at risk of GBVAW during war. The intrafamilial violence in rural Colombia, accepted by *campesinas* as the normal state of affairs, made them strong rather than vulnerable.

Merger's framework finds interesting coincidences with the Colombian conflict that could explain the GBVAW experienced by *campesinas*. Merger's (2016: 93) definition of women as a weapon of war links this concept 'to the strategic ends of an armed group' and describes 'sexual violence [as] perpetrated systematically, publicly, on a mass scale'. This description fits perfectly the actions of paramilitaries against their enemies. However, when looking deeper, it becomes clear that a coincidence of terms does not mean that her explanation suits the specificities of the GBVAW experienced by *campesinas*.

Conceivably, the biggest difference between these authors is their flexibility: Merger's framework recognises that each conflict is dissimilar to the next, and key aspects outside the control of women – culture, internal politics and economics – may influence the causes behind GBVAW. But what becomes evident now is that GBVAW against Colombian women during war does not fit any theory or framework because the actions against women are as particular and unique as the war itself. Therefore, to arrive at a clear understanding of the political economy of GBVAW in Colombia, one must analyse first the roots of the conflict, and then the Colombian men.

Unquestionably, political economy's demanding framework and the contribution of True's and Merger's principles opened up an entirely new spectrum of possibilities, not just to recognise factors but also to link issues previously not associated with GBVAW. Religious bias, patriarchal values, moral canons, societal gender roles and geographical specificities, all intrinsic to a nation's culture, influence greatly the type of woman who enters war scenarios. As such, there are significant behavioural differences in how urban and rural populations respond to turmoil in their lives. It is also well known that the latter are always a step behind urban development; their cultural change is neither swift nor decisive. Colombia's war took place precisely in the most underdeveloped rural areas of the country. Long before the war began, *campesinas* lived under the rule of men's authority, their world was already small, limited to care activities, and with no possessions or rights. In essence, they were invisible. Given their precarious circumstances, *campesinas* entered the conflict not just vulnerable but deeply undervalued – the perfect profile to become targets, mere casualties of war. So what propelled these women to become actors rather than just victims? The explanation is as complex as the conflict, but what is indisputable is that these women tore down five traditional paradigms.

- **First paradigm: sexual violence destroys women.** *Campesinas* stood up quietly but decisively against violence, and were responsible for what Stewart (2010: 2) calls 'complex networks of pro-peace movements'. They suffered greatly as a result of sexual abuse, yet their social and political reaction is what sets them apart. Perhaps the intrafamilial violence intrinsic to their lives may be behind their strength. Rural women should not be invisible in Colombia, for their achievements during the war can be measured by the numbers of national laws enacted on their behalf.
- **Second paradigm: conflict does not affect gender roles.** A very unusual fact in this war is that patriarchal norms worked harder against rural men than against *campesinas*. The failure to protect women drove men to self-destruct productively and socially. Their power is their greatest weakness as well, for an absurd paradox in rural men's definition of masculinity is *women*. Paramilitary forces quickly understood their feebleness and turned women into effective weapons of war that swiftly destroyed rural masculinity and entire communities.
- **Third paradigm: economic policies are neutral in terms of gender and GBVAW.** Elson and Cagatay's (2000) thesis about the non-neutrality of economic policies on social issues is applicable to gender in this conflict. The *Apertura* also joined forces with the conflict, and negatively impacted women. The extensive nature of agribusinesses renewed old alliances between landowners and paramilitaries to extend their plantations, a relationship that gave rise to violent displacement driven by the economic interests of a few. The weapon of choice to force men out was women.
- **Fourth paradigm: public policies are neutral in terms of gender or GBVAW.** In armed conflicts, political factors usually ignore the gender content in public policies. Decentralisation – which also joined forces with the war – impacted rural women via different forms of GBVAW. Fiscal resources and political power moving to local and regional governments reinforced paramilitary control over specific areas of the country. Not only did the quality of social services diminish rapidly, but also perpetrators freely enforced more archaic patriarchal values on women in towns under their hegemony.

Decentralisation fortified the power and financial base of paramilitary forces; their authoritarian rule turned women into objects of reproduction or pleasure for commanders and troops.

- **Fifth paradigm: rivalry between gender roles stems from competitive globalisation.** In Colombia's war, rivalry between gender roles does not stem exclusively from competitive globalisation. In fact, this kind of rivalry is mostly seen among displaced men and women, and its effect is even more ruthless. High demand for care services in urban Colombia propelled former *campesinas* into the labour market. The lack of demand for rural men's abilities crushed their masculinity once more, and that is the reason behind the GBVAW endured by displaced *campesinas* living in urban areas.

## Final thoughts

Most of the conclusions of this Colombian case analysis diverge from those commonly perceived by gender equality advocates and experts. Decisively choosing to view women as actors rather than just victims and going beyond historically accepted explanations for the war by including economic and social perspectives led to unexpected final thoughts.

Traditional feminists would reject from the very start any analysis that focuses on men to explain what happens to women. Many believe that the study of men's situation will not contribute to advancing women's struggle for equal rights. This study is proof of the contrary. Colombian rural women's astonishing shift from victim to crucial actors in the conflict could not be fully understood, nor realised, without the contribution of men's weaknesses.

These women experienced all the possible dimensions of gender-based violence at the hands of three different types of perpetrators: the most brutal and inhumane paramilitary forces; the FARC, which neglected the rights of female combatants in spite of its equalitarian gender discourse; and national military forces that failed miserably to honour their vow to protect the population when perpetrating heinous crimes against women. And yet, rather than simply surviving like victims do, *campesinas* rose up to become crucial actors who drove change for the entire Colombian society – a vital accomplishment that few have recognised.

Unquestionably, when it comes to war and its undertones, Colombia continues to be unique. This analysis of the political economy of violence against women during war proves that the nation's rural women are also quite unique. Important paradoxes separate them from preconceived notions portraying women as defenceless, weak victims lost in the aftermath of the war. The first one is the strength of *campesinas*, who, despite heinous abuse from known and unknown men, took their lives into their hands, without any help, support or guidance, to forge their own future. The second and most unexpected paradox is their fortitude as proof that, in Colombia, GBVAW was not a method to control women, but rather the weapon of choice to force men into submission. The third, hidden and very surprising, is that, although the wounds still live in women's bodies, the real casualty of this war is men's masculinity.

Unaided and quietly, these women influenced change in an entire nation, not just for themselves but for future generations of rural and urban women alike. Today, the strength and voices of *campesinas* have already achieved what urban women still hope for. Their courage has moved them from victims to vital actors in this long war, but their achievements should not stop in Colombia. They are a message to the world about the need to look beyond the obvious when it comes to the study of women and what affects their lives.

## Notes

1 The FARC is known as the oldest guerrilla group in the world, founded in 1964, and was the largest insurgency in the country.

2 The 'Final Accord' is how this study will refer to the 2016 peace agreement signed between the Colombian government and the FARC. It includes compromises on land reform, political participation, anti-drug policies, etc. A six-person committee is charged with supervising compliance; only one member is a woman.

3 The Colombian Liberal Party resembles the American Democratic Party. The Conservative Party is ideologically close to the Republican Party.

4 The term 'guerrilla' includes different guerrilla groups, historically varying between three and nine different revolutionary forces, all with left-wing ideologies.

5 This study will indiscriminately use the term *campesinas* in reference to rural women; therefore, both terms refer to the same group of women.

6 Information on homicides, forced disappearances and kidnappings is available, but this research is unable to use it because the Victim Registry includes both direct and indirect victims for these three victimising factors. For instance, there are 166,592 victims of forced disappearance, a figure that includes those forcibly disappeared (direct victims) as well as those within their family circle (indirect victims). Similarly, the registry does not provide further data on the indirect victims' gender.

7 The legal age for marriage without parental consent and the nation's sexual consent age is fourteen years. However, the range structure used in the collection of data caps the definition of girls at eleven years old. Therefore, for this analysis, girls will be split into eleven and under and twelve to seventeen.

8 Both UN Security Council (2012: 6) and UN Women (2012) corroborate this belief in their reports on Colombia's war.

9 In the year 1999, Colombia's GDP fell by 4.2 per cent (Banco de la República, 2016).

10 Oxford Dictionary definition of 'casual' at http://bit.ly/1igMXbd

11 This stereotype stems from the idea of patriotism, which emerged when armies ceased to be led by warlords and became professional organisations. There are two distinct notions in this concept: the nation, which is a family-like structure that must be preserved and reproduced (Wills, 2005: 74); and the fatherland, which represents the ultimate sacrifice in order to protect the nation. Women were assigned the conservation and reproduction of the nation, and men were expected to be willing to die for the fatherland. In this way, the professionalisation of armies led to a reinforcement of gender roles that still continues today (ibid.).

12 Care tasks focus on providing for the individual's physical, social and emotional well-being; society has traditionally assigned these tasks to women (López Montaño et al., 2015).

13 The percentages of answers from men and women do not add up to 100 per cent because participants were allowed to choose more than one reason for joining the FARC.

## References

Acosta, C. L. 2015. 'Mujeres, Violencia Sexual, Desplazamiento Forzado y Restitución de Tierras en el Departamento del Magdalena 1999 a 2012', *Criterios* 8 (2): 207–58.

Banco de la República. 2016. *Indicadores Económicos*. Bogotá: Banco de la República, http://bit.ly/1UY9hlO

Call, C. T. 2012. *Why Peace Fails: The Causes and Prevention of Civil War Recurrence*. Washington DC: Georgetown University Press.

Castrillón, G. Y. 2016. '¿Víctimas o Victimarias? El Rol de las Mujeres en las FARC', *Revista Opera* 16, http://bit.ly/2oUxaTq

CGR. 2015. *Primera Encuesta Nacional de Víctimas*. Bogotá: Contraloría General de la República (CGR), http://bit.ly/2nbPryg

CNMH. 2012. *El Placer: Mujeres, Coca y Guerra en el Bajo Putumayo*. Bogotá: Taurus & Pensamiento for Centro Nacional de Memoria Histórica (CNMH).

CNMH. 2013. *Basta Ya!* Bogotá: Centro Nacional de Memoria Histórica (CNMH), Comisión Nacional de Reparación y Reconciliación.

CNRR. 2011. *Mujeres que Hacen Historia: Tierra, Cuerpo y Política en el Caribe Colombiano*. Informe del Grupo de Memoria Histórica. Bogotá: Comisión Nacional de Reparación y Reconciliación (CNRR).

Colombia Reports. 2015a. 'Understanding Colombia's Conflict: Inequality', Colombia Reports, 7 January, http://bit.ly/2nAbP3v

Colombia Reports. 2015b. 'Who Commits Most Sex Crimes in Colombia's Conflict', Colombia Reports, 20 April, http://bit.ly/2nrLLlJ

Congreso de la República. 1988. *Ley 30 de 1988 – Otorga Facultades al*

*Presidente de la República*. Law 30. Bogotá: Gobierno de la República.

Congreso de la República. 2002. *Ley 731 de 2002 – Normas para Favorecer a las Mujeres Rurales*. Law 731. Bogotá: Gobierno de la República.

Congreso de la República. 2011. *Ley 1448 de 2011 – Víctimas y Restitución de Tierras*. Law 1448. Bogotá: Ministry of the Interior, http://bit.ly/2fstRCK

Corte Constitucional. 2015. *Auto 009: Prevención de la Violencia Sexual en el Marco del Conflicto*. Sala Especial de Seguimiento Sentencia T-025 de 2004. Bogotá: Gobierno de la República.

Crandall, R. 1999. 'The End of Civil Conflict in Colombia: The Military, Paramilitaries, and a New Role for the United States', *SAIS Review* 19 (1): 223–37.

Cueter, N. 2015. 'Caught between the War on Drugs and Guerrilla Warfare: Colombia's Road to Peace'. Master of Arts in Liberal Studies (MALS) thesis, Georgetown University.

DANE. 2015. *Tercer Censo Nacional Agropecuario*. Bogotá: Departamento Administrativo Nacional de Estadística (DANE), Gobierno de la República, http://is.gd/nENfxm

DANE. 2017a. *Exportaciones: Junio 2017*. Boletín Técnico. Bogotá: Departamento Administrativo Nacional de Estadística (DANE), Gobierno de la República, https://bit.ly/2H2BoVy

DANE. 2017b. *Presentación Resultados de Pobreza 2016*. Presentación. Bogotá: Departamento Administrativo Nacional de Estadística (DANE), Gobierno de la República, http://bit.ly/2wObGoW

Defensoría del Pueblo. 2014. *El Conflicto Armado y el Riesgo para la Mujer Rural. Sistema de Alertas Tempranas*. Bogotá: Torre Gráfica.

DNP. 1984. *Política sobre el Papel de la Mujer Campesina en el Desarrollo Agropecuario*. Documentos Conpes 2109. Bogotá: Departamento Nacional de Planeación (DNP), Gobierno de la República.

DNP. 2013. *Lineamientos de Política Pública para la Prevención de Riesgos, la Protección y Garantía de los Derechos de las Mujeres Víctimas del Conflicto Armado*. Documentos Conpes 3784. Bogotá: Departamento Nacional de Planeación (DNP), Gobierno de la República.

DNP. 2015a. *Saldar la Deuda Historica con el Campo. Marco Conceptual*. Bogotá: Departamento Nacional de Planeación (DNP), Misión para la Transformación del Campo, Gobierno de la República, http://bit.ly/1RlxgFC

DNP. 2015b. *El Campo Colombiano: Un Camino Hacia el Bienestar y la Paz*. Bogotá: Departamento Nacional de Planeación (DNP), Misión para la Transformación del Campo, Gobierno de la República.

Elson, D. and Cagatay, N. 2000. 'The Social Content of Macroeconomic Policies', *World Development* 28 (7): 1347–64, https://bit.ly/2ArJnZG

ENC. 2015. *Mujer Militar: Igualdad y Liderazgo*. Bogotá: Ejercito Nacional de Colombia (ENC), Gobierno de la República, http://bit.ly/2nCFfv4

Enloe, C. 2004. 'The Politics of Masculinity and Femininity in Nationalist Wars' in Enloe, C., *The Curious Feminist: Searching for Women in the New Age of Empire*. Berkeley: University of California Press.

Game, A. and Pringle, R. 1984. *Gender at Work*. London: Allen and Unwin.

Gates, S., Håvard, H., Håvard, M. and Håvard, S. 2012. 'Development Consequences of Armed Conflict', *World Development* 40 (9): 1713–22.

González, F. 2004. 'The Colombian Conflict in Historical Perspective' in García-Durán, M. (ed.), *Accord*,

*Alternatives to War: Colombia's Peace Processes*. London: Conciliation Resources and CINEP.

Guzmán, G., Fals Borda, O. and Umaña Luna, E. 1962. *La Violencia en Colombia: Estudio de un Proceso Social. Vol. I.* Bogotá: Tercer Mundo.

Herrera, N. and Porch, D. 2008. '"Like Going to a Fiesta": The Role of Female Fighters in Colombia's FARC-Ep', *Small Wars and Insurgencies* 19 (4): 609–34, http://bit.ly/2vzeXSu

Ibáñez, A. M., Gáfaro, M. and Calderón, V. 2011. 'Desplazamiento Forzoso, Participación Laboral Femenina y Poder de Negociación en el Hogar: ¿Empodera el Conflicto a las Mujeres?' Documentos CEDE 45. Bogotá: Universidad de los Andes.

INML. 2015. *Violencia Sexual en Colombia*. Bogotá: Instituto Nacional de Medicina Legal y Ciencias Forenses (INML), Gobierno de la República.

Londoño, L. M. and Nieto, Y. F. 2006. *Mujeres no Contadas: Proceso de Desmovilización y Retorno a la Vida Civil de Mujeres Excombatientes en Colombia. 1990–2003*. Bogotá: La Carreta Editores.

López Montaño, C. 2011. 'Diseño y Formulación de Políticas para las Mujeres Desplazadas' in *El Reto Ante la Tragedia Humanitaria del Desplazamiento Forzado: Superar la Exclusión Social de la Población Desplazada*. Bogotá: CODHES.

López Montaño, C., Rodríguez Enríquez, C., Rey de Marulanda, N. and Ocampo, J. A. 2015. *Bases para un Nuevo Modelo de Desarrollo con Igualdad de Género*. Bogotá: CiSoe and ONU Mujeres.

Mantilla, S. 2012. 'Economía y Conflicto Armado en Colombia', *Latinoamérica* 55 (2): 35–73, http://bit.ly/1WokhVN

Meger, S. 2016. *Rape, Loot, Pillage: The Political Economy of Sexual Violence in Armed Conflict*. Oxford: Oxford University Press.

Ministerio de Defensa Nacional. 2010. *Política en Derechos Sexuales y Reproductivos, Equidad y Violencia Basada en Género, Salud Sexual y Reproductiva, con Énfasis en Vih*. Bogotá: Programa Integral contra la Violencia de Género, http://bit.ly/2mWqKpC

NRC. 2015. *Global Overview 2015: People Internally Displaced by Conflict and Violence*. Oslo: Internal Displacement Monitoring Centre, Norwegian Refugee Council (NRC).

Otero, S. 2006. 'Colombia: Las Mujeres en la Guerra y en la Paz. Lo Femenino de las FARC y de las AUC', ReliefWeb, 21 March, http://bit.ly/2nnumvY

Otis, J. 2015. 'Colombians Accuse US Soldiers and Officials of Sexual Assault', *Time*, 15 April, http://ti.me/1b1oak6

RUV. 2017. 'Red Nacional de Información', Registro Único de Víctimas (RUV), Gobierno de la República, https://bit.ly/2uZlZNI

Stewart, F. 2002. *Horizontal Inequalities: A Neglected Dimension of Development*. Oxford: Centre for Research on Inequality, Human Security and Ethnicity (CRISE).

Stewart, F. 2010. 'Women in Conflict and Post-conflict Situations'. New York: Development Cooperation Forum, UN Economic and Social Council.

True, J. 2010. 'The Political Economy of Violence against Women: A Feminist International Relations Perspective', *Australian Feminist Law Journal* 32 (1): 39–59, https://bit.ly/2gbH4zB

True, J. 2012. *The Political Economy of Violence against Women*. Oxford and New York: Oxford University Press.

UN Security Council. 2012. *Report of the Secretary-General on Conflict-related Sexual Violence*. General Assembly 66.

Geneva: United Nations (UN) Security Council.

UN Women. 2012. *Addressing Conflict-related Sexual Violence: An Analytical Inventory of Peacekeeping Practice.* New York: United Nations (UN).

US Library of Congress. 2013. *Colombia: A Country Study.* Fifth edition. Washington DC: Federal Research Division, Library of Congress.

Vélez, C. I. 2013. 'Más Mujeres Quieren Ingresar a la Vida Militar', *El Colombiano*, 20 August, http://bit.ly/2nEoNtq

Verdad Abierta. 2013. 'La Historia de las FARC', *Verdad Abierta*, 3 October, http://bit.ly/1GHrDB2

Vergel, C. 2012. 'Entre Lutte Armée et Féminisme: Quelques Reflexions à Propos des Femmes Combattantes en Colombie', *Revista Derecho del Estado* 29.

Wills, M. E. 2005. 'Mujeres en Armas: ¿Avance Ciudadano o Subyugación Femenina?', *Análisis Político* 54: 63–80, http://bit.ly/2grjf3J

World Bank. 2016. 'World Development Indicators', World Bank, http://bit.ly/1Cd8EkQ

Yagoub, M. 2014. 'How Colombia's Drug Trade Constructed Female Narco-beauty', *Colombia Reports*, 5 February, http://bit.ly/1MqYOuA

# 4 | CONTESTING TERRITORIALITY: PATRIARCHY, ACCUMULATION AND DISPOSSESSION. 'ENTRENCHED PERIPHERALITY': WOMEN, POLITICAL ECONOMY AND THE MYTH OF PEACE BUILDING IN NORTH EAST INDIA

*Roshmi Goswami*

## Introduction

In recent times, the Colombian peace talks and the process itself have generated tremendous interest and attention worldwide, especially among women peace activists and advocates. It has been well documented and acknowledged that sexual violence was used as a weapon of war by all sides, and that women and children, particularly from Afro-Colombian and indigenous groups, bore the brunt of the conflict.[1] But the acknowledgement and commitment to redress move beyond sexual violence. In articulating the violations of conflict as violations of justice and by including a range of remedies to address infringements, from violence against women to discriminatory land ownership and access, the Colombian peace accords signal a move to deal with the root causes of conflict and their attendant violence, and include redress for both direct and structural causes of violence.

Indeed, the quest for justice or the desire for 'just peace', framed differently in different contexts, is an aspirational goal of peace builders across the world as well as in communities emerging from armed conflicts and wars. Lederach's (2003) pioneering and extensive work on conflict, which emphasised peace as embedded in justice, consisted in seeking constructive change or a process of transformation for violent conflict – the elements of which include the building of relationships and social structures through a radical respect for human rights. For Galtung (1969), peace building is integrally connected to addressing structural violence or indirect violence – violence caused by certain social structures or social institutions that prevents people from meeting their basic needs. Although structural violence is said to be invisible, it has a number of influences that shape it, including discriminatory laws, racism and gender inequality. The absence or negation of structural violence is what Galtung defines as positive peace, differentiating it from what he calls negative peace, which is the absence of personal or direct violence. Grounding these ideas in realities and referring particularly to factors that limit access to healthcare in the context of Haiti, but which are applicable universally, Farmer et al. argue that social inequalities lie at the heart of structural violence and that structural violence is structured and stricturing for it constricts the agency of its victims and 'tightens a physical noose around their necks', thereby determining how material and social resources are allocated and experienced (2006).

Building on these analyses, Gready and Robins (2014) suggest transformative justice as an alternative approach. They argue that transformative justice is a concept that can clearly be applied anywhere and at any time to address concerns such as structural and everyday violence that are often exacerbated in a post-conflict or peace-building period. The salient feature of transformative justice is transformative change that emphasises local agency and resources; prioritises process rather than preconceived outcomes; and challenges unequal and intersecting power relationships and structures of exclusion at both the local and global level. They argue that the focus of a transformative justice approach will be on intersections between economics and power; on discrimination and exclusion; and on changing the future rather than returning to the past.

These analyses of structural violence resonate and synchronise with the lived experiences of women, while the emphasis and commitment to justice that they necessitate are especially critical for them. Decades before Galtung and others, feminists developed a broad understanding of peace and violence, positing that there can be no peace if there is oppression and no stability without justice. Feminist discourse has clearly held the view that physical violence against women in the context of armed conflicts and wars is closely linked to the status of women's rights in peacetime, which include their socio-economic rights. Central to the feminist analysis is the concept of patriarchy as an oppressive and hierarchical system, which is essentially structural violence often enacted as personal violence. The feminist analyses, underpinned by the lived experiences of women and notions of justice, remain focused on patriarchy as a system of oppression and form the basis of the more recent political economy approach. Arguing that violence is a continuum enabled by the hierarchical social arrangements in both the private and public spheres, a feminist political economy approach seeks to reconceptualise justice on the basis of women's lived experiences (True, 2014). Persistent advocacy by women's rights activists and women human rights defenders has resulted in some level of focus on sexual violence. While this is necessarily an exclusive focus on rape and other forms of direct sexual violence, it fails to recognise the full range of abuses committed against women and girls and what women suffer in situations of violence (Schmid, 2012), and also what women aspire to in a moment of political transition. Indeed, the Colombian process has raised the bar for negotiations around sexual violence ensuring dignity,[2] and, more importantly, it brings in issues that capture the on-the-ground realities and priorities of women's lives.

The endemic conflicts in Asia and their peace negotiations do not reflect a high standard for issues concerning women. The resistance or apathy to gender justice is also often couched in the much touted 'uniqueness of Asian values' argument. Additionally, the conflicts are very complex, involving different stakeholders with varying social dynamics. A 2013 study shows that the South and South East Asia regions have some of the world's longest armed struggles, lasting multiple generations and averaging at around forty-five years per struggle, and that the armed struggles are mostly subnational conflicts or armed conflicts over control of a subnational territory within a sovereign state (Parks et al., 2013). These long-enduring conflicts have been extremely devastating, compromising security and justice and steadily corroding the lives and social fabric of the communities in the affected areas. Within the national context these conflicts are invariably situated in remote regions of the state, which are peripheral both in terms of location and in power sharing. Primarily peopled by communities often referred to as 'minorities', their contributions to national politics as well as to the national economy are invariably perceived to be insignificant or peripheral (Goswami, 2017).

A political economy method of analysis shows that, as political and economic power are part of the same authority structure, the economic, political and social realms are all interconnected and power operates not only through direct coercion but also through the structured relations of production and reproduction that govern the distribution and use of resources, benefits, privileges and authority within the home and transnational society at large (True, 2014). A feminist political economy lens further adds that violent conflict, which often results from struggles to control power and productive resources, normalises violence, spreads it throughout societies, and involves celebrating masculine aggression and perpetuating impunity for men's violence against women. It highlights that if women are unable to gain access to physical security, social services, justice and economic opportunities, their particular vulnerability to violence continues in peacetime (ibid.). This chapter attempts to bring out aspects of the ways in which political, economic, social and ideological processes have intersected to impact and shape gender-based violence in the subnational conflicts of North East India and continue to do so in the present period of 'protracted peace'. Using a political economy approach, the chapter draws out the structural basis and systems that anchor gendered unequal political and economic power sharing that perpetuate violence, while also presenting a diversity of women's lived experiences. While surfacing the changes that women seek in their quest for justice, the chapter concludes by highlighting the need to recast women's resistance in the region and in conflict contexts in general in transformative terms, moving beyond direct violence to addressing hierarchical sociopolitical and economic arrangements and resource sharing in both the private and public spheres.

## Landscapes

### The peripheral context and women

The enormously diverse north-eastern part of India, which originally comprised seven states, is often clubbed together as one unit, which in itself is hugely contradictory and continues to be contested. The commonalities relate to it being a region of protracted subnational conflicts spanning several decades, and to it being the resource-rich periphery or hinterland of the Indian mainland. The conflicts – as diverse as the region itself – have ranged from political and civil struggles for self-determination and aggrieved groups contending for a greater or fairer share of power or a stake in the system, to interethnic conflicts over fractured identities or scarce and dwindling resources (Goswami et al., 2014). My own knowledge – which is based on experience and scholarship, as well as extensive fieldwork coupled with expertise on women's human rights, particularly in the context of conflict – provides a compelling picture of the region. Questions of identity and ethnicity have been central and have added layers of complexity, both within the parameters of the conflicts as well as in the various 'peace arrangements'. The political goals of the armed conflicts have ranged from greater political autonomy and political rights to extreme positions in the past, such as calls for outright secession from India. Contestations over the control and optimal utilisation of natural resources (land, water and minerals), while less openly articulated, have been core to many of the conflicts and continue to be critical present-day fault lines. The response of the Indian state has varied over the years but has essentially been one of dominance and control – whether by the overt repressive measures and direct violence of earlier times or through the more subtle, resource-extractive 'development' mantra of the present. In such a context there is much cynicism, even around the intent and viability of India's much touted 'Look East' foreign policy, which was initiated in 1991 in order to see the region not as a periphery but as a thriving and integrated economic hub linking South Asia and South East Asia.

Subnational conflicts generally remain unrecognised officially by states and their existence is an issue of intense debate and political disagreement. Similarly, in North East India the persistent non-acknowledgment of these conflicts by the Indian state, or its categorisation of the problem as one of law and order, has kept the levels of violence high and the situation outside the purview of international humanitarian law and internationally accepted normative standards of justice and human rights (Goswami, 2017). Over the decades, as new demands and new groups have emerged, the original causes of the conflicts – economic and political inequalities, entrenched social injustices, gross human rights violations or unequal power structures – have become submerged under an overarching umbrella of ad hoc, short-term political arrangements. This includes economic relations of violence as a subterranean but thriving war/conflict economy that has grown progressively; in many instances the earlier conflicts have metastasised into complex economic alliances. The overt military presence of earlier times has undoubtedly decreased, but decades of extensive militarisation have left their scars. Security concerns in general continue to restrict access and information but covertly also enable economic gain and profiteering among a select few, in activities ranging from the dubious extraction of the diverse resources of the region to the arms trade, and including cold-blooded economic gains from fake encounter deaths (Bhattacharjee, 2015). While more in-depth research is needed to reveal the nexus between the different 'power brokers', feedback from women's rights and human rights groups working on the ground as well as my own experiences show that vested interest stakeholders include state officials, politicians, the military, non-state armed groups, arms dealers, corporations and various types of 'facilitating agents'.

As in the rest of the world, women have borne the brunt of the heightened militarisation – whether specifically targeted by security forces or rival militant groups, or because of the continuum of violence from the public to the private. The impact has been debilitating and far-reaching, with violations ranging from sexual violence, displacement and loss of support bases and livelihoods to disappearances and extra-judicial killings of family members, lack of all forms of human security and the constant sense of fear and dread (van Lierde, 2011). Alternatively, while the different 'peace moments', peace negotiations and agreements provide important opportunities for conflict transformation, masculinised securitisation has either increased greatly or continues to be the dominant focus (Goswami, 2017).

Several questions can be raised about how peace is conceptualised in these peripheries. Are these peace processes aimed at ensuring justice by ending violence and deep-rooted social and political inequalities as well as gender inequalities and exclusion of the 'peripheral other'? Or are they mere 'settlements' within a patriarchal framework that simply continue the entrenched inequalities and in some instances bring in greater complexities? The present context in the so-called 'peripheral' North East Region of India provides for an interesting gendered analysis of the political economy of conflict. Using illustrations from three different contexts and time frames in the region and a gender lens, this chapter attempts to:

- reveal the consequences of entrenched gender inequalities in the narratives of armed struggles, human rights and peace building in the region;
- analyse whether there is any understanding of the structural causes and long-term impacts and consequences of conflict-related sexual violence and the different ways in which social, political, economic

and ideological processes have intersected to impact and shape conflict-related gender-based violence (True, 2014) and what attention is being paid to these; and

- determine whether the content, form and politics of the peace processes of any of the three different contexts provide any evidence of an understanding and attempt at 'social transformation' or gender justice, and if not, why?

Finally, it attempts to highlight what women on the ground really want and the need therefore to recast women's resistance in transformative terms to realise these aspirations.

## Territoriality and challenges to the emerging nation state

### The Naga conflict: patriarchal power games, women's bodies and the othering of the periphery

The Indo-Naga conflict is one of the longest running, not just in India but in all of South Asia. Having resisted the forced inclusion of the Naga Hills into British India in 1881, during the mobilisation for Indian independence the Nagas petitioned the Simon Commission 'to leave us alone to determine for ourselves as in ancient times'. Thereafter, the Naga National Council (NNC), formed under the leadership of Angami Zapu Phizo, declared the Naga region an independent state on 14 August 1947. Prior to this, in a historic meeting Mahatma Gandhi assured the Naga leaders that no force would be used against them and that the Nagas were free to stay out of the Indian National Council. A plebiscite called on the issue of Naga independence in 1951 had 99 per cent of the Nagas give their verdict in favour of independence. The Naga resistance was an affront to the brand-new power of the emerging Indian nation state, which responded with a massive and brutal show of force. The Armed Forces (Special Powers) Act was enacted in 1958 to deal with this. This Act was supposed to be a temporary special measure but it equipped the armed forces with unbridled powers, totally cramping the fundamental rights of citizens, and it is still in operation today.

What followed were years of extensive and intense counter-insurgency operations by the Indian state; these included combing operations, arbitrary detentions and the burning down of whole villages, all marked by extreme levels of violence and brutality. Naga women were especially and strategically targeted – raped, sexually abused and brutalised to teach the 'insurgents/rebels' a lesson as well as to break them down psychologically. The Nagas were known to be extremely protective about their women and children. Historically, as head-hunting warrior tribes constantly at war with their neighbouring villages, each tribe had a fairly elaborate defence structure and hierarchy to protect women and children. Only the most able and bravest warriors formed the inner core of defenders assigned this task. To be able to break through this formidable defence and reach the women was considered the greatest victory for the aggressors and absolute defeat – both physical and psychological – for the defending tribe. It was a measure and assessment of masculinities – patriarchal notions of personhood – pitted one against the other. In addition, women were also looked upon as the most 'prized possessions' and as the keepers of the tribe's culture and identity. By violating the women, the aggressors conveyed a message of trampling on the tribe's inner core of being. Many of the instances of brutalisation also took place inside or in the vicinity of churches, which were sacred sites held in immense reverence and awe by the recently converted Nagas. These violations deeply hurt and crippled the Naga psyche. For the Indian state and its security forces, the intensity of the sexual violence was determined in part by the 'othering' of the people from the peripheries. As they were clearly different in appearance, food habits, culture and religion from 'mainland India', the 'othering' of the Nagas was easy.

The periods of violence were also punctuated by a series of 'peace initiatives', which were at best 'band aid' insincere attempts towards a political solution. These simply fuelled the resistance further, making it more complex with the formation of the National Socialist Council of Nagaland (NSCN) in 1980, which splintered into the Isak–Muivah faction (NSCN-IM) and the S. S. Khaplang faction (NSCN-K) in 1988, but all with an avowed objective of establishing a Nagalim (greater Nagaland) covering all Naga-inhabited areas. Finally, in 1997, the NSCN-IM and the Union government entered into a ceasefire agreement and have since held over eighty rounds of dialogue to resolve the conflict. A similar ceasefire agreement was signed with the NSCN-K in 2001.

Alongside attempts at reconciliation among the different Naga tribes, intra-tribal feuds and fresh demands for greater autonomy continue. Civil society organisations such as the apex tribal council, Naga Hoho, the church[3] and women under the aegis of the Naga Mothers Association

(NMA) have played remarkable roles in brokering peace and stopping fratricidal killings among the different armed factions. While the NMA's role in determining the terms of the ceasefire agreement is especially laudable, it has also moved beyond the immediate cessation of violence to questioning deeper structural issues of violence against women and continues to advocate for women's more substantive engagement in state building. Questioning power and control has also been taken up more recently by other sections of civil society, particularly youth organisations and business associations; the latter formed an action committee called Against Corruption and Unabated Taxation (ACAUT) to oppose rampant and multiple tax collection by Naga rebel groups and to question their ongoing aggression and control. The NSCN, however, maintains that, as a people-mandated revolutionary group, it has the right to tax people and continue to reap the economic benefits of war.

With no clear outcome, the peace negotiations between the Indian state and the NSCN-IM have indeed been excruciatingly protracted. After eighty rounds or so of talks, a Naga Framework Agreement (NFA) with the Indian government was arrived at in 2015. This long-awaited Naga peace agreement, however, has been shrouded in deep secrecy, with no clarity on what it actually contains or the actual status of the controversial Naga unification demand.

The Mizo conflict: patriarchal controls, apathy and 'spirit wounds'

Before the formation of the state of Mizoram in 1987, the Mizo or Lushai Hills was a district in the state of Assam. But, like the Naga struggles, the Mizo aspirations for autonomy and self-rule also pre-date Indian independence, although they came to a head in the 1960s. Every fifty years or so a cyclical ecological phenomenon locally called Mautam or 'bamboo death' occurs in the region, during which a certain species of bamboo flowers attracts a plague of rats that plunder crops and granaries, resulting in famine. The devastating famine of 1959 was met with neglect and apathy by the Assam government, deepening the resentment and discontent of the Mizos. A famine relief team that was formed ultimately morphed into the Mizo National Front (MNF). Focused on Mizo nationalism with self-determination as its main objective, the MNF led a secessionist movement aimed at establishing a sovereign Christian nation for the Mizos. This Mizo independence movement lasted until the peace accord or the Memorandum of Settlement was signed in 1986.

The movement was met with extremely brutal and hard-hitting counter-insurgency operations by the Indian state. The Assam Disturbed Areas Act 1955 and the Armed Forces (Special Powers) Act 1958 were invoked, proclaiming the entire Mizo district as 'disturbed'. This enabled and provided impunity for arbitrary arrests, detentions and the killing of innocent persons, brutalisation and extreme humiliation of the men, plundering of villages, and rampant rape and sexual abuse of women. But the most significant, infamous and memorable operations were air strikes by the Indian air force using incendiary bombs on civilian territory and its own citizens. This was unprecedented anywhere in the country and rare in any other part of the globe.

The other, more deeply subversive, operation – one that brought about far-reaching structural changes and remains a memory of 'collective distress' – was the introduction of the 'grouping of villages' scheme under the provisions of Defence of India Rules 1962 and the Assam Maintenance of Public Order Act 1953. The massive regrouping of villages into larger units, purportedly for more efficient management, was carried out by eviction and coercive resettlement under supervision of the military. It was undertaken to subdue MNF volunteers and cut off the food supply and access to shelter for the rebels as well as to disrupt and break community cohesion. Under the grouping policy, nearly 80 per cent of the rural population was shifted from their villages and resettled along the highways. Resistance was met brutally with gross human rights violations. Women were raped, crops that people had toiled for months to grow were torched, old villages were burned, and the new settlements kept under the control of the security forces. The grouping resulted in traumatic upheaval, with the Mizo community suffering what is referred to as a 'spirit wound'. Communities were broken up, people were forced into different camps and often agreement papers were signed at gunpoint, people helplessly watching the torching of their homes, precious belongings and granaries and the killing of their livestock (Nunthara, 1981). About 5,200 villages were affected by the regrouping and whole populations were made subservient to the power and authority of the security forces. There was heightened surveillance, the breakdown of traditional knowledge, and no access to forests beyond permitted limits. Consequently, an entire community of self-sufficient farmers became totally dependent on the government. For the Mizos, this has been one of their most traumatic and painful experiences, one that has left behind very deep psychological wounds and has had a long-term impact on the social fabric of the otherwise cohesive Mizo society. For women who had already been sexually violated, the regrouping added another dimension of trauma and loss of familiar support bases.

Like the Naga movement, women from all walks of life were targeted, including heavily pregnant women. The brutal gang rape of two young women by security forces in 1966 is a well-remembered case. On a fateful night, in retaliation for an MNF attack on a convoy of the Indian army, villagers were herded together and their homes set on fire by the army. Two women, the daughters of prominent community leaders, were held separately in a hut where soldiers took turns in raping them. Recently, after almost fifty years, compensation of 500,000 rupees each was announced by the central government for the two survivors. But it was too little too late for the severely traumatised women, who can no longer lead a normal life, like most of the violated women of the period. The entire Mizo community – and women in particular – suffered silently, as there was no institution where the victims could seek justice or redress. It was these crimes and violations that prompted various women's groups to come together to form the powerful Mizo Hmeichhia Insuihkhawm Pawl (MHIP), which vowed to work for and fight for the collective rights of Mizo women.

Enthused by the MNF's call for *Zalenna* or Freedom for Mizoram, both young and old Mizo women joined the freedom movement in large numbers, enrolling in the Mizo National Volunteers (MNV). They mostly received training in basic nursing rather than in combat, but they formed the backbone of the movement by providing food and serving as messengers, carrying strategic information. As large numbers of unmarried women volunteered in the MNF, women were held in great suspicion by Indian military personnel and endured much harassment. My research documented a volunteer recalling how, before she became a fully fledged member of MNF, she was repeatedly summoned by the Indian security forces, humiliated in public with her hands and feet tied up. The repeated humiliation pushed her into joining the armed struggle.

### The Assam movement: the youthful romance of resistance, disillusionment and women

The death of a parliamentarian in the state of Assam in 1978 necessitated a by-election. During the preparation of the electoral rolls, a dramatic increase in the number of registered voters was noticed. Subsequent media reports and a statement of concern by the Election Commissioner himself over the massive numbers of illegal settlers and voters triggered a strong response from student bodies and sections of civil society. Thus began a mass student movement called the Assam Agitation or Assam Andolan, which demanded a revision of the electoral rolls followed by disenfranchisement and deportation of illegal voters. In the mass mobilisation of civil society, people joined in the thousands, with women from all walks of life being particularly active and visible. The question of Assam's economic exploitation and its use as a hinterland was added to the initial grievances and the movement blockaded shipments of crude oil and other natural resources from the state to the mainland. The Indian state dealt with the agitation severely and the movement itself, though conceived primarily as a non-violent protest, led to an extremely violent fallout.[4]

Simultaneously, a section of Assamese youth decided to launch an armed resistance to what it perceived as state terrorism and economic exploitation. In 1979, they formed the United Liberation Front of Assam (ULFA),[5] which is a self-proclaimed revolutionary political organisation engaged in a liberation struggle for the establishment of a sovereign, socialist Assam. As it sought to establish a united Assamese identity irrespective of ethnicity, caste, class, tribe or religion, it was tremendously appealing to the otherwise marginalised multi-ethnic communities of Upper Assam and managed to have strong support bases in both rural and urban Assam. Once again, women played an important role and were central to establishing this identity. Notwithstanding its strong initial support, the ULFA, unlike the Naga and the Mizo resistance movements, was never considered to be an all-Assamese movement. And over the years, as the ULFA veered away from its initial objective of challenging the economic hegemony of the Indian state and increasingly became associated with extreme acts of brutality, violence and economic extortion, whatever support it had nosedived.

The violence of the ULFA has been matched by the violence and aggression of the Indian state's series of counter-insurgency operations. Family members, especially women and sympathisers of the ULFA, bore the brunt of these operations. In a clear message of superior strength and as a warning to those supporting or providing shelter for the militants, 'combing and search operations' by the security forces were often accompanied by sexual violence, extreme intimidation and looting. Almost all the reported cases were in far-flung rural areas of the state – the peripheries of the periphery. Interviews with women ex-combatants show that many women who were only marginally involved with the ULFA became committed members and combatants following actual atrocities or due to the fear of atrocities (Goswami, 2015).

The ULFA has dallied with a call for peace at different moments, particularly with the formation of a People's Consultative Group (PCG) in 2005. The late Dr Mamoni Raisom Goswami, the eminent feminist writer, played a pivotal role in thawing the ULFA resistance and urging them towards peace negotiations. The PCG held three rounds of dialogue with the Union government over a period of one year but the process collapsed. Finally, peace negotiations took a more definitive direction in 2009 after the arrests of top ULFA leaders and greatly facilitated by eminent citizens of Assam.[6] Despite opposition to the peace talks by one section of the ULFA, the peace negotiations that began in May 2010 – with one woman member in the ULFA team – have been ongoing since then.

## Outside the patriarchal edifice of peace settlements

### The peripheral 'other' and sexual violence

Despite increased international attention to sexual violence and the growing status of India as a responsible global player on a range of issues, in the 'peripheries' of the country justice for sexual violence perpetrated by state security forces remains elusive. Sexual violence by non-state armed groups and individuals remains invisible, and, more importantly, issues of sexual violence continue to remain outside the purview of the patriarchal structures and terms of reference of peace talks and peace negotiations (Goswami, 2017).

Sexual violence has a grievous and corrosive effect on society, intimidating and terrorising not just the victim but also families and the entire community. In most cases it is an act of domination grounded in a complex web of gendered socio-cultural preconceptions and is politically driven (Goswami, 2017). In conflict contexts, it is essentially an assertion of power and superiority perpetrated by those who have power against a targeted population that does not, and, in many instances in the three contexts cited, it is an example 'of making punishment a spectacle' (Foucault, 1995).

Sexual violence in the region has been deployed to establish the dominance and supremacy of the Indian state (Goswami et al., 2014). It has been used to torture and humiliate people into submission, as well as to punish and humiliate an enemy group or a community that had opposed or challenged the idea of a homogeneous unified Indian nation state. Post-independence, the armed movements in the peripheral North East Region of India were an affront to the idea of the nation state and nationalism. In addition, social, cultural and economic marginalisation of the peripheries, plus the perception of the peripheries as the other, also contributed to the high incidence of violence in the region by state security forces.

Among the various instances of sexual violence and torture that took place during the Naga struggles, the Oinam Hill Village incident that occurred during Operation Bluebird by the Indian security forces stands out in its level of brutality and is strongly etched in the memories of the Naga people. On a fateful day in 1987, suspected armed rebel cadres attacked an outpost of the Indian military in broad daylight, killing nine soldiers. The unprecedented counter-insurgency operation launched by the Indian security forces was accompanied by rape, torture, arson, vandalisation of public and private property, illegal detention, and so on. The whole population of Oinam village was detained in an open area for many days. Women were openly raped and molested and two pregnant women were forced to give birth in full view of the Indian security forces.

Similarly, during the twenty years of armed rebellion, the Mizo Hills, a far-off peripheral territory of the Indian state, witnessed horrific sexual violence and punitive measures perpetrated by the Indian security forces. Sexual violence was a form of extreme torture, and, for those women who experienced it, the torture has remained a painful and private memory. In research I conducted in the 1990s as part of a women's rights organisation, North East Network, women survivors in Mizoram spoke about their ordeal for the first time – some twenty years or so after the incident. For the women, there was no closure to the two-decades-old pain and horror, as there has never been any support to deal with those memories. While the women spoke, the men stood by, extremely embarrassed by the outburst and public display of emotions in an otherwise rather stoic community – and also perhaps for having failed to 'protect' their women.

Sexual violence manages to denigrate and destroy the communities targeted because social and cultural structures are so deeply intertwined with constructed ideas of gender and notions of women's purity/impurity or of women being the property of men. For the men of the tribal communities of North East India, communities that are deeply bound by the cultural and social mores of tradition and customary practices, sexual violence against the women of their communities is the ultimate humiliation and destroys their constructed and highly prized masculinity.

The Indian armed forces, however, are not the only perpetrators of sexual violence. Although it has been relatively easy to uncover sexual violence by state security forces, it has been far more difficult to identify or get people to talk about sexual violence by the armed rebels. Although such cases are fewer in number, the patterns followed are similar. The protracted peace process and peacetimes among the Nagas, for instance, have created concentric circles of peripherality, and in that 'peripheral other' women continue to be the most vulnerable other. Apart from individual instances of sexual violence and torture by non-state groups in incidents resembling the Oinam case, women's rights activists from the state of Manipur have talked about rapes of women having taken place in remote villages of the periphery by militant outfits, either to establish supremacy over a rival group or to teach an entire village a lesson. In addition, in the few cases documented by the North East Network, there emerge two categories of women who seem to have been targeted – women whose community is socially, ethnically or economically peripheral to the dominant militant group and strong independent women who have dared to question excesses or peace dividends enjoyed by a privileged few, or who express dissent or simply assert their individuality.

While all women are adversely affected in situations of protracted armed conflict, for a woman perceived to be associated with a militant group, either as an active combatant or a sympathiser, the violations are especially brutal, although the general response is different. In Assam, there have been appreciable protests by human rights groups and civil society organisations against sexual violence, yet when it involves a woman combatant the response differs. In the ongoing peace talks between the ULFA leaders and the Indian government, there is a clause on the disappeared members of the outfit but none for the survivors of sexual violence. In interviews conducted with women members of the ULFA, it is clear that, for the woman combatant, victimhood is closely intertwined with notions of agency and justice and therefore needs to be understood and addressed taking that complexity into account. A middle-aged woman is a constant visitor to a state-designated ULFA camp where the members of the outfit live as the peace negotiations proceed. Her eight-month-pregnant daughter, who was a ULFA cadre, was brutally gang-raped and killed by security forces in an act that was justified as being 'in the line of duty'. The level of brutality, however, also reveals a deeper, more insidious and misogynist justification – that of teaching a lesson to a woman who has transgressed social norms in choosing to be associated with a militant group. For the mother of the militant woman, an important aspect of justice is that there is a symbolic recognition of her daughter's role in the armed struggle, and her frequent visits to the ULFA camp are to negotiate that (Goswami, 2017).

### The militarised canvas: brutalised communities, sexual violence and the culture of impunity

Sexual violence in North East India has been facilitated particularly by implementation of the Armed Forces Special Powers Act of 1958 (AFSPA), which was first used in 1960 to curb the Naga struggle as a temporary measure, but has remained in operation in different parts of the region for over six decades. When initially promulgated, the NNC was the lone resistance movement in the region, but since then armed groups have multiplied, debunking the argument that AFSPA is necessary to curb and contain armed movements. Strong advocacy for its repeal has continued, the most notable being the recently ended unprecedented sixteen-year protest fast of Irom Chanu Sharmila, who was in detention and force-fed for those sixteen years (from 5 November 2000 to 9 August 2016). An analysis of the use of AFSPA clearly indicates that it is essentially the lawless use of excessive force and that it has created a legal regime that has resulted in impunity for the armed forces, allowing them the use of any strategy or tactic without the constraints of legal principles or constitutional safeguards. In the so-called disturbed areas where AFSPA is in operation, structures and processes tend to be overwhelmed by the authority and power of the army, since the Act shields the security forces from arrest and criminal prosecution through provisions of statutory immunity that require the concerned executive authority to grant prior sanction for prosecution. The Act grants extraordinary powers to any military officer, including any commissioned officer, warrant officer, non-commissioned officer and any other person of equivalent rank in the military forces, to use lethal force if deemed necessary; to arrest without a warrant, using such force as may be necessary, including killing; and again without a warrant, to enter and search any premises on mere suspicion.

International human rights bodies including the CEDAW (Convention on the Elimination of All Forms of Discrimination Against Women) committee have repeatedly called for a repeal or review of AFSPA. These positions were reinforced nationally in 2013 by the Justice J. S. Verma Committee, which voiced the concern that 'systematic or isolated sexual violence, in the process of Internal Security duties, is being legitimised by the Armed Forces Special Powers Act'. The committee recommended wide-ranging measures to address this reality and review continuance of the Act. Stressing that women in conflict areas were entitled to all the security and dignity afforded to citizens in any other part of the country, the committee recommended bringing sexual violence against women by members of the armed forces or uniformed personnel under the purview of ordinary criminal law; taking special care to ensure the safety of women who are complainants and witnesses in cases of sexual assault by the armed forces; and instituting special commissioners for women's safety and security in all areas of conflict in the country. However, army officials defended the Act, saying that removing the requirement for sanction in cases of violence against women, as recommended by the committee, would have a 'de-motivating' effect on army personnel.[7] On the contrary, it is obvious enough that a very high risk of abuse is inherent in powers that are formulated very broadly and in very vague language.

In the present context of negative peace, where levels of direct violence by state forces have decreased, of greater concern is the culture of impunity and militarised violence that this Act has perpetuated in the region. Based on an incisive piece of research conducted in Nagaland, Kikon (2017) argues that the Indian state is deeply implicated in escalating the culture of sexual violence and impunity in Nagaland because the impunity that AFSPA provides to the Indian security forces has legitimised such a culture. But the government of India is yet to accept its role and responsibility in the destruction of property, the psychological trauma and loss of lives in the Indo-Naga conflict and the breakdown of the social fabric of Naga society. Kikon's research supports my argument that the protracted peace process of the Naga struggle has only escalated violence against women. Kikon points out that the culture of impunity that has seeped into Naga society allows perpetrators of sexual violence to escape justice, while their victims are trapped between exhortations by women's advocacy groups not to suffer quietly and the social stigma attached to sexual violence that puts the blame solely on the woman. Indeed, for a community that has known sexual violence to be used as a weapon of dominance, it is totally incongruous that comments such as 'men can smell the sexual signals that girls give out and they attract men and get raped' are made by that same community (ibid.:104).

Naga women today are essentially caught between different sites of power and heightened patriarchal control by the community, the church and the state. Years of militarisation have had a lasting effect on Naga society, tearing communities apart, heightening inequalities inherent in traditional norms and practices, and creating new 'saviours' and new power imbalances. Families disintegrated as the majority of men went underground to join the armed struggle, leaving women to sustain and hold the family together. While religion and the church provided comfort and support to many of these women, they also gradually became an indisputable alternative seat of power and patriarchal control. This is equally true for the women of Mizoram. Apart from the women who lost their men to the resistance, many of the MNF women themselves also turned to the church to deal with their disappointments and trauma. Some even justify the lack of space for women's political participation by saying that work for God is far superior to political work. Thus, despite the fact that both these communities today have considerable numbers of woman-headed households single-handedly grappling with and managing a range of socio-economic challenges, this has not necessarily changed the positions or perspectives of women themselves. Rather, patriarchal values and controls and notions of moral chastity have increased greatly. It is not surprising, therefore, that in cases of survivors of sexual violence and teenage pregnancies in Naga society, 'it is the hymen-centric moral and cultural code' (Kikon, 2017: 105) that is perpetuated and aggressively reinforced.

### The continuum of violence: the public and the depoliticisation of the private

The naturalisation of patriarchal power, territorial claims over the female body and increased violence in the private come together in Kikon's account of a fifteen-year-old survivor of sexual violence who was repeatedly sexually abused by her father, a cadre of an armed Naga outfit living in the ceasefire camp (2017). Both the Naga and Assam protracted peace processes have resulted in thousands of disarmed and seemingly disempowered men languishing in the designated camps awaiting an uncertain future but asserting power and control in the private sphere. Documentation by the North East Network (Hazarika and Sharma, 2014) also shows the great vulnerability of women to domestic violence perpetrated by surrendered militants in Assam who are not languishing in camps but have become extremely powerful with the surrender packages and settlements that they signed with the Indian state. If domestic violence in general remains grossly under-reported, when it involves an intimate partner who is also an armed and macho ex-militant then the possibility of it being reporting is nil.

Feminist discourse has long held that making a distinction between the public and the private sphere depoliticises the domestic sphere. So unless justice is reconceptualised on the basis of women's lived experience, the everyday violence that women experience will remain marginal and invisible. As Kikon highlights: 'Every Naga woman has experienced humiliation and insults from the men on the basis of her womanhood but these men are not outsiders or strangers. They are their "respected" uncles, cousins and in some cases their fathers or brothers who never fail to remind them about the pre-destined inferior roles that have already been slated out for them' (Kikon, 2002: 174–82). She further contends that, in the present context of the Nagas, the two institutions that mostly get away with sexual violence and reinforce the impunity provided by the AFSPA are the family and armed groups.

The young survivor's story aptly supports the feminist position that violence is comprehensively tackled only when the structural issues that underlie and enable it are addressed. Different dimensions surfaced as the incident was reported to the police by the girl's aunt, as the aunt and the father belonged to rival armed groups. Thus the case travelled between different legal jurisdictions – insurgent courts, customary family meetings, and state police stations. Redress eluded the young girl as the complex dynamics of patriarchal institutions in the public sphere completely depoliticised the private. Political and family rivalry were intertwined and the state agencies were reluctant to address an 'internal' matter that also involved rival armed groups. Kikon rightly points out that this case is of critical importance because the act of sexual violence transgressed the boundaries of the family, the political and the legal jurisdiction of the rival armed groups as well as the state agencies. And yet, finally, none of the institutions attempted to hold the perpetrator accountable for the private violation and get justice for the young girl (Kikon, 2017).

But the violations are not just an internal matter. With a conclusive resolution still eluding the two-decade-old peace talks, Naga society today is in a protracted peace process caught up in what seems to be a permanent state of impermanence. On the other hand, in both the Naga and Assam contexts the benefits of economic progress has created concentric circles of peripherality as the privileged middle class begins to enjoy the dividends of peacetime. Such a fragile context requires agility and high alertness to political manoeuvres, possibilities and affiliations, however flawed or temporary these may be. And gender justice is the first thing to be bartered away either for the sake of morality or for political and economic expediency. The fact that women are not perceived as individuals but rather as the valuable property of a family or the carriers of a community's cultural identity makes this easy to do.

The same logic underpins action that is often taken by non-state actors. While state agencies hesitate to act, the armed groups in the region are notorious for dispensing their own forms of justice. In cases of sexual violence in particular, competing authorities that involve both state and non-state actors often present their own versions of justice. In many instances, perpetrators of sexual violence – civilians or combatants – have been sentenced to capital punishment when tried and found guilty in the tribunals of the armed groups. Not all women oppose these actions but a sizeable section does, pointing out that these attempts by the armed groups are merely face saving with no justice for the victim. In a well-publicised case of sexual violence by cadres of NSCN-IM there was a standoff between the women's organisation Totimi Hoho and the armed group, with the women demanding that the perpetrators be handed over to the state police for prosecution while the armed groups maintained that the violators would be dealt with by its own police.

Women also draw attention to the high levels of class and ethnic bias in responses or in the trials conducted by the armed or unarmed non-state actors. When the perpetrator belongs to the same tribe or community there is great leniency,[8] but when it is someone outside the acceptable ethnic circle the reaction can be extremely violent, as the 2015 Dimapur lynching incident showed.[9] It is highly likely, therefore, that the rage that led to the accused's death was not due to wanting justice for the rape survivor but more the result of outrage at the temerity of an outsider laying claim to a woman's body, which is the community's property. As a result of years of militarisation, what has emerged today is the attitude that the non-Naga is a distinct enemy, while the myth that Naga men automatically uphold justice and honour and do not indulge in sexual violence is a collective denial of gender-based violence in Naga society.

*Sacrosanct traditions: customary laws and the woman question*

Globally, there is now a substantive body of research and analysis that seeks to understand violence against women in diverse settings, including conflict zones, private homes and the family. What, however, is not adequately analysed are the structural inequalities of households or communities, the political and economic structures that underpin gender inequalities and increase women's vulnerability to violence. Beyond the all-encompassing hold of the patriarchal Christian church, both the Nagas and the Mizos are also inherently governed by their customary laws and practices, many of which are sites of deep structural inequality as they sustain unequal gendered power relations. An important premise of both the Naga and the Mizo peace negotiations has been a commitment to respect and protect these customary practices. Today, Mizoram and Nagaland are each permitted by Article 371(A) of the Indian constitution to frame their own laws that align with customary laws.[10] Men may choose to be unshackled by some of the positive norms and codes of conduct set out in customary laws, but women have to uphold without question all that is 'traditional'. Among other things, the customary laws of both these highly patriarchal communities deny women land and inheritance rights and a role in decision making. These customary laws and practices embody what Galtung refers to as cultural violence, as they are cited to justify or legitimise structural violence and deny women their personhood.

Traditionally, both Naga and Mizo women have been restricted by the gendered norms of culture and custom, with an extremely well-defined sexual division of labour and identity. Mizo women participated in large numbers in the Mizo resistance movement, but as far as the discourse of the MNF movement and Mizo nationalism was concerned, this resistance was perceived primarily as being organised and led by men, while the contribution of women remained sidelined and invisible. The portrayal of women merely as victims of sexual violence is often highlighted, but to date the contribution and participation of women have been systematically excluded in the larger discourse of the MNF movement. The women question – victim or agent – did not feature at all in the agenda during the peace negotiations with the Indian state; rather, total protection of all customary laws and practices, including those that are gender discriminatory, was a non-negotiable clause. So while the Mizo peace agreement signed with the Indian government protected Mizo customary practices in the post-conflict phase, Mizo women under the aegis of the MHIP have had to fight a long and tough battle for inheritance rights and the right to political participation, which has resulted in some degree of victory. Formerly, Mizo women were severely constrained in showing any forms of dissent, even in cases of extreme domestic violence. Under Mizo customary laws, a Mizo man could divorce his wife by simply uttering the words *Ka Mei Che* (I divorce you). A divorced woman had to immediately leave her marital home and all her belongings, even if everything was jointly acquired by both wife and husband. She also had no right to her children, and sometimes not even visitation rights. Any dissent or questioning by women often resulted in men divorcing them. Through the concerted efforts of the MHIP, however, this was changed with the Mizoram Divorce Ordinance (MDO) in 2008, which was subsequently adopted as the Mizo Marriage, Divorce and Inheritance Act in 2014.

Likewise, despite Naga women's great contribution and sacrifice for the Naga cause, Naga customary laws deny women inheritance rights and participation in political decision making. Sociological studies, however, indicate that there is no homogeneous body of customary laws among the Naga community; rather, such laws are plural in nature, differing from tribe to tribe and from village to village. Very often, however, the male-led Naga tribal bodies interpret customary laws uniformly, with the aim of denying women their rights.

As Galtung emphasises, transformation must be able to respond to life's on-the-ground challenges, needs and realities. For Naga women under the aegis of the NMA, the challenge has been to bring about change in their extremely gender-discriminatory customary laws relating to inheritance and land rights as well as to achieve success in their long battle for inclusion in political decision making.[11] As feminist analysis has shown time and again, the physical violence that women experience during wars and conflicts is closely linked to their status and rights during peacetime, including their socio-economic rights within their own communities. Violence is then a continuum enabled by hierarchical social arrangements in both the public and the private sphere. A feminist political economy approach therefore seeks to reconceptualise justice on the basis of women's lived experiences (True, 2014). As the protracted Naga peace negotiations reach their final stage and the community looks to chart a new roadmap for the community for the future, women's struggle for political and economic participation and for power and resource sharing acquires critical significance. A lack of political and economic power takes away the personhood of a Naga woman and makes her especially vulnerable to violence and voiceless against any violations. In November 2016, an exciting chapter in Naga political and feminist history seemed to have opened up. The Nagaland Assembly initially passed the Nagaland Municipal (First Amendment) Act in 2006, providing for 33 per cent of seats to be reserved for women in urban local bodies. But as the NMA urged the government to hold elections with the quotas, the government – under pressure from tribal men – took recourse through the special constitutional provisions under Article 371(A) and passed a resolution that such a reservation for women would conflict with customary law. The High Court upheld the state government's position and the NMA appealed to the Supreme Court, where a final order is pending.

For the first time, there seems to be unanimity among Naga men from all the different and sometimes adversarial tribes on one issue – opposition to reserved places for women, citing customary laws and norms. As soon as the dates for civic elections were notified, various tribal bodies called for a boycott of the elections if reserved seats for women were allowed. What followed was extreme aggression, arson, violence and intimidation. Many women were forced to withdraw their nominations. Under pressure from family and their community, women too were polarised. The position of the revered rebel leaders has also been ambivalent: while they are sympathetic to the women, who have always been their strongest support base, they have not come out with any definitive public statement. For the few Naga women who have broken ranks with their own communities and stand by their position, this is a struggle that goes beyond electoral representation and is about power sharing and gender justice.

## Women's eternal quest: justice and dignity

*Structural social arrangements and women's imagined justice for sexual violence*

The conflict contexts in North East India – particularly among the Naga and the Mizo – illustrate how the complexities of justice, inequalities and transitions are especially intractable when it comes to gender. The recent Naga situation throws up important points about what lies at the core of women's struggles in politically contested contexts and transitions. How do women imagine justice? How do they negotiate and manoeuvre their multiple and often conflicting identities? And how do they balance justice with social and political commitments in communities involved in protracted armed struggles and resistance? Clearly, the Naga women's imagined justice for sexual violence would imply an acknowledgement of women's personhood and justice premised on notions of equality, and not seen through the patriarchal lens of protecting property and bodies. It is increasingly acknowledged that, to ensure justice, especially in post-conflict transitions, affected people must have access to political procedures and a voice in decisions that affect their lives.

Aguilar (2011: 128–9) highlights that an essential step in identifying the different dimensions of women's experience during and after conflict is to understand 'gender deficits and gaps in legal, economic and political structures that existed before the conflict: the dynamics of power and control over economic resources; the gender dimension of the economic system within communities and families; and the cultural factors that determine social and economic status in specific contexts'. In the Mizo context, for instance, the village regrouping scheme was doubly disempowering for women, as, among other disadvantages, it took away women's power and control over economic production and valued knowledge of local contexts. At the community level, the challenging of customary laws by Naga and Mizo women is a critical step towards correcting the gender deficits and gaps in age-old economic and political structures.

Scholars across a range of related and overlapping fields identify structural violence as a critical issue. Drawing on the analyses of Galtung (1969) and Farmer et al. (2006) and applying them to transitions, Evans (2016), for instance, elaborates that social injustice and structural violence are in fact synonymous and denote a condition in which violence occurs – not because it is precipitated by the direct actions of specific individuals against other specific individuals, but rather because of structural social arrangements embedded in the political and economic organisation of the social world. This arrangement, as Farmer et al. (2006) argue, is both structured and stricturing, constricting the agency of its victims and violent because it causes injury of a deep nature. For sustainable peace in this region of protracted conflicts, it necessitates the dismantling of power hierarchies between the federal and peripheral state structures that determine production and reproduction and govern the distribution and use of resources, authority and benefits. For women, the dismantling of power hierarchies needs to go beyond the obvious. Feminist discourse has long advocated an intersectional approach that explores the way in which gender intersects with other identities to produce both opportunities and oppression or multiple forms of discrimination. For Naga and Mizo women, the social arrangements of their respective communities are embedded in structured customary laws and practices that have been stricturing their agency as full members of their communities. So, while justice for sexual violence is important, in a moment of political transition acknowledging and correcting systemic and entrenched discrimination are essential steps in implementing guarantees of non-discrimination, gender equality and just peace. In the present post-conflict and protracted peace context, ensuring a strong gender focus in the dynamics of power and control over economic resources is of vital importance and could be the fulcrum of women's activism in addressing structural violence.

### Political economy of gender justice: the need for a transformative approach

An emerging approach that is more closely linked to the realities, needs and expectations on the ground in a post-conflict period is that of transformative justice which entails a 'shift in focus from the legal to the social and political, and from the state and institutions to communities and every-day concerns' (Gready and Robins, 2014: 340). Elaborating what transformative justice involves and contrasting it with transitional justice, Gready and Robins propose that perhaps a transformative approach is more relevant to address the needs and realities of peace process contexts. It is certainly more relevant to women, because 'transformative justice is not the result of a top-down imposition of external legal frameworks or institutional templates, but of a more bottom-up understanding and analysis of the lives and needs of populations' (ibid.: 340). Transformation, then, is not limited simply to political settlements but includes a range of approaches that bring in social, political and economic dimensions.

Transformative justice, in particular in a post-conflict context, is therefore of special significance for women and other marginalised communities, because, in its essence, it implies a process of transformation of oppressive hierarchies and discriminatory social structures and the possibility of positive peace. As Chinkin (2009) states, notwithstanding the huge challenges, a post-conflict moment or a society emerging from conflict can also present a strategic opportunity to bring about transformation in all areas of women's lives. In these post-war periods, for a very brief moment, a small window of opportunity opens up in which a range of measures, including legislative and policy measures, can be developed and institutionalised in order to protect and advance women's human rights as well as to engage seriously with issues of reparations, human security, accountability, peace and justice, and social and political agency.

All three contexts are evidence of the way in which gender inequalities deeply impair women's access to a range of rights, which are exacerbated during conflict and often neglected in the post-conflict phase. Women are doubly victimised due to entrenched inequalities as well as by the impact of the conflict. Not only do systems of wars and armed conflicts exacerbate existing structural inequalities and vulnerabilities, they also have far-reaching human rights implications for women. Therefore, to address the impact on women exclusively through the lens of direct sexual violence is insufficient as it ignores the gendered dimensions of conflict. What is important is to repeatedly foreground the fact that gender inequalities are a continuum in women's lives. As Schmid (2012) argues, during conflicts women suffer not only existing discrimination and violations but also multiple and interrelated human rights violations. She shows, for instance, that a woman losing her husband or children not only suffers the direct violations of civil and political rights (e.g. the killing or disappearance of her loved ones) but often also endures dire economic, social and cultural consequences by becoming the sole caregiver in the household. Women are also disproportionally affected by denials and discrimination with regard to issues such as accessing land tenure, property, education or healthcare (ibid.). In the author's interviews with the ULFA women, they talked about the 'violence' of peacetime – of their inability to break out of the socio-economic deprivations and entrenched gender inequalities that they had to grapple with as civilian women. And the Naga women's current struggle for representation in decision making at this important political moment in Naga history is a collective imagining of the future and a call for rectification of denials and discriminations.

As Aguilar (2011) argues, 'true social transformation' can be achieved only with the fulfilment of economic, social and cultural rights, as these rights are crucial to women breaking the circle of exclusion that makes them a target of direct violence. The Colombian government's and the FARC rebels' pledge to both improve access to land for women and ensure that perpetrators of sexual violence, including rape, will not be eligible for amnesty is therefore an extremely important milestone.

Like most well-known and well-documented peace processes, those in North East India are characterised by being top-down, male-led and essentially power-driven transactions. Nowhere is this more evident than in the recent Naga context. The key thrust of women, peace and security globally is the need to change this approach. Women have critiqued not only wars and conflicts but also the essentially male-led and male-dominated transactions that occur during political transitions, when either women's rights are bartered in the interests of political expediency or the pervasive existing gender inequalities and biases in society limit women's meaningful participation on every level and at every stage of the peace negotiations and post-conflict transitions. The reality from these three North East India contexts also underscores the need to move out of this patriarchal transaction mode and aim at something that is truly transformative. This would necessarily entail a focus on local needs and priorities by ensuring that the voices of the marginalised are heard, that participation and ownership are enhanced, that process as well as outcome is prioritised, and that unequal and intersecting power dynamics are challenged. And, as such, the Naga women's struggle for women's reserved places and their right to political decision making is of paramount importance at this juncture of Naga history.

Gready and Robins' arguments resonate with the feminist discourse that making a distinction between the private and the public depoliticises the domestic. This has led to the marginalisation and invisibility of everyday violence perpetrated against women – notably violence occurring in families and communities – which are rooted in structural causes. Judicial processes, while important, reduce women to their injury in a violation- and perpetrator-centred way, rather than discussing the gendered power relations that lead to violations. Denial of a range of rights for women under Naga and Mizo customary laws is a manifestation of gendered power relations. Casting rights in explicitly transformative terms entails acknowledging and seeking to challenge inequalities linked to power and hierarchy (Gready and Robins, 2014), and the importance of this cannot be overstated. It also requires accepting that human rights are defined by struggle and born of experiences of deprivation and oppression.

What would a transformative justice approach look like for women situated at different stages of the conflict continuum in a region that is fast becoming a place for endless economic possibilities for the present political dispensation? It would necessitate changing all that reinforces existing social and economic hierarchies of power and including affected communities – particularly women – as agents in shaping the new agenda for change through policy and practice. Above all, it would call for reviewing and redefining a kind of women's resistance that goes beyond the narrow limits of ethnicity, class, religion and political affiliations. Finally, for the region itself, a transformative justice approach with a focus on addressing socio-economic injustices and the structural roots of present injustices would be a more effective and yet more nuanced way of removing stereotyped peripherality and the discriminatory 'othering' of peoples and individuals.

## Notes

1 See Cecilia López Montaño and María-Claudia Holstine (this volume) for a quite different insiders' analysis.

2 In August 2014, Decree 1480 was adopted, establishing 25 May as the National Day for the Dignity of Women Victims of Sexual Violence caused by the Internal Armed Conflict, as a measure of collective reparations.

3 In July 1997, the Baptist church organised the Atlanta Peace meet where the NSCN leadership accepted initiatives to start an unconditional dialogue process.

4 See the Nellie massacre in February 1983.

5 According to the government of India, the ULFA is classified as a terrorist organisation banned under the Unlawful Activities (Prevention) Act of 1990. Concurrently, the government started military offensives against it, named Operation Bajrang (November 1990), Operation Rhino (September 1991),

Operation All Clear (December 2003) and Operation Rhino 2 (October 2001), led by the Indian army. The anti-insurgency operations still continue today under the Unified Command Structure.

6 It was led by eminent intellectual Dr Hiren Gohain, who formed a state-level convention, 'Sanmilita Jatiya Abhivartan', which called on both New Delhi and the ULFA to come forward to the negotiation table without any preconditions or delays.

7 Lieutenant General Harwant Singh, former Deputy Chief of Staff for the army, wrote: 'No military personnel would want to get involved in false civil cases and spend the next few years doing the rounds of civil courts where all false evidence from the hostile local witnesses will be marshalled against them.'

8 For instance, in August 2007, four college students abducted and raped a woman from Showuba village near Dimapur. The four were arrested after a complaint was filed at a local police station. The Showuba village council court tried the youths and let them off after imposing a fine of fifteen rupees each (Banerjee, 2014: 150).

9 In March 2015, a huge mob broke through the main gates of the Dimapur central jail and dragged a non-Naga man accused of raping a Naga girl out of the jail, beat him up, paraded him naked, lynched him and hanged his body from the town's clock tower while the police remained helpless spectators.

10 Article 371(A) of the constitution states: 'Notwithstanding anything in this Constitution, no Act of Parliament in respect of religious or social practices of the Nagas, Naga customary law and procedure, administration of civil and criminal justice involving decisions according to Naga customary law, ownership and transfer of land and its resources, shall apply to the State of Nagaland unless the Legislative Assembly of Nagaland by a resolution so decides.'

11 Nagaland is the only state in the country that has never had a woman member of the legislative assembly. While every village and tribe has its own women's wing, there are no women on the village council and the apex decision-making body of Naga tribes, the Naga Hoho, has no women's representatives either.

## Bibliography

Aguilar, G. O. 2011. 'Asserting Women's Economic and Social Rights in Transitions' in Aguilar, G. O. and Gómez, F. I. (eds), *Rethinking Transitions: Equality and Social Justice in Societies Emerging from Conflict*. Cambridge: Intersentia.

Amnesty International. 1990. *India, 'Operation Bluebird': A Case Study of Torture and Extrajudicial Executions in Manipur*. New York: Amnesty International.

Banerjee, P. 2012. 'Women, Conflict, and Governance in Nagaland' in Samaddar, R. (ed.), *Government of Peace: Social Governance, Security and the Problematic of Space*. London and New York: Routledge.

Banerjee, P. 2014. 'New Conundrums for Women in Northeast India, Nagaland and Tripura' and 'Women, Violence and North East India', *Economic and Political Weekly* 49 (43–44).

Baruah, S. 2007. 'Postfrontier Blues: Towards a New Policy Framework for Northeast India'. Policy Studies 33. Washington DC: East-West Center.

Baruah, S. 2014. 'Routine Emergencies: India's Armed Forces Special Powers Act' in Sundar, A. S. (ed.), *Civil War and Sovereignty in South Asia:*

*Regional and Political Economy Perspectives.* New Delhi: Sage.

Bell, C. and O'Rourke, C. 2007. 'Does Feminism Need a Theory of Transitional Justice? An Introductory Essay', *International Journal of Transitional Justice* 1 (1): 23–44.

Bhattacharjee, K. 2015. *Blood on My Hands: Confessions of Staged Encounters.* Noida, India: HarperCollins.

Chakravarti, U. 2017. 'Introduction' in *Fault Lines of History: The India Papers.* New Delhi: Zubaan.

Chinkin, C. 2009. 'The Protection of Economic, Social and Cultural Rights Post-conflict'. Paper commissioned by the Office of High Commissioner for Human Rights, www2.ohchr. org/english/issues/women/docs/ Paper_Protection_ESCR.pdf (accessed 3 May 2019).

Coomaraswamy, R. 2015. *Preventing Conflict, Transforming Justice, Securing the Peace: A Global Study on the Implementation of United Nations Security Council Resolution 1325.* New York: UN Women.

Das, P. 2013. 'The History of Armed Forces Special Powers Act' in Chadha, V. (ed.), *Armed Forces Special Powers Act: The Debate.* New Delhi: Lancer's Books.

Dey, S. K. 2013. 'Human Rights Issue and Insurgency due to Bamboo Flowering: A Case Study of Lushai Hills District of Assam', *Excellence: International Journal of Education and Research*, November.

Economic and Political Weekly. 2017. 'Naga Women Fight Back', *Economic and Political Weekly* 52 (3).

Evans, M. 2016. 'Structural Violence, Socioeconomic Rights, and Transformative Justice', *Journal of Human Rights* 15: 1–20.

Farmer, P. E., Nizeye, B., Stulac, S. and Keshavjee, S. 2006. 'Structural Violence and Clinical Medicine', *PLoS Medicine* 3 (10): 1686–91.

Foucault, M. 1995. *Discipline and Punishment: The Birth of the Prison.* Translated by A. Sheridan. New York: Penguin Random House.

Galtung, J. 1969. 'Violence, Peace, and Peace Research', *Journal of Peace Research* 6 (3): 167–91.

Goswami, R. et al. 2005. 'Women in Armed Conflict Situations. Guwahati: North East Network.

Goswami, R. et al. 2014. 'General Recommendation 30: Women in Conflict Prevention, Conflict and Post-conflict Situations' in *India: 4th and 5th NGO Alternative Report on CEDAW.* New Delhi: National Alliance of Women.

Goswami, R. 2015. *Of Revolution, Liberation and Agency: Aspirations and Realities in the Lives of Women Combatants and Key Women Members of the United Liberation Front of Assam(ULFA).* New Delhi: Heinrich Boll.

Goswami, R. 2017. 'The Price of "Revolution": Who Determines? Who Pays?' in Chakravarti, U. (ed.), *Fault Lines of History: The India Papers.* New Delhi: Zubaan.

Gready, P. and Robins, S. 2014. 'From Transitional to Transformative Justice: A New Agenda for Practice', *International Journal of Transitional Justice* 8: 339–61, www.york.ac.uk/ media/cahr/documents/IJTJ-2014- Gready-339-61.pdf (accessed 3 May 2019).

Hazarika, A. and Sharma, S. 2014 *Armed Struggle, Identity and the State.* Guwahati: North East Network.

Hluna, J. V. and Tochhawng, R. 2012 'Outbreak in the Mizo Hills: Reason and Responsibilities' in *The Mizo Uprising: Assam Assembly Debates on the Mizo Movement, 1966–1971.* Cambridge: Cambridge Scholars Publishing.

Hmingthanzuali. 2016. 'Memories, Trauma and Resistance: Mizo Women's Narratives on Rambuai'. Unpublished article.

Hoenig, P. and Singh, N. 2014. *Landscapes of Fear: Understanding Impunity in India*. New Delhi: Zubaan.

Iralu, K. D. 2000. *Nagaland and India: The Blood and the Tears*. Kohima: Eastern Publications.

Iralu, K. D. 2005. 'The Fifty-four-year Indo-Naga Conflict' in Hussain, M. (ed.), *Coming Out of Violence: Essays on Ethnicity, Conflict Resolution and Peace Process in North-East India*. New Delhi: Regency Publications.

Karmarkar, R. 2014. 'Manipur's Horror: When Operation Bluebird Stuck Terror', *Hindustan Times*, 5 November.

Kashyap, S. G. 2017. 'Opposed to 33% Reservation for Women, Naga Bodies Call for Boycott of Civic Polls', *Indian Express*, Guwahati, 5 January.

Kikon, D. 2002. 'Political Mobilization of Women in Nagaland: A Sociological Background' in Fernandez, W. and Barbora, S. (eds), *Changing Women's Status in India: Focus on the Northeast*. Guwahati: NECRC.

Kikon, D. 2017. 'Memories of Rape: The Banality of Violence and Impunity in Naga Society' in Chakravarti, U. (ed.), *Fault Lines of History: The India Papers*. New Delhi: Zubaan.

Kotwal, D. 2000. 'The Naga Insurgency: The Past and the Future', *Strategic Analysis* 24 (4): 751–72.

Lasuh, W. and Nuh, V. K. (eds). 2002. *The Naga Chronicle*. New Delhi: Regency Publications.

Lederach, J. P. 2003. *The Little Book of Conflict Transformation*. New York: Good Books.

Longvah, S. 2014. 'Territorial Dimension in the Naga Peace Process', *International Research Journal of Social Sciences* 3 (5): 41–5.

Luithui, L. and Haksar, N. 1994. *Nagaland File: A Question of Human Rights*. New Delhi: Lancer International.

Manchanda, R. 2005. *Naga Women Making a Difference: Peacebuilding in Northeastern India*. Washington DC: Women Waging Peace Policy Commission.

Menamparampil, T. 2008. 'The Role of Religious Leaders in Peace Initiatives' in Fernandez, W. (ed.), *Search for Peace with Justice: Issues around Conflicts in Northeast India*. Gauhati: Northeastern Social Research Centre.

Misra, U. 2000. *The Periphery Strikes Back: Challenges to the Nation State in Assam and Nagaland*. Shimla: Indian Institute of Advanced Study.

Misra, U. 2005. 'Towards a Resolution of the Naga Issue' in Hussain, M. (ed.), *Coming Out of Violence: Essays on Ethnicity, Conflict Resolution and Peace Process in North-East India*. New Delhi: Regency Publications.

Moloney, A. 2016a. 'Women's Voices Heard Clear and Loud in Colombia's Peace Deal', Thomson Reuters Foundation, 28 September.

Moloney, A. 2016b. 'No Amnesty for War Rapists: Colombia Peace Talks Turn to Women's Rights', Thomson Reuters Foundation, 25 July.

Nag, S. 2001. 'Tribals, Rats, Famine, State and the Nation', *Economic and Political Weekly* 36 (12): 1029–33.

Nagaland News. 2012. 'SC Directs Nagaland Govt. to Respond on 33% Women Quota', *Nagaland News*, 20 November.

Nagaland Post. 2012. 'Assembly Stands by Art.371(A); Rejects Women Reservation', *Nagaland Post*, 23 September.

Nunthara, C. 1981. 'Grouping of Villages in Mizoram: Its Social and Economic Impact', *Economic and Political Weekly* 16 (30): 1237–40.

Nunthara, C. 1989. 'Impact of Grouping Scheme on Traditional Organization' in *Impact of the Introduction of the Grouping of Village in Mizoram*. New Delhi: Omsons Publications.

Parks, T., Colletta, N. and Oppenheim, B. 2013. *The Contested Corners of Asia: Subnational Conflict and International Development Assistance*. San Francisco: The Asia Foundation, https://asiafoundation.org/resources/pdfs/ContestedCornersOfAsia.pdf (accessed 3 May 2019).

Roluahpuia. 2015. 'Memoirs of a Mizo Rebel', *Northeast Review*, 22 May.

SAHRDC. 2015. 'Armed Forces Special Powers Act: A Study in National Security Tyranny'. New Delhi: South Asian Human Rights Documentation Centre (SAHRDC), http://themanipurpage.tripod.com/letters/humanrhts.html (accessed 15 May 2015).

Schmid, E. 2012. 'Women's Freedom from Want after Armed Conflicts: Does the Inclusion of Economic, Social and Cultural Rights in Transitional Justice Help Women?', *NJA Law Journal (Special Issue)*.

Shimray, A. S. A. 2005. *Let Freedom Ring: Story of Naga Nationalism*. New Delhi: Promilla and Co.

Srivastava, D. 2013. 'Rights-based Critique of AFSPA' in Chadha, V. (ed.), *Armed Forces Special Powers Act: The Debate*. New Delhi: Lancer's Books.

True, J. 2014. 'The Political Economy of Violence against Women: A Feminist International Relations Perspective', *Australian Feminist Law Journal* 32 (1): 39–59, www.researchgate.net/publication/241764665_The_Political_Economy_of_Violence_Against_Women (accessed 3 May 2019).

van Lierde, F. 2011. *We the Widows of the Gun*. The Hague: Cordaid.

Woch, K. 2016. 'In Support of Implementation of 33% Women Reservation in Nagaland Municipal Elections 2016', *Morung Express*, 6 September.

# 5 | REIMAGINING SUBVERSION: AGENCY AND WOMEN'S PEACE ACTIVISM IN NORTHERN UGANDA[1]

*Yaliwe Clarke and Constance O'Brien*

## Introduction

This chapter provides an analysis of the micro-politics of women's community peace initiatives in Northern Uganda. It examines both the gendered socio-economic and political shifts that occurred as a result of the war as well as the ways in which women's agency attempted to subvert patriarchal norms. It further interrogates the extent to which women peace activists addressed structural violence within an existing liberal peace-building framework.

Data was gathered from in-depth interviews with seventeen people (fifteen women and two men) who founded and/or worked in community peace organisations in Northern Uganda between 1998 and 2011. The findings reveal that shifts in patrilineal family networks that resulted from the war opened up the possibility for women peace activists to become important nodes of material support. Women were able to initiate several peace groups; set up small group saving schemes; harvest crops from abandoned fields; engage in petty trade; and access support from international humanitarian organisations to help provide for the livelihoods of the most vulnerable. It is significant that these initiatives were being undertaken despite ongoing sexual and gender-based violence. At the same time, internal displacement destabilised the clan system, resulting in major shifts in patrilineal ties and a loss of social control. By looking after orphaned children, grandchildren and other members of the extended family, women's maternal roles expanded at a time when there were minimal social economic resources available.

Critical insights are offered as to how women's peace-building efforts claimed 'spaces' that were previously held by men, who were the dominant material providers and protectors of the family. It would seem that there were some shifts in political economic arrangements during the war and that the resulting peace-building efforts of women peace activists contributed to a contestation of various forms of patriarchy.

The following section interrogates the conceptual underpinnings of liberal peace efforts that framed women's peace activism in Uganda.

## Neoliberal peace building and feminism: a framing argument

The Fourth World Conference on Women in Beijing in 1995 and the ratification of the Rome Statute of the International Criminal Court resulted in an increase in the public profiling of women and women's organisations working for peace. The 1995 Beijing Platform for Action included sections on 'violence against women' and 'women and armed conflict'. In each section there is explicit mention of forms of sexual violence that take place during armed conflict, such as 'murder, systematic rape, sexual slavery and forced pregnancy'. It included a call for these kinds of violence to be prevented or addressed in broad efforts for peace and security, especially in relation to the rights of women.[2] This was followed by the passing of United Nations Security Council Resolution 1325 on Women, Peace and Security in October 2000, and the further championing of largely rhetorical international pressure to include 'women' in formal peace processes. These international instruments focus on the prevention of violence against women during war as well as on women's efforts to bring about peace.

In her 2007 book *From Where We Stand*, Cynthia Cockburn argues that '[t]he sex- and gender-specific experiences of women in war is often neglected, misrepresented or exploited in the media, by politicians, and the anti-war movement'. Other studies draw on 'women's peace work' and theorise gendered meanings of peace (Barry, 2005; Cheldelin and Eliatamby, 2011; Moser and Clark, 2001; Pankhurst, 2003). This analysis was preceded by feminist critiques of neoliberal interpretations of peace and armed conflict in the early 1990s emanating predominantly from a political science perspective (Steans, 1998; Tickner, 1992; Whiteworth, 1994). According to Zaum:

> liberal peacebuilding has been used to describe external peacebuilding interventions that share several characteristics: first, they are conducted by liberal, Western states; second, they are motivated by liberal objectives such as responding to large-scale human rights violations or being conducted under an international responsibility

to protect; and third, these interventions promote liberal-democratic political institutions, human rights, effective and good governance, and economic liberalization as a means to bring peace and prosperity to war-torn countries. (Zaum, 2012: 121)

Liberal peace is derived from a combination of realist and liberal thinking dominant in international relations as well as policy frameworks of international development organisations such as the United Nations (UN) and World Bank (Campbell et al., 2011; Heathershaw, 2013; Pugh et al., 2008; Richmond, 2006; 2012). Even though it aspires to broad goals of human security, there is a narrow focus on positivist interpretations of security that centre on homogenised Western ideas of democracy (Richmond, 2006). There is little meaningful engagement with local cultures and welfare needs that fall outside neoliberal economic prescriptions.

In recent years, liberal peace has been framed in terms of indigenous communities' own approaches to building peace that go beyond judicial processes and ideas about rights as framed in universal human rights discourse. Heathershaw (2013: 280) refers to this as a 'liberal-local hybridity'. He argues that it still remains competitive rather than co-constructive. There is yet to be an alternative theoretical approach to peace building where 'political authority is reconstituted across multiple geographical scales'.

Feminists (Hendricks, 2011; Hudson, 2012; Scully et al., 2010), on the other hand, highlight the fact that neoliberal peace does not address patriarchal structural violence that is embedded in the very idea of the state. Race, class and gender are modes of exclusion and domination that form part of the development of capitalism with its categories of difference and inequality. For the global South, histories of colonialism cannot be separated from the formation of the state and versions of development expressed in national development plans, including those of post-conflict reconstruction and peace building. Confortini (2010: 4) argues that even 'recent restructurings of capitalism, often termed "globalisation", have meant further intensification and rationalisation of modes of domination, subordinating peoples and lands on a transnational scale and realigning social relations to better meet the needs of capital'.

Despite considerable knowledge about the centrality of deconstructing patriarchy, liberal peace frameworks continue to centre masculine realities (Campbell et al., 2011; Heathershaw, 2013). For example, Doyle and Ikenberry's comprehensive survey of scholarship on war and peace conducted in 1997 contains six gender-related index entries but devotes only about one-tenth of its survey to gender. The words 'women' and 'gender' occasionally show up as a passing note. This scant attention to women's standpoint is reflected in UN peace processes: from twenty-one major peace processes held since 1992, only 2.4 per cent of signatories were women.[3] Furthermore, no women have been appointed chief or lead peace mediators in UN-sponsored peace talks. So far, only one woman has joined the African Union's (AU's) mediation team (Graça Machel was one of three mediators in the AU team during the Kenyan crisis in 2008). Olonisakin and Okech's edited book on *Women and Security Governance in Africa*, published in 2011, states that peace-building efforts in Africa have struggled to take women's lived realities of (in)security into account.

One has to note that a mere inclusion of 'women' in the discourse and in the practice of peace building does not necessarily mean a disruption of neoliberalism. Pratt and Richter-Devroe state that:

> The liberal peacebuilding agenda that is privileged by the UN and gender advocates working at/through the UN represents a limited strategy for those women's movements engaged in a more radical agenda of social and political transformation. Women's 'resistance' to global capitalism and forms of colonialism (rather than peacebuilding per se), for example, is not supported by the 1325 agenda, although women might find their involvement in such initiatives empowering, perhaps even more so than participating in the 1325 gendered peace agenda. (Pratt and Richter-Devroe 2011: 498)

A review of UN documents ten years after the passing of 1325 revealed that critiques of militarism, military budgets and military priorities were curtailed and reformulated into positive calls for women's participation and a gender perspective on peace and security (Gibbings, 2011: 532). This is a worrying trend, given 'that African militarism has generated more insecurity than security, often terrorising rather than protecting local populations, dominating the political sphere, blurring the boundaries between civilian and military, and thereby undermining all non-military forms of political and institutional authority and accountability' (Mama and Okazawa-Rey, 2012).

According to Mama and Okazawa-Rey, mainstream security discourse and practice pays minimal attention to 'the contradictory ways in which women are affected by the complex relationship between gendered capitalist processes and militarism, and the manner in which women negotiate their lives through both' (2012: 97). Besides militarism, the vestiges of colonialism and the politics of ethnicism continue to bedevil the possibilities of peace.

An overview of Uganda's socio-economic and political history provides some critical insights that could inform our understanding of women's trajectory of 'emancipation' in such a context.

### The challenges of the historical political-economic context and Ugandan women's 'emancipation'

Since independence in 1962, Uganda has experienced contested peace (in central Uganda and some parts of Southern Uganda) alongside armed conflict in the West Nile, the northern districts of Gulu and Kitgum and some parts of the Apac District (Sathyamurthy, 1986; Saul, 2004). Local populations have suffered extreme violence at the hands of rebel groups, government military and policing forces. The roots of the war can be traced back to the early 1900s when the British colonial administration signed an agreement with the Buganda Kingdom – a move that gave one ethnic group political and economic leverage over other ethnic communities and kingdoms (Karugire, 1980; Sathyamurthy, 1986).

According to Branch (2011), British colonial interpretations of ethnic identity pitched dominant ethnicities in the north against those in the south. The British colonial method of indirect rule fostered negative stereotypes about certain ethnic groups which in turn fuelled extreme political tension. In fact, the colonialists supported the development of the Acholi as a homogeneous ethnic identity and appointed chiefs in the north to advance British administrative attempts at centralisation. As Branch aptly states:

> The national dimension of an Acholi political identity was thus formed in the dynamic relationship between the educated Acholi class and British administrative strategies in the context of processes of state formation in the Uganda Protectorate ... From the beginning, therefore, Acholi political identity had two dimensions: an internal dimension based around competing claims to an authentic tradition

and leadership within Acholi society, at first fought out between the appointed chiefs and the lineage-based *rwodi-moo*, elders, and others; and a national dimension, as Acholi represented themselves as Acholi on the national political stage in order to compete in Uganda's tribalized national politics. (Branch 2011: 52–3)

In contrast to these male-dominated, ethnically polarised chiefdoms, women's missionary initiatives were multilingual, multi-ethnic and multi-religious. For example, the Uganda Women's Council, formed in 1946, was established by 'African, European, and Asian women who wanted to create an organisation made up of women of all ethnicities, races, religious backgrounds, and political affiliations to take up issues of mutual concern' (Brown, 1988: 20; see also White, 1973: 47, cited in Tripp, 2004: 143). This was in contrast to tribally defined political parties that were largely set up through socio-political networks that tried to resist the British system of indirect rule. It is thus likely that the local elite in the north comprised mostly men in chiefdoms and political parties with a few women who held leadership positions in religious and small-scale community organisations at council and municipal levels.

Amone and Muura (2014) state that there was significant investment in education and infrastructure in the more 'productive' southern part of Uganda, with little or no such investment in the north, which was considered to be 'a source of labour'. This meant that the demand for labour in the south stimulated a flow of migrant labour from Kitgum, Gulu and parts of West Nile to the central region. With hardly any education and low literacy in English, these migrants were often employed as casual labourers or low-ranking personnel in government, private companies, the army or police. Migrant labourers were closely monitored so that their ethnic origins were not lost. With the passing of the Vagrancy Ordinance in 1925, migrant workers who had no work were required to return home to their 'tribe' (ibid.). Thus the north had become little more than a reserve for migrant labour and military recruitment. This form of militarised and ethnicised rule depended on a burgeoning male elite comprised of colonial administrators, missionaries, parish priests and (British-appointed) chiefs. They were mostly men, with varying degrees of conformity and resistance to British rule. Women were also part of this elite, albeit in a less central way.

Thus, the structural features that define contemporary Acholi society and politics are historically rooted in this uneven regional development of Uganda. Lopsided patriarchal economic expansion strategies and state structures of indirect rule under colonialism resulted in deep regional disparities. At independence, the British handed over the country to a politically divided society in which the king of Buganda, representing southern communities, formed a weak alliance with Milton Obote, who was politically aligned to communities in the north (Mutibwa, 2008; Saul, 2004). In 1966, Obote broke away from an alliance with the Buganda Kingdom and assumed political authority of the whole country. During his first presidency, Obote relied heavily on the state army, in which one commander, Idi Amin, held political sway (Ngoga, 1998). With Amin's military takeover in 1971, all ministers were sworn into the army as officer cadets, making them subject to military discipline (Decker, 2014: 43). Mutibwa (2008) and Saul (2004) describe Idi Amin's presidency from 1971 to 1978 as a period in which militarism was further institutionalised through the merging of the government and the army.

With this rising militarisation of the state grew a new socio-economic 'class' of military men and their female companions (Decker, 2014: 43). Due to previous colonial recruitment practices, most soldiers were from ethnic communities in the north, coming from the West Nile, and were known as 'Nubians'. Those who were not part of this class struggled on the margins of a militarised political economy. In Decker's (ibid.: 87) study, women who lived in Kampala explained that their husband's salaries were too low to support their families. In addition, their men mysteriously disappeared, being taken by the secret police or going into hiding, leaving women to fend for themselves through income-generating activities.

With the takeover of state power by the National Resistance Movement in 1986, political power shifted back to the south. This intensified the leadership crisis in the north that had begun during the 1970s and 1980s and later developed into a profound social crisis (Branch, 2011: 56–62). For twenty years (1986–2006), the Acholi region suffered from the war, with subsequent rebel groups, most notoriously the Lord's Resistance Army (LRA), taking up arms against the government and attacking the civilian population. At the same time, government troops were guilty of gross human rights violations. It is estimated that more than 2 million Acholi were living in camps for internally displaced persons (IDPs) for several years of the conflict.

By the time Uganda became a British protectorate in 1894, there were several voluntary women's associations started by Christian missionaries and wives of colonial administrators and businessmen (Tripp, 2004). Formal education for girls was their initial focus. This early investment in education saw the first school established in 1898 and the second in 1905 and resulted in women entering diverse spaces of influence, beginning with leadership within churches and later in the civil service (ibid.). 'By the 1930s women were sitting with men on Church Councils and were being elected to Diocesan Educational Boards, and to the Church Synod and various other bodies' (Allen, 1930, cited in Tripp, 2000: 34). In fact, the earliest national women's association was the Protestant Mothers Union, which was founded in 1906 in Budo by British missionary wives. In 1908 it was opened up to Ugandan women who were wives of male students at Kings College in Budo. By 1930, women were represented on all committees of the Native Anglican Church. Another large organisation was the Girl Guides, formed in 1921 by Foster Smith of the Church Missionary Society. The Uganda Women's League was formed in 1938. In 1939, the Uganda Women's Emergency Organisation was formed in response to the consequences of the war. The Catholic counterpart of the Protestant Mothers Union was established much later, in 1959. After the Second World War, there was an increase in female missionaries and civil servants, especially in the field of education and community outreach. This included assisting the Department of Community Development in 1946 to set up community development clubs (Tripp, 2004: 127).

Despite a clear public political commitment to gender equality after Yoweri Museveni took over in 1989,[4] with legal reform and quota systems for women in parliament, the government did not directly address the ways in which the war destabilised women's socio-economic reliance on subsistence agriculture, particularly in rural areas. Forced displacement and the threat of abduction and sexual violence, mostly experienced by women, impacted on women's ability to grow crops. This inadvertently reduced women's activity in subsistence agricultural work, particularly crop production, which forms the basis of the economy in Northern Uganda.

Most female workers in Uganda are either unpaid family farmworkers, accounting for 80 per cent of all unpaid workers, or self-employed in the informal sector. According to the National Agricultural Advisory Services (NAADS), a government programme to support agricultural production, men tended to concentrate on the production of cash crops of coffee, cotton, tobacco and, more recently, cereals. Women concentrated on food crops, mainly for consumption, while simultaneously providing much of the labour for cash crop production (Ellis et al., 2005).

The gendered nature of agricultural production is clearly evident in the way in which socio-economic uses of land underwent significant changes during the war. These shifts have not been sufficiently documented in mainstream accounts. In urban centres, women found it difficult to obtain formal work and hence increasingly resorted to informal trade and entrepreneurship as a means of survival. At the same time, there were also shifts in men's economic influence, especially among men in rural areas of the north who were either displaced, had lost their cattle, and/or had reduced access to land.

### The micro-politics of Ugandan women's peace-building efforts

According to Tripp, 'The women's movement in Uganda made an unexpectedly swift and visible entrance onto the political scene shortly after Yoweri Museveni's National Resistance Movement took over in 1986' (2000: xiii). She describes the women's movement as a relatively autonomous political force in the country, one that challenged 'clientelistic (i.e., ethnic and religious) bases of mobilization that have plagued the country since independence'. Women's activism around issues of legal rights, peace, reproductive education and health issues, credit schemes, disabled women and land rights became established and grew exponentially after 1986. According to Mulumba, 'Women's involvement in peace efforts in Uganda's most recent history dates back to 1985 when Tito Okello seized power in a coup. At this time the National Council of Women organized over 2,000 women to demonstrate on the streets of Kampala for peace and against the mistreatment of women by the military' (2002: 113–14).

A government-led formal peace negotiation process[5] to address the conflict in Northern Uganda started in 2006 after twenty years of armed rebellion. The peace talks between the government of Uganda and the LRA took place in Juba, Southern Sudan, with the support of the government of South Sudan. Women such as Betty Bigombe, a former minister of state in charge of the Northern Uganda Reconstruction

Programme, undertook initiatives to end hostilities as early as 1995. She went into the bush for face-to-face peace talks with the leader of the LRA, Joseph Kony (Tamale, 1999: 48–51). In December 2004, Betty Bigombe mediated talks between the government and the LRA rebels. In 2008, these talks stalled when the rebels withdrew within a few days of signing the ceasefire agreement (Quinn, 2009).

In 2006, women's organisations formed a coalition aimed at ensuring that women's perspectives and demands would be taken into consideration during the talks. This process was called the 'Juba Peace Caravan'. According to Nabukeera-Musoke:

> In November 2007, the Coalition ran the Women's Peace Caravan through the districts of Kampala, Luwero, Masindi, Kona Kamdini (the meeting point for women peace groups from Teso, Lira, Pader and Kasese), Gulu and Kitgum. With over 100 women activists at the start of the journey, the caravan aimed at raising awareness and mobilizing Ugandans to support the peace process and to strengthen solidarity with the war-torn communities of Northern Uganda. (2012: 12)

Various authors attest to the fact that women's peace work has not been taken too seriously, especially considering their exclusion or peripheral status at government-led peace talks (Atim, 2010; Apio-Julu, 2004; Ocheri, 2011; Okot, 2010). According to Selle (2008: 3), government-led negotiations were headed by Dr Ruhakana Rugunda, the Minister of Internal Affairs in Uganda at the time. The chief mediator was Riek Machar, the vice president of Sudan. The government negotiation team of 2008 comprised only men, with one or two women members of parliament who acted as observers. There were only two female LRA representatives, and they had a limited role in the negotiation process (ibid.).

According to Okot's (2010: 43–6) research on women and peace building in Gulu District, women tended to be involved in traditional peace building at clan level. They prepared food for gatherings, provided traditional beers and sang and danced (all prescribed feminine roles). Some elderly women were accorded the opportunity of providing words of wisdom in settling disputes and/or giving blessings to the 'returnees' or ex-rebels (Selle, 2008; Atim, 2010; Apio-Julu, 2004). Other women's groups were formed as a response to immediate livelihood needs that were caused by the armed conflict. Ocheri's (2011) doctoral research on formerly abducted children who became mothers revealed the complex questions of 'rehabilitation' that face militarised societies in which both women and men were active participants in the war. According to Ocheri (ibid.), these young mothers reconstructed their own framing of their 'post-bush' life and livelihoods.

In response to an increase in the number of widows and orphans, the National Association of Women's Organisations in Uganda (NAWOU) started a childcare centre and assisted in the resettlement of women ex-prisoners of war. Uganda's Women's Effort to Save the Orphans (UWESO) also sought to respond to the needs of children orphaned by the war. UWESO was founded in the Luwero District and is now active in about thirty-six districts in Uganda.

Thus, it is clear that women undertook various peace-building strategies that conscientised communities and provided much-needed services. However, the women peace activists who were interviewed as part of Yaliwe Clarke's doctoral research may not have been sufficiently interrogated in terms of patriarchy and liberal peace building.

The major driving force for their peace activism was the devastating impact that the war had on vulnerable women and children (who were traumatised, violated, mutilated and/or orphaned); the absence of immediate substantive, humanitarian assistance; the possibility of these women's agency, given the inability of men to perform their roles and functions; and new contestations around the land issue. All of these issues made it possible for some reimagining and reinterpretation to occur.

### Women's creative reinterpretation of peace: living beyond survival

One sub-sample of Yaliwe Clarke's doctoral research focused on seventeen founding members or staff of six women's community peace organisations in Northern Uganda. Nine of these key informants were women who lived in towns and founded peace groups during and just after the war. All except one were working as teachers or civil servants at the time when they founded the organisation and lived in a house or owned land near or within a town to which people had fled for refuge. Almost all of them are active and held fairly high-ranking positions in faith-based organisations such as the Mothers Union, the Catholic church, or the Acholi Religious Leaders Peace Initiative. The average age of the key informants at the time when the data was collected (December 2013 to February 2015) was forty. All the women spoke of having either witnessed or experienced various forms of violence, including abduction, forced marriage and rape, as well as economic neglect from their husbands and/or extended family members. In addition, nine focus group discussions were held in order to corroborate the narratives gained from the key informants and informants from seven large support organisations were consulted.

Some organisations did not have a large membership (for example, WAN), or they no longer held regular activities in the community (PVP and WOPI-U) and therefore it was not easy to access beneficiaries. Organisations that were relatively functional – that is, they had offices, employed staff and had regular contact with communities – were WAN, KIWEPI, WOPI-U and KICWA.[6] All of these organisations were deliberately founded to respond to the needs of the communities.

The following sections highlight some of the key findings from the seventeen key informants. These are presented according to four main themes:

- shifts in patriarchy: abduction, displacement and the erosion of family structures;
- war as an opportunity for women's agency and the subversion of patriarchy;
- subverting economies of patriarchy: microcredit and land; and
- women's agency in re-socialising masculinities.

### Shifts in patriarchy: abduction, displacement and the erosion of family structures

Most informants explained that women founded various organisations because the war destabilised men's (heteronormative) dominance over social and material stability.[7] A combination of forceful recruitment of men into fighting forces, rape and forced marriage of girls and women, and the looting of cattle and other property contributed to a destabilisation of masculine identities among the Acholi and Langi societies (Dolan, 2009; 2002; Esuruku, 2011; Kizza et al., 2012). Harris's (2012) research on family structures and gender/age systems and social change in Northern Uganda suggests that, before the war, men held 'explicit power as occupiers of the superior position in the gender hierarchy', while older women held implicit power within households and the patrilineage as mothers, aunts and sisters-in-law. Men's power was associated with their role as fathers, uncles

TABLE 5.1 Profile of seventeen staff and founders of six women's peace organisations

| Organisation | Informants | Gender | Age | Highest education | Marital status | Religion | Ethnicity |
|---|---|---|---|---|---|---|---|
| **KIWEPI** | KIA (founder) | F | 57 | Below tertiary | Widow | Muslim | Acholi |
| | KIC (founder) | F | Late 50s | Bachelor's degree | Widow | Catholic | Acholi |
| | KIL (founder) | F | 44 | Certificate in education<br>Secretarial diploma<br>Bachelor's degree in business administration | Married | Christian | Acholi |
| | KIX (staff) | F | 30 | Degree in adult and community education | Married | Catholic | Acholi |
| | KIB (staff) | F | Early 20s | Degree in public administration<br>Undertaking master's degree in business administration | Single | Catholic | Acholi |
| | KID (staff) | M | 29 | Degree in public administration and management<br>Master's degree in public administration and management | Single | Catholic | Acholi |
| | KIH (intern) | F | Mid-20s | Unknown | Married | Catholic | Acholi |
| **KICWA** | KIY (founder) | F | 59 | Unknown diploma/certificate in counselling | Widow | Protestant | Acholi |
| | KIU (volunteer) | F | 25 | Degree in public administration and management | Married | Catholic | Acholi |
| | KIZ (staff) | M | 38 | Unknown | | Protestant | |

*(continued)*

TABLE 5.1 *(continued)*

| WOPI-U | KIJ (founder) | F | 53 | Completing master's degree in education, planning and management | Divorced | Anglican | Langi |
|---|---|---|---|---|---|---|---|
| | KIS (founder) | F | 55 | Graduate (first woman to graduate in sub-county) | Married | Catholic | Langi |
| | KIW (founder) | F | 43 | Degree in accounting | Married | Muslim | Langi |
| | KIE (staff) | F | 30 | Degree in development studies<br>Certificate in administrative law | Married | Anglican and Catholic | Langi |
| PVP | KIK (founder) | F | 63 | Tertiary (unknown) | Widow | Christian | Acholi |
| WAN | KIN (staff and founder) | F | 30 | Bachelor's degree in development studies | Married | Unknown (possibly Christian) | Acholi |
| Live Again | KIT (founder) | F | 51 | Master's degree in education, administration and planning | Unknown | Christian | Acholi |

*Source:* Yaliwe Clarke, PhD research in progress (2015).

and elders of patrilineal clans. The ownership and control of land were central to this power. Boys and young men were relied upon for lineage continuity as well as for social and economic support in old age. With displacement, violence and loss of livelihoods, these dominant masculine roles and positions were significantly destabilised (Dolan, 2009). This history of the war was recounted by both female and male informants, bearing in mind that relatively few males were part of the study. All referred to having witnessed the high recruitment of men by fighting forces. They also pointed out that more men than women were likely to be killed if they refused to adhere to the demands of the fighting forces. Others reported that more men stayed in rural areas to protect their land and cattle. For example, a founder of WOPI-U explained that many men stayed behind in rural areas in an attempt to fulfil their role as protector of land and property, while women moved into towns with their children to seek protection:

> If you moved along the road as people are being displaced and running, you see a woman running with a mattress on her head, with a saucepan, a child on her back and holding the other children's hands. At times you would look around and not see a man with her. She's travelling for the protection of the children and where she is travelling now she has to look for how to feed the children. Most men first remain back in the villages ... And that is one of the reasons these women are carrying this responsibility rather than the men. (Key Informant J, founder and board member, WOPI-U, Lira, December 2013)

Mass violence and displacement caused substantive changes in both men's and women's economic and political spheres of influence. Research undertaken by Dolan (2009; 2002), Finnström (2006) and Harris (2012) indicates that the National Resistance Army of Museveni and the LRA, as well as the Ugandan (government) army, were all known to steal cattle, loot property, rape, abduct and/or kill and maim people. The mass loss of cattle and the abduction mostly of boys and young men further resulted in the destabilisation of masculine authority (Annan et al., 2011; Dolan, 2002). Masculine authority was also undermined in the mid-1990s when the Ugandan army forced approximately 2 million people in rural Acholiland into 'protected villages' (i.e. IDP camps). Government army officials used this as an opportunity to further victimise Acholi communities and prevent them from supporting the LRA (Finnström, 2006, cited in Harris, 2012). With no land to till or cattle to herd, most men resorted to excessive consumption of alcohol and gambling (Dolan, 2002).

Research on suicide rates among men in IDP camps in Northern Uganda (Kizza et al., 2012) revealed that most suicide cases were a result of men's loss of dignity and their sense of social worth. Older men felt that they had been made redundant while younger men attempted to recover their status by abandoning school, opting for early marriage and struggling to provide for their families. 'They were trapped in an identity vacuum in which they were neither men nor children – a dilemma they tried to solve through risky social behaviour' (ibid.: 10). Their self-esteem was further affected when they realised that their wives and daughters were selling sex to survive. Some were forced to witness their women and daughters being raped by government soldiers or by the LRA. In some instances, men were further humiliated when they themselves were raped by government soldiers (Dolan, 2002: 74–5). Figure 5.1 illustrates the displacement of men and women as a result of the war in

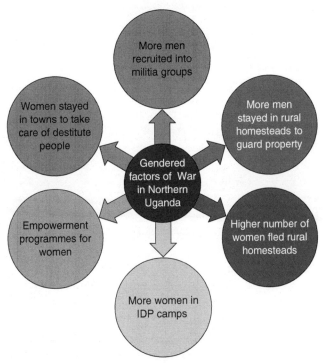

**Figure 5.1** Gender flux: displacement of men and women

Northern Uganda. The subsequent effects of abduction and the erosion of family structures mobilised women to collective peace efforts.

### War as an opportunity for women's agency and the subversion of patriarchy

Findings from this doctoral study indicate that women's power was marginally increased as a result of the war, which, in turn, transformed the social conditions that shaped gender norms, predominantly among Acholi and Langi communities. There was a broadening of older women's previously implicit power as mothers, aunts and sisters-in-law or diviners. Widowhood, forced marriage and an increase in the number of orphaned children meant that women suddenly experienced an increase in their material and maternal responsibilities, inadvertently increasing their sphere of influence in the clan. This expansion of material – as opposed to discursive – power occurred within and beyond their fathers' or husbands' lineage. The study specifically revealed the ways in which the war affected women's place within extended families, especially with regards to their abduction and children born in captivity:

- Women and girls abducted and/or separated from their families for several years were forced to marry members of militia groups whose children they bore from rape.
- Children born in captivity faced various possibilities, namely:
  - those who lost touch with their biological fathers or were rejected by their stepfathers were taken in by their mother's paternal clan; and
  - those who were separated from their families and/or were rejected by their mother's paternal clan ended up being supported by other women.

All women who founded community peace organisations referred to an urgent need to assist large numbers of destitute children within their families or the communities in which they lived. One founder member 'adopted' eight children:

> Right now I have eight. My one has now left; she has now matured and she's doing her own thing. But my dependants – I have four grandchildren I picked from my sisters I am helping them with. Then one son from my brother and then other non-relatives I just picked and just got them on board. I have currently eight. (Key Informant J, founder and board member, WOPI-U, Lira, December 2013)

In 2003, the aforementioned participant was supporting thirty-six people.

> Yes, that was beside the normal family members I had thirty-six members and then the land where I am staying now – I had already bought it but I had not yet developed it so I pushed them, three other families, to stay there. So it was a difficult period because: one – you had to feed and maintain these people; and two – you had to reassure them that things would settle in time ... People were worried. They left part of the family there, half of them is here; that was a bit of a difficult time ... they lost their properties. (Key Informant J, founder and board member, WOPI-U, Lira, December 2013)

Thus, given this situation, many women replaced men's previous dominant role as material provider and protector of the family. Furthermore, the everyday chaos of overcrowded IDP camps meant that there was an inevitable mixing of clans and sub-clans within a confined space, resulting in shifts in patrilineal ties as well as a general loss of social control. Women somehow managed to support families by adopting various initiatives despite the ongoing sexual and gender-based violence:

> And so you have all these responsibilities of caring for children, caring for the sick, fetching water, fetching firewood, doing all that and the war is disturbing you, is distorting all the arrangements for you to do this work because the expectation at the end of the day is that if food is to be brought to the table it is you who is to bring it ... And for the women because life became so difficult in the camp they had to move back home to see if they could get the leftover cassava or potatoes or whatever and in the process they were raped and in the process they were hit by the land mines. All these women suffered; it was in the process of trying to make their families survive ... to have food. And so for us as women that is something which is unique and I think that is so for every woman. (Key Informant K, founder, PVP, Gulu, December 2014)

One particularly vulnerable group of women were those who were abducted and returned with children born during captivity. According to Annan et al. (2011: 883), up to 26 per cent of female youth aged between fourteen to thirty-five were abducted during the war. They were mainly recruited to become 'wives' of men in the LRA and mothers of abducted children, some of whom were not their own. Those who were forcibly married (up to 25 per cent) experienced coercive sexual relationships 'characterised by shared domicile, domestic responsibilities, exclusivity, and sex carried out under threat' (ibid.: 884). The longer the time in captivity, the higher the chances of repeated sexual and gender-based violence in the form of rape and forced marriage. Of the six organisations included in the study, the Women's Advocacy Network (WAN) was founded solely by women who were formerly abducted. The study found that, as a result of the abductions, the boundaries of the clans, families and communities became porous within the war context. The war economy relied on abductions to both literally and figuratively reproduce child soldiers. Patrilineage ties became diluted and disrupted as a result.

The women's ability to found peace groups in the midst of such stigma, violence and social flux reveals their resilience in crafting individual and collective options for themselves and the communities around them. This ability to navigate their lives through precarious situations is both a form of resilience and agency (Vigh, 2003: 136, cited in Utas, 2005). From a feminist perspective, agency also implies subverting or contesting patriarchal social configurations and framing:

> a sense of oneself as one who can go beyond the given meanings in any one discourse, and forge something new, through a combination of previously unrelated discourses, through the invention of words and concepts which capture a shift in consciousness that is beginning to occur, or through imagining not what is, but what might be. (Davies, 1991: 51)

The study found that a form of reimagining peace occurred in the way women activists dealt with the trauma of men's displacement and loss of property during the war. For example, women started organising various peace groups and providing for the material and social well-being of others in need. They took on new social positions that contested men's power and shifted certain patriarchal constructs of femininity – they became dominant providers of material resources and claimed their need for ownership of land.

### Subverting economies of patriarchy: microcredit and land

One prominent way in which women were able to support communities was through microcredit schemes and small-scale income-generation activities. In the early stages of formation of the peace groups, peace-building efforts began with the collection of food from friends and family. This later developed into more institutionalised approaches, such as the establishment of small businesses in juice making, tailoring, trading in food, rearing of animals, wine making, mushroom growing and bee keeping, among other activities. Some of these businesses later developed into savings or microfinance/microcredit schemes that allowed women to work in groups, save collectively, and share financial risks.

> We had cases of women who wanted to be market vendors, we started with them. And then those who were able to grow what little income they got, they moved to certain higher levels and they were able to earn better income. And later on they were able to tell us, now I am settled, my husband has come back, my children are now going to school. If I was getting a 5 per cent interest, now I'm getting like 20 per cent and something like that. We had some women who were doing well who actually impressed us. (Key Informant K, founder member, PVP, Gulu, December 2014)

They described the expansion of their ability to provide for people around them as contributing towards peace. Several organisations in Kitgum that were not core to the study – such as KIWEPI, KICWA and others – combined the income-generation projects with savings schemes often termed 'village savings and loan associations' (VSLAs) that were mostly funded and coordinated by CARE International. VSLAs formed part of a broader programme called the Sustainable Comprehensive Response for Vulnerable Children and their Households (SCORE). As of 2013, CARE had helped facilitate the establishment of 27,222 VSLA groups in rural Uganda, representing over half a million people. The report states that up to 52 billion Ugandan shillings, about US$19 million, had been saved (Lowicki-Zucca et al., 2014). On the one hand, the international donors' role in facilitating numerous projects for the most vulnerable is highly commendable, but on the other it also furthered patriarchal economies.

Nevertheless, this doctoral study found that the benefits of income generation were linked to the alleviation of poverty as well as to longer-term benefits of capacity building, empowerment and consciousness raising that went beyond mere survival.

[A]t least when a person is economically stable she is able to do many things ... and that gives us a peace of mind. You are not worried about what to eat tomorrow, what to wear and what to do, you are settled ... [O]ther people need to be able to have peace of mind to be able to think positively, because if I am not sure of what I am doing the next minute or what would happen the next minute to me then why should I go ahead and plan for that? That also interferes with what one is able to do. (Key Informant J, founder and board member, WOPI-U, Lira, December 2013)

The women explained that the benefits were evident in changes to their social positioning. They had an improved capacity to take care of their families and deal with the trauma of displacement as well as other psycho-social impacts. Women's involvement in these peace collectives shifted their status in a positive way both socially and economically. Thus, their involvement in income generation was perceived as a practical attempt to address the ravages of war, in ways that addressed the various needs of women.

And then right now, in those days we also initiated some income-generating activities, we trained women on making bread, making wine from the local resources available at home and then training them [in] tailoring and some aspects of life skills that can sustain them and mushroom their growing, those things they can do at home within their compound ... [B]ut then as people went back home from the camps we changed, our vision actually changed; we were looking at the development aspect, women out there should be empowered, because we were working directly with the women affected by the war ... [W]e've given them goats and then this training on tailoring has also continued and then there's the aspect of human rights, training on gender-based violence which affects women ... then there is also a component of reproductive health. (Key Informant W, founder, WOPI-U, Lira, December 2013)

Overall, it seems that income-generation projects and saving schemes nourished local forms of association. The extent to which they fostered associational life that recognised and transformed oppression through collective consciousness and resistance is difficult to assess. Amina Mama (2014: 37–8) is rather sceptical as to whether women living in war contexts or the aftermath of war can actually address the broader structural roots of oppression, yet this study gives credence to the fact that some shifts had occurred. The attempts at microcredit schemes played a vital survivalist role that was essential for their livelihoods. However, women were still denied access to and ownership of land. They generally do not inherit land from their fathers as they take on their husbands' clan names when they marry.

In the Acholi sub-region, land acquisitions are particularly sensitive, occurring in the wake of long-standing displacement of the majority of the population and the resultant confusion about boundaries. Their resettlement has been further complicated by speculation about the presence of oil (Sjögren, 2014). The vast, fertile and possibly oil-rich land in Acholi has attracted the attention of prospective investors, willing and able to take advantage of an impoverished population. In addition to the many local land disputes, the region has recently witnessed an increasing number of controversial purchases, leases and allocations. All of this has fuelled anxiety and tension.

Land ownership has thus remained a major issue for women even in the post-conflict context. The study found that formerly abducted women had major difficulties in reintegrating into the community since no land was allocated to them.

> [A]s women if you leave home … you don't have your share of land at home, you are expected to have a share at your husbands' place, now you only … access the land, you don't have any ownership over that land and then as soon as your husband dies it's either your children who can take over that land but not you, [or] you can go and then the children have that land. Now while the children grow up somebody maybe an uncle of the children, a brother-in-law is always in control of that land. (Key Informant W, founder, WOPI-U, Lira, December 2013)

Many mothers of children born in captivity had lost contact with the father of their child and were not able to easily find or be accepted by the child's paternal clan. Members of militia groups tended not to use their clan name in order to hide their true identity. This made it even harder for mothers to trace their children's paternal clan after they returned from the 'bush'. Other women refused to have their forced marriages to rebels recognised. According to these women, the traditional processes of bride-price payment and other ceremonies that introduced non-lineage members into the family were not followed and thus the marriage to rebels could not be considered socially legitimate. There were thus many 'fatherless' children who were unable to claim ancestral allegiance from their paternal clan. With no knowledge of or contact with their biological father's lineage, these children often had no legitimate claim to their father's land.

> The land conflict – we realised that as we visit them the issue of land here is a very hot issue in the sense that traditionally the women do not have access or control over land; you can only control land through your husband or through a brother or somebody but not directly as a woman. So we were trying to appeal to the clan leaders to sympathise with the child mothers and try to portion them land ... And we were trying to appeal to them to portion some of the land to the child mothers so that they could do some of their farming from home. Because, traditionally they are supposed to farm from where they are married ... they have clashed over land. (Key Informant Z, founder, KICWA, Kitgum, February 2015)

Thus, it would seem that patriarchal norms relating to land were still 'non-negotiable'. Within such a context, woman nevertheless continued to interrogate aspects of patriarchy, albeit in a non-critical manner. For example, the findings of this doctoral study show how women initiated projects that affirmed and valorised non-abusive masculinities while at the same time unconsciously re-inscribing dominant masculinities.

### Women's agency in re-socialising masculinities

Acholi men, like all others, have been socialised into the dominant patriarchy. According to the women in this study, building peace at the micro-level entails women having an equal opportunity in making decisions and not being subjected to male dominance:

> For someone to realise about peace, two things [gender equality and peace] should go together ... If they don't go together then I don't think things will go well. That is why in this land things are not going well because in culture they say a woman is under a man so must always be under a man and a decision must always be made only by a man. And a man is ever right; when he says something it must be taken so automatically that one does not bring peace because a man might say something which depresses a woman ... But when you say a woman is given time to actually express ourselves and her decision is also taken into account that is when we say OK I think there is peace. A woman talks, the husband talks, or men talk and women talk ... But

here culture is still tying us down. It's tying us down. (Key Informant Y, founder, KICWA, Kitgum, February 2015)

There was an awareness of both patriarchal (structural) and cultural oppressions beyond that, which the war either reinforced or (re)created. Some women activists argued that the roots of violence in the community are linked to Acholi customs of manhood during and after the war. In this regard, one peace group in Lira, Women's Peace Initiative–Uganda (WOPI-U), implemented a community-based awareness project on gender-based violence called SASA!. SASA!, which means 'now' in Kiswahili, was in fact designed by two Kampala-based organisations – Raising Voices and the Centre for Domestic Violence Prevention (CEDOVIP). They trained more men than women in using a methodology that aimed at creating 'a critical mass committed to and able to create social norm change' (Abramsky et al., 2014).

A founder member of the women's peace group referred to the benefits of including men in the SASA! project:

In our recent SASA! project the majority of our community activists are men and I want to say it is wonderful because if you want to address SGBV [sexual and gender-based violence], approach it from the men, who are the perpetrators ... I want to share an experience of one of them giving a testimony. Of how the SASA! training alone has transformed him; he used to be a drunkard, very violent and every time he reaches home everybody including the woman runs for the hills but every evening during the two weeks training, we gave them fifty shillings out of pocket so in the next meeting with them, he gave a testimony that for the first time he gave the fifty thousand to the wife but before that he used to not give money to his wife and the woman asked him, 'What is this for?' And to make sure that he was telling us the truth, the brothers came to find out how their brother got transformed, 'Who are these people who have transformed our brother?' And so basically, and this is just to elaborate, much as the women, the men are difficult people, but when you bring them on board they are very resourceful and they are really dependable people. And you know since they are more outgoing they reach out to the community more than the women; that's what I see. (Key Informant S, founder of WOPI-U, Lira, December 2013)

The SASA! initiative points to an actual change in the violent masculine behaviour of a community member with whom the peace group worked. Whether or not such change can or will be sustained is dependent on a variety of factors. The SASA! project is fairly new and not all informants were directly involved in the project.

According to Abramsky et al.:

> The central focus of the intervention is to promote a critical analysis and discussion of power and power inequalities – not only of the ways in which men and women may misuse power and the consequences of this for their intimate relationships and communities, but also on how people can use their power positively to affect and sustain change at an individual and community level. (Abramsky et al., 2014: 3)

Two other groups – KIWEPI and WOPI-U – established projects aimed at changing masculinities in the domestic sphere through men-only projects that valorised men who perform 'peaceful' masculinities. At the time of the study, the programmes aimed to transform certain 'irresponsible' masculinities that the war seemed to have (re)created or reinforced. For example, in 2009, KIWEPI began a project titled 'Male-Engage', which grew out of a women's empowerment project. According to a male staff member who coordinated KIWEPI's women's empowerment programme at the time of the study, KIWEPI's core management team realised that women's empowerment would not be complete if men were not 'brought on board'.[8] He gave an example of KIWEPI's village saving scheme in which it was useful to have both husband and wife in the same scheme. This ensured that men were aware of the principles of saving and therefore could not easily undermine their wives' efforts to save. Apart from deliberately inviting men to join saving schemes, KIWEPI partnered with CARE International and began 'educating' the community, especially men, on the importance of women's empowerment programmes and men's role as partners with women in the home and the community. In conversation with communities with whom they worked, KIWEPI's interpretation of 'peaceful' masculinities included five themes: men who are not violent in the home; men who do not abuse alcohol; men who financially support the family; men who assist with household chores; and men who allow their wives to make some decisions in the home. Community members were able to vote for men who demonstrated that they lived up to all of these five core themes. They were awarded special recognition through an award ceremony in which they were officially named as *Lacor Makwiri* – role model men:

*Lacor Makwiri* should be of the following qualities. One, his children should all be attending school, there should be nothing like school dropout. Two, his household should not experience food insecurity, food should be enough in that household. Three, he should not be a person who is violent each and every time battering the woman, and all that is, those are some of the things they came up with. He should also not drink irresponsibly, like coming back home at midnight. *Lacor Makwiri* is not like that ... They should have the necessary health facilities, the latrine should be there at home, the rubbish pit, the shelter for bathing, the shelter for animal and poultry should be separate from the human, from the human habitat. That is how he is defined, the role model man. Then afterwards, they nominated names after the campaign, the community went into secret ballot voting, that is how the 39 role model men were selected, ya. (Key Informant D, KIWEPI, Kitgum, 19 December 2013)

It would appear that women's attempts at re-socialising masculinities were circumscribed largely by their immediate experiences of gender-based violence and the lack of material provision, which excluded a deeper analysis.

## Conclusion

This chapter highlights the complexities and nuances that under-pin women's peace initiatives in Northern Uganda. These women displayed a sense of agency and resilience in their efforts to establish community support groups and organisations that addressed the socio-economic and psychological impact of the war with very few resources at their disposal. The women who initiated these peace groups had sufficient social linkages to be able to address immediate humanitarian needs, albeit on a small scale. While one has to concede that there was some 'reimagining of their realities', which can be traced through their narratives, there is little evidence of a deeper conceptualisation of their peace efforts. It is clear that women in this study did not directly address the political and ethnicised roots of the war but focused instead on the immediate pressing needs of the most vulnerable. Their modus oper-andi showed features of a 'coping economy' (Peterson, 2008), which later turned into a mere survivalist mode. They targeted the needs of families that had been reconfigured due to war, attempted some renegotiation of ethnic/clan boundaries, without much success, and played a role in the recasting of more 'peaceful masculinities'. Central to all these attempts at 'social repositionings' was a heavy reliance on micro-savings and income-generation projects that would provide for the material needs of families and the most vulnerable in the community. Despite these multilevel efforts to repair the social fabric of this war-torn society, the land issue remained unassailable. Patriarchal clan systems and customs denied women ownership of land. Thus, while they made some gains in occupying previously masculinised spaces, such as being material providers, they were blocked from shifting the power dynamics inherent in land ownership.

In drawing this chapter to a close, it becomes evident that the women peace activists started off with informal activities to address basic needs resulting from the impact of the war and progressed to more strategic networking with international organisations to provide relief. Furthermore, their agenda shifted towards structural rearrangements, starting with microcredit savings schemes, contesting land ownership, and addressing violent masculinities and ruptured clan systems.

Further research and analysis would be needed to show the inter-sections between the patriarchy and Uganda's neoliberal political economy, as well as entrenched ethnic divisions between Northern Uganda and the rest of country. As Confortini says, there is need for more 'feminist curiosity' about how:

> patriarchy – in all its varied guises, camouflaged, khaki clad, and pin-striped – is a principal cause both of the outbreak of violent social conflicts and of the international community's frequent failures in providing long-term resolutions to those violent conflicts. (Confortini 2010: 4)

## Notes

1 Research for this chapter was funded by the Social Science Research Council (SSRC).

2 See a copy of the Beijing Platform for Action at www.un.org/womenwatch/daw/beijing/platform/violence.htm (accessed 4 May 2019).

3 See 'Facts and Figures on Peace and Security' on the UN Women website at www.unifem.org/gender_issues/women_war_peace/facts_figures.html (accessed 25 February 2013).

4 He encouraged the creation of Uganda's first set of gender policies in 1989. The Ugandan Gender Policy established a policy framework for gender quotas to be included in political party structures. The National Resistance *Movement* (formally referred to as the National Resistance *Army* that overthrew Idi Amin) was the first to implement a fairly successful quota system for women (Tamale, 1999).

5 'Peace process' here refers to a formal state-led negotiation and

reconciliation process that is paralleled by a number of other mechanisms to address the conflict, including the Amnesty Law, International Criminal Court, and the African traditional mechanism of *Mato Oput*. Since these mechanisms are parallel to the peace negotiation process, it is important to mention them as each mechanism largely affects the progress of the others.

6 The organisations are KICWA – Kitgum Concerned Women's Association; KIWEPI – Kitgum Women's Peace Initiative; PVP – People's Voice for Peace; WAN – Women's Advocacy Network; WOPI-U – Women's Peace Initiative–Uganda.

7 Here we use Pierre Bourdieu's theory of masculine dominance, which defines it as a social world that lends itself to objectification that is entirely constructed around an androcentric world view – an archaeological history of masculine unconscious 'which constitutes women as symbolic objects whose being (*esse*) is being-perceived (*precipi*), [and] has the effect of keeping them in a permanent state of bodily insecurity, or more precisely, symbolic dependence' (2001: 66).

8 Interview, December 2013.

## References

Abramsky, T., Devries, K., Kiss, L., Nakuti, J., Kyegombe, N., Starmann, E. and Michau, L. 2014. 'Findings from the SASA! Study: A Cluster Randomized Controlled Trial to Assess the Impact of a Community Mobilization Intervention to Prevent Violence against Women and Reduce HIV Risk in Kampala, Uganda', *BMC Medicine* 12 (12): 122.

Allen, M. 1930. 'The Women and Girls of Uganda', *Uganda Church Review* 20 (October–December).

Amone, C. and Muura, O. 2014. 'British Colonialism and the Creation of Acholi Ethnic Identity in Uganda, 1894 to 1962', *Journal of Imperial and Commonwealth History* 42 (2): 239–57.

Annan, J., Blattman, C., Mazurana, D. and Carlson, K. 2011. 'Civil War, Reintegration, and Gender in Northern Uganda', *Journal of Conflict Resolution* 55 (6): 877–908.

Apio-Julu, I. C. 2004. 'Women's Roles in Conflict Resolution: A Case Study of the Acholi, Northern Uganda'. Master's thesis, Makerere University, Kampala.

Atim, O. B. 2010. 'Armed Conflicts and Women's Empowerment in Northern Uganda: A Case of LRA Conflict in Gulu and Kitgum Districts, 2003–2008'. Master's thesis, Makerere University, Kampala.

Barry, J. 2005. *Rising Up in Response: Women's Rights Activism in Conflict.* Boulder CO and New York: Urgent Action Fund.

Bourdieu, P. 2001. *Masculine Domination.* Stanford: Stanford University Press.

Branch, A. 2011. *Displacing Human Rights: War and Intervention in Northern Uganda.* Oxford: Oxford University Press.

Brown, W. 1988. *Marriage, Divorce and Inheritance: The Uganda Council of Women's Movement for Legislative Reform.* Cambridge African Monographs 10. Cambridge: African Studies Centre.

Campbell, S., Chandler, D. and Shabaratnam, M. (eds). 2011. *A Liberal Peace?: The Problems and Practices of Peacebuilding.* London: Zed Books.

Cheldelin, S. I. and Eliatamby, M. (eds). 2011. *Women Waging War and Peace: International Perspectives* on *Women's Roles in Conflict and Post-conflict Reconstruction*. London: Continuum.

Cockburn, C. 2007. *From Where We Stand: War, Women's Activism and Feminist Analysis*. London: Zed Books.

Confortini, C. 2010. 'Feminist Contributions and Challenges to Peace Studies' in *The International Studies Encyclopedia*. Chichester and Malden, MA: Wiley-Blackwell and International Studies Association.

Davies, B. 1991. 'The Concept of Agency: A Feminist Poststructuralist Analysis', *Social Analysis: The International Journal of Social and Cultural Practice* 30: 42–53.

Decker, A. C. 2014. *In Idi Amin's Shadow: Women, Gender, and Militarism in Uganda*. Athens OH: Ohio University Press.

Dolan, C. 2002. 'Collapsing Masculinities and Weak States: A Case Study of Northern Uganda' in Cleaver, F. (ed.), *Masculinities Matter! Men, Gender and Development*. London: Zed Books.

Dolan, C. 2009. *Social Torture: The Case of Northern Uganda, 1986–2006*, Vol. 4. New York: Berghahn Books.

Doyle, M. and Ikenberry, J. G. (eds). 1997. *New Thinking in International Relations*. Boulder CO: Westview Press.

Ellis, A., Manuel, C. and Mark, B. C. 2005. *Gender and Economic Growth in Uganda: Unleashing the Power of Women*. Washington DC: World Bank.

Esuruku, R. S. 2011. 'Beyond Masculinity: Gender, Conflict and Post-conflict Reconstruction in Northern Uganda', *Journal of Science and Sustainable Development* 4 (25): 25–40.

Finnström, S. 2006. 'Wars of the Past and War in the Present: The Lord's Resistance Movement/Army in Uganda', *Africa* 26 (2): 200–20.

Gibbings, S. L. 2011. 'No Angry Women at the United Nations: Political Dreams and the Cultural Politics of United Nations Security Council Resolution 1325', *International Feminist Journal of Politics* 13 (4): 522–38.

Harris, C. 2012. 'Gender–Age Systems and Social Change: A Haugaardian Power Analysis Based on Research from Northern Uganda', *Journal of Political Power* 5 (3): 475–92.

Heathershaw, J. 2013. 'Towards Better Theories of Peacebuilding: Beyond the Liberal Peace Debate', *Peacebuilding* 1 (2): 275–82.

Hendricks, C. 2011. *Gender and Security in Africa: An Overview*. Oslo: Nordiska Afrikainstitutet.

Hudson, H. 2012. 'A Double-edged Sword of Peace? Reflections on the Tension between Representation and Protection in Gendering Liberal Peacebuilding', *International Peacekeeping* 19 (4): 443–60.

Karugire, S. R. 1980. *A Political History of Uganda*. Nairobi: Heinemann.

Kizza, D., Knizek, B. L., Kinyanda, E. and Hjelmeland, H. 2012. 'Men in Despair: A Qualitative Psychological Autopsy Study of Suicide in Northern Uganda', *Transcultural Psychiatry* 49 (5): 696–717.

Lowicki-Zucca, M., Walugembe, P., Ogaba, I. and Langol, S. 2014. 'Savings Groups as a Socioeconomic Strategy to Improve Protection of Moderately and Critically Vulnerable Children in Uganda', *Children and Youth Services Review* 47: 176–81.

Mama, A. 2014. 'Beyond Survival: Militarism, Equity and Women's Security' in Foeken, D., Dietz, T., de Haan, L. and Johnson, L. (eds), *Development and Equity: An Interdisciplinary Exploration by Ten Scholars from Africa, Asia and Latin America*. Leiden: Brill.

Mama, A. and Okazawa-Rey, M. 2012. 'Militarism, Conflict and Women's

Activism in the Global Era: Challenges and Prospects for Women in Three West African Contexts', *Feminist Review* 101 (1): 97–123.

Moser, C. N. and Clark, F. 2001. *Victims, Perpetrators or Actors?: Gender, Armed Conflict and Political Violence*. London: Zed Books.

Mulumba, D. 2002. 'The Women's Movement and Conflict Resolution in Uganda' in Tripp, A. M. and Kwesiga, J. C. (eds), *The Women's Movement in Uganda: History, Challenges, and Prospects*. Kampala: Fountain Publishers.

Mutibwa, P. 2008. *The Buganda Factor in Uganda Politics*. Kampala: Fountain Publishers.

Nabukeera-Musoke, H. 2012. 'Women Making a Difference to the Juba Peace Negotiation Process'. Unpublished paper. Kampala: Isis-WICCE.

Ngoga P. 1998. 'Uganda: The National Resistance Army' in Clapham, C. (ed.), *African Guerrillas*. Kampala: Fountain Publishers.

Ocheri, E. A. 2011. 'An Exploration of Intra-bush and Post-bush Experiences of Formerly Abducted Child Mothers in Northern Uganda: Issues in Rehabilitation, Resettlement and Reintegration'. PhD thesis, Makerere University, Kampala.

Okot, A. C. 2010. 'Women and Peacebuilding: The Case of Women Involvement in Peace-building Process in Gulu District'. Master's thesis, Mackerere University, Kampala.

Olonisakin, F. and Okech, A. (eds). 2011. *Women's Security Governance in Africa*. Dakar and Nairobi: Pambazuka Press.

Pankhurst, D. 2003. 'The "Sex War" and Other Wars: Towards a Feminist Approach to Peace Building', *Development in Practice* 13 (2–3): 154–77.

Peterson, V. S. 2008. '"New Wars" and Gendered Economies', *Feminist Review* 88: 7–20.

Pratt, N. and Richter-Devroe, S. 2011. 'Critically Examining UNSCR 1325 on Women, Peace and Security', *International Feminist Journal of Politics* 13 (4): 489–503.

Pugh, M., Cooper, N. and Turner, M. (eds). 2008. *Whose Peace? Critical Perspectives on the Political Economy of Peacebuilding*. London: Palgrave Macmillan.

Quinn, J. R. 2009. 'Getting to Peace? Negotiating with the LRA in Northern Uganda', *Human Rights Review* 10 (1): 55–71.

Richmond, O. P. 2006. 'The Problem of Peace: Understanding the "Liberal Peace"', *Conflict, Security and Development* 6 (3): 291–314.

Richmond. O. P. 2012. *A Post-liberal Peace*. London and New York: Routledge.

Sathyamurthy, T. V. 1986. *The Political Development of Uganda 1900–1986*. Aldershot: Gower.

Saul, J. S. 2004. 'The Unsteady State: Uganda, Obote, and General Amin' in Mohan, G. and Zack-Williams, T. (eds). *The Politics of Transition in Africa*. Trenton NJ: James Currey.

Scully, P., McCandless, E. and Abu-Nimer, M. 2010. 'Gender Violence and Gender Justice in Peacebuilding and Development', *Journal of Peacebuilding and Development* 5 (3): 3–6.

Selle, L. 2008. 'Women Participation in Peace Building in Northern Uganda: A Case of Gulu District'. Master's thesis, Mackerere University, Kampala.

Sjögren, A. 2014. 'Scrambling for the Promised Land: Land Acquisitions and the Politics of Representation in Post-war Acholi, Northern Uganda', *African Identities* 12 (1): 62–75.

Steans, J. 1998. *Gender and International Relations: An Introduction.* Cambridge: Polity Press.

Tamale, S. 1999. *When Hens Begin to Crow: Gender and Parliamentary Politics in Uganda.* Kampala: Fountain Publishers.

Tickner, A. J. 1992. 'Hans Morgenthau's Principles of Political Realism: A Feminist Reformulation' in Grant, R. and Newland, K. (eds), *Gender and International Relations.* Milton Keynes: Open University Press.

Tripp, A. M. 2000. *Women and Politics in Uganda.* Kampala: Fountain Publishers.

Tripp, A. M. 2004. 'A New Look at Colonial Women: British Teachers and Activists in Uganda, 1898–1962', *Canadian Journal of African Studies/ La Revue Canadienne des Études Africaines* 38 (1): 123–56.

Utas, M. 2005. 'Victimcy, Girlfriending, Soldiering: Tactic Agency in a Young Woman's Social Navigation of the Liberian War Zone', *Anthropological Quarterly* 78 (2): 403–30.

Vigh, H. E. 2003. 'Navigating Terrains of War: Youth and Soldiering in Guinea-Bissau'. PhD thesis, Institute of Anthropology, Copenhagen.

White, C. D. 1973. 'The Role of Women as an Interest Group in the Ugandan Political System'. MA thesis, Makerere University.

Whiteworth, S. 1994. *Feminism and International Relations.* New York: St Martins Press.

Zaum, D. 2012. 'Beyond the "Liberal Peace"', *Global Governance* 18 (1): 121–32.

## 6 | THE PRISM OF MARGINALISATION: POLITICAL ECONOMY OF VIOLENCE AGAINST WOMEN IN SUDAN AND SOUTH SUDAN

*Fahima Hashim*

### Introduction

Violence against women is a global phenomenon that is manifested in different forms, and Sudanese and South Sudanese women are no exception to this. They have been subjected to many forms of violence, varying from structural and physical to mental. Contributing factors and proxies such as family, local community and the state have precipitated violence against women. Regardless of the various forms of violence, Sudanese women attain positions that vary depending on their differing socio-geographical, ethnic, cultural and religious backgrounds. This chapter aims to identify the main socio-economic, political and cultural factors contributing to the emergence and perpetuation of violence against women in Sudan. It examines the role of political Islam and the state in justifying and promoting these forms of violence and also explores the various manifestations of resistance and organisations against policies and legislations that sustain violence against women.

Despite the great complexity and complications, different forms of violence in Sudan and South Sudan have been met with resistance from various forces, such as women's organisations, women in politics and women in exile. Resistance has resulted in both success and failure, which will be addressed in this chapter.

Using the premises of feminist political economy that highlight the masculine nature of the integrated political economic authority structure (True, 2010), this chapter attempts to map out the various forms of structural violence faced by women in the North and South of Sudan.[1] Using this theoretical framework, relevant literature and my own lived experiences, the chapter explores the socio-cultural norms, patriarchal family and marriage institutions and institutional violence depicted in the force of Islamisation laws and policies that hinder women's economic contributions, as well as violence in conflict, sexual violence, displacement and racism.

## Background: state failure

Violence, civil wars and political instability compounded by dogmatic interpretations of Islam have plagued Sudan since its independence from the British in 1956. Such turbulence was a direct result of the postcolonial state, which was built on a history of colonial exploitation of the area's resources rather than its development. The British bequeathed power to an elite group who came predominately from the Islamised and Arabised elements of riverine social groups and formulated a very narrow form of state identity based exclusively on their interpretation of Islam and on Arabism. This identity ignored other social, cultural, religious and linguistic components of the country, which led to their overt marginalisation and exclusion from major decision making. The separation of South Sudan in 2011 was but one result of the narrowly defined state identity forged by the centralised state through physical and ideological force. As a result, women from all walks of life have been negatively affected by the failures of Sudanese state formation, especially under the rule of the current government, from 1989 to the present.

Since its independence in 1956, Sudan has witnessed an upsurge of armed ethnic and regional movements that have resulted in massive suffering and have caused widespread displacement and large numbers of refugees in the South (Idris, 2013). The protest in the South challenged the newly independent Sudanese state, which was controlled by the Arabised and Islamised elites who strove to define and impose a certain understanding of citizenship rights and responsibilities that ignored the multicultural and social reality of Sudan (ibid.).

Between 1898 and 1956, Sudan was ruled by an Anglo-Egyptian administration. Despite being administered as one country, the British followed widely divergent policies in governing North and South. This dual system 'reinforced Arabism and Islam in the North and encouraged southern development along indigenous African lines, while introducing Christian missionary education and the rudiments of Western civilisation in the South. For the British, Sudan was effectively two countries in one' (AfDB, 2011). Moreover, the concentration of economic, political and administrative development in the North at the expense of the South created severe socio-economic and political discrepancies between the two regions and affected the relationship between the people of the North and the South (ibid.). There were, in fact, many factors deriving from unequal development that affected the possibility of building one nation, and education was a major one. Access to education in the South was restricted to missionary education, which 'discouraged southern Sudanese from engaging in politics, political debates and action'. By contrast, northern Sudanese had 'the opportunity to have political platforms and exposure to the outside world' (ibid.).

During the period of Anglo-Egyptian rule, issues of women's development in the southern region were left to be controlled and decided by tribal norms and customary laws. This process affected girls' enrolment in school. The position of women was determined by their reproductive role and economic contribution, which were based on women's agricultural work and marriage. When reaching the age of marriage, girls in southern Sudan became the family wealth; as such, women had no choice but to follow the family's decision (Hall and Ismail, 1981; Badri, 2009). It was difficult to retain female teachers to maintain the continuity of girls' education in the South due to early and forced marriage. The gap between girls' education in the North and South was affected by the 'divide and rule' policy of the colonial administration; this affected levels of education attained by girls in the South, which remained limited in comparison to the North. Realisation of this came during the 1940s with the rise of a national movement calling for an independent Sudan (Hall and Ismail, 1981; Badri, 2009). By the time women in the North were obtaining their political rights for the first time, women in the South still had little access to education and were suffering from poverty within a situation of regional instability, a situation that lasted until the first peace agreement in 1972 (Hall and Ismail, 1981; Badri, 2009).

Today, Sudan has an estimated population of 40 million (almost 50 per cent female and 50 per cent male), with about 32 per cent urban, 68 per cent rural and 7 per cent nomads (SIHA Network, 2015). Islam is the predominant religion, particularly in the North, while Christianity and animist traditional religions are more prevalent in the South and in some areas of the southern Blue Nile and western regions. Sudan is a republic with a federal system of government. There are multiple levels of administration, with twenty-six states, ten of which are in South Sudan (ibid.).

The elements that constitute national identity in Sudan are complex. The population is composed of a multitude of ethnic groups and inhabitants speaking more than 130 languages and dialects (SIHA Network, 2015). An Islamic-African-Arab culture has emerged over the years and has become predominant in the North. The Arabic language is spoken in most parts of the country (ibid.).

South Sudan consists of more than sixty ethnic groups with eighty local languages. The population is predominantly Christian, with a few Muslims and the remaining number practising traditional tribal beliefs (UNDP, 2015). People living in rural areas represent 83 per cent of the country's population, and cattle culture is an essential element of society. As a result, ownership of a herd of cattle is a key marker of wealth and cattle raiding was the main catalyst of intercommunal violence before the current political conflict erupted in 2013 (ibid.).

Over the past twenty years, Sudan's economy has undergone a rapid and turbulent transition to a full-blown market economy, departing from a legacy of state control and indicative planning (Almosharaf, 2014). Loans from a global Islamic banking sector and the imposition of an Islamic banking system have played a crucial role in these changes (ibid.). This has impacted on women in the market economy and has led to the privatisation of education and health. It has also disenfranchised the non-Muslim population.

Sudan scored 0.490 and ranked 165 out of 188 countries in the 2016 Human Development Index (HDI). Sudan's macro-economic context, according to the World Bank, is that of a lower-middle-income country with a gross domestic product (GDP) of US$72,065.90 in 2013, rising to US$95,585.40 in 2016. Its GDP growth was 4.4 per cent in 2013, increasing to 4.7 per cent 2016, and it had an annual inflation rate of 30.0 per cent in 2013, decreasing to 16.9 per cent in 2015. The agriculture and livestock sectors currently contribute less than 40 per cent of Sudan's GDP. After the discovery of oil in the South in late 1999, Sudan became completely dependent on oil revenue, which contributed more than 50 per cent of government revenue and comprised 95 per cent of its exports (BTI, 2018).

The unemployment rate was estimated in 2016 at 19.3 per cent. Disparities also appeared between rural and urban areas in the level of social exclusion, with development more concentrated in the centre while the west, south and east remained relatively deprived (BTI, 2018). 'This has contributed to, and been enhanced by, the growth of conflict particularly in the west and south. In Darfur, the rebel movements have explicitly referenced their political and economic exclusion due to ethnic and racial discrimination by central Nile ethnic groups' (ibid.).

As highlighted in an International Monetary Fund (IMF) report:

> There are many factors that account for persistent poverty in Sudan but the main factors include:
>
> - The long and drawn out civil conflicts in southern, western and eastern Sudan that have diverted resources from development to fighting wars, impaired social capital and good governance and destroyed human and physical capital …
> - The urban bias of development policies and programs in the past that neglected efforts to broadly increase the productivity of rural factors of production, particularly in the sphere of rain-fed agriculture;
> - The lack of a coherent poverty reduction effort and a sustained reform to promote shared growth and diversify the economy. (IMF, 2013)

These factors were further compounded by 'an unsustainable external debt [and] the long economic international sanctions' (IMF, 2013).

It can be concluded that poverty in Sudan is predominantly in rural areas and among those whose income derives from farming and livestock. The incidence of poverty is marginally lower (44.2 per cent) among the small percentage of households headed by women (17.3 per cent) compared with households headed by men, which have an incidence rate of 47.2 per cent (BTI, 2018).

Public healthcare provision is limited and of poor quality. And while education provision for all age groups (inclusive of women and girls) has expanded, the quality has declined. In both healthcare and education, there is also some limited but expensive provision beyond the reach of the majority of the population. According to Round 2 of the Sudan Household Health Survey (SHHS2) in 2010, the infant mortality rate in Sudan was sixty per 1,000 live births while the under-five mortality rate was eighty-three per 1,000 live births during the five-year period before the SHHS2. Estimates of neonatal/post-neonatal and child mortality rates were calculated using the direct method and were thirty-four and twenty-six per 1,000 live births respectively (Government of Sudan, 2012).

The number of women in the workforce has increased, although this has largely been driven by necessity and on average women earn less than men (BTI, 2018). Women now comprise 29.4 per cent of the labour force and, in some universities, there is a higher percentage of women students than men. Sudan scored 0.591 points in the United Nations Development Programme's 2014 Gender Inequality Index. While this is a slight improvement over previous years, Sudan is still on the same level as Mozambique and the Democratic Republic of Congo (ibid.).

### The status of inequality: women's economic, social and cultural position

Women's economic status continued to deteriorate despite equal distribution of wealth and power, social justice and the right to equal participation in public life being enshrined in the interim constitution of 2005. Economic and social plans still fail to consider women's needs and barely take account of women's significant participation in the economy (Elrayh, 2014).

The position of women in Sudan varies in accordance with the socio-economic, political, cultural and geographic differences in the country, and therefore it is always difficult to talk about Sudanese women in North and South as a unified group. Patriarchy is the common domain, while the state and society are affected by the imposition of political Islam and ethnic discrimination.

The right to education is enshrined in the current bill of rights in the interim constitution of 2005. While this is a key means for women's advancement, it remains unfulfilled through lack of political commitment, leaving 50.6 per cent of women illiterate. The deteriorating economic situation of families and customary beliefs about gender roles have also played their part in denying women's and girls' right to education, as males are given preference (Elrayh, 2014).

Despite noticeable progress in efforts to address gender inequality, formal and non-formal educational institutions do not consistently promote gender equality in all aspects of social, economic and political life. While women in Sudan are economically active and gender attitudes are changing, significant variations exist across states and between rural and urban environments.

Sudan's literacy rate is 58.6 per cent, which is comparatively low by international standards. Literacy rates are generally higher in urban areas compared with rural areas. While the rate of urbanisation is very high, this is mainly accounted for by the capital, Khartoum, which in 2008 (the latest census) had a population of 4.27 million; in comparison, Nyala in South Darfur, the second-largest city in the country, had a population of 443,000 people (UN-HABITAT, 2014). The literacy rate for women is lower than for men: 53.1 per cent compared with 64.1 per cent. However, there has been an increase in the number of literate women, which has led to an improvement in the social and working conditions of women in recent years. The ratio of women to men in tertiary education is 1.1:1.0 (the gender parity index), although the ratio of girls to boys in primary education is 0.9:1.0. In secondary education, both sexes are equally represented. Overall, educational enrolment is low although there has been a rise in the numbers of students in higher education, especially among women. However, the quality of education at all levels has generally fallen, which has encouraged the growth of private education for those able to afford it (BTI, 2018).

The effect of the absence of legal provisions for implementing the constitution's positive discrimination clause is that only a small number of women assume high-ranking positions in state institutions and the private sector. According to Elrayh (2014), the estimated percentage of women graduates in higher education is 58 per cent. However, only 26 per cent of them find their way into the formal sector. Of the 90 per cent of Sudanese who live below the poverty line, 65 per cent are women (ibid.).

## The space between us

Along the path of Sudan's history, women both in the North and South have had no opportunity to get together or integrate in order to help build one nation. Despite being part of a single nation, they followed different trajectories in dealing with gender identity, religion and patriarchy.

### South Sudanese women's marginalisation

Women in South Sudan are shaped by the social and economic context of being one of the world's least developed countries, devastated by decades of conflict (1955–72 and 1983–2005). The population is

48 per cent female and 52 per cent male; the global average is 51 per cent female and 49 per cent male. A majority of its population is very young, with 72 per cent under thirty years of age. It has the highest rates of maternal mortality in the world: one in seven women are at risk of dying from childbirth or pregnancy (Makuei et al., 2018). Education rates are profoundly low, with only 27 per cent of the adult population literate, and there is a marked gender discrepancy, with 40 per cent of men but only 16 per cent of women over fifteen years of age being literate. UNICEF estimates that 70 per cent of children aged six to seventeen years have never been enrolled in school. Cultural norms and traditions, especially in rural areas, marginalise women from being involved publicly or having any political or social activities (ibid.).

Prior to the peace agreement, during the conflict of 1983–2005, gender-based violence involving both physical and mental abuse was widespread in South Sudan. There was a focus on sexual violence, especially the rape of women and men, which occurred against a background of traditional practices including 'girl compensation' and forced prostitution or sexual slavery that were lived realities for the women of South Sudan. Moreover, domestic violence was an accepted norm in society. Early marriage was and still is a common trend, with 45 per cent of girls married before they are eighteen years old and 7 per cent of girls married younger than fifteen years of age. Polygamy is another norm and divorce is extremely difficult for women to obtain. Traditionally, only men can ask for divorce and the wife's family has to pay back the bride price (UNDP, 2015).

Southern Sudanese women, as well as women in the North, are not homogeneous and their social position is shaped by ethnic cultural traditions. The southern woman's recognised place is the home, where she becomes a wife and a mother. Further, the ideal woman is one who is hardworking, cares for her family and is submissive (Hall and Ismail, 1981). However, women in the South are not segregated from men in their social life, unlike women in the predominantly Muslim North. Yet they are faced with different problems and challenges, such as lack of education, poverty and conflict. In spite of the reproductive role of women in the South, they represent an important economic force in agriculture, food production and cattle herding. However, little research and very few studies had been carried out in South Sudan before the eruption of the first conflict in 1955 (ibid.).

Since the signing of the comprehensive peace accord (CPA), South Sudan has at least formally recognised the importance of the role of women and their contribution to peace negotiation processes, albeit small. The country has therefore enacted explicit laws and policies on gender equality, with the transitional constitution and 2011 bill of rights providing guarantees for the equality of men and women. It recognises the historical inequalities between women and men in South Sudan and sets a 25 per cent affirmative action quota for women in legislative and executive bodies and in political participation. As a result, women currently comprise 26.5 per cent of the National Legislative Assembly (No Safe Place, 2017).

### Women of northern Sudan: the privileged

Like many Muslim societies governed by Islamic law since the Ottoman Empire (1821–85), North Sudan is fundamentally patriarchal in nature and is exclusively controlled by men, whose key role is to maintain the household economically and socially. However, women's subordinate position in the North began to change when the British started to recognise girls' education during the 1920s. This followed efforts made by Sheikh Babiker Badri in 1907 to start a school for girls to provide formal education and teach his own daughters and relatives (seven girls), which the British refused to support. British colonisation led to a major shift in the country's economy as it introduced capitalism and transformed the country into a supplier of raw materials for British industries and a market for European manufactured goods.

The British had a gender discriminatory policy in education in the North, mainly training men as workers while educating girls to become good wives. Despite this, however, education for girls was used as a vehicle towards emancipation (Hall and Ismail, 1981; Badri, 2009; Hale, 1996). In the 1920s, a considerable number of girls enrolled in schools with class sizes varying between forty and sixty students. By 1925, five girls had been trained at the teacher training institute in Omdurman, which had opened in 1923, to work in elementary schools in the North (Hall and Ismail, 1981; Badri, 2009). By the early 1930s, the colonial administration began considering health work and teaching as women's work, seemingly improving women's economic status. Therefore, women tended to be employed as nurses, midwives and community health workers. This employment was considered suitable and was socially acceptable, albeit with some reluctance. During the Second World War, the British needed nurses; however, with the restrictions of Sudanese social norms and Islam concerning the mixing of women and men in the North, the British authorities recruited female prostitutes who turned out to be good in nursing. This, however, made nursing unwelcome work for respectable Sudanese women (Spaulding and Beswick, 2016). By 1926, four midwives had graduated, their ages ranging from forty to sixty years. Seven nurses graduated in the mid-1930s, later joined by two women from the South by the late 1930s (Hall and Ismail, 1981).

When the British established midwifery training in late 1920s, only older women (aged forty to seventy), married and with children were accepted and recruited. Young, unmarried, committed women were not welcomed by society until later and the British avoided recruiting them, afraid that they would be labelled 'perverted' (Brown, 2017). Some women from the South were recruited to be trained as midwives; however, they were segregated from working with midwives from the North as the British trainers were afraid that the South Sudanese women would learn the practice of female genital mutilation (FGM) (ibid.).

In the late 1930s and early 1940s the country was in turmoil, with calls for independence followed by the formation of political parties (Ali, 2015). This helped northern women to start organising and forming their own trade unions; these were mainly the women teachers' and nurses' trade unions, which were initiated in the late 1940s (Ahmad, 2014). By the early 1950s, some women began joining the Communist Party, which at that time was the only political party that opened its doors to women. Soon after this, the Women's Union was formed and became the first umbrella organisation for Sudanese women to work collectively (ibid.).

### Violence against women: prevalence and manifestations

The most widely used definition of violence against women is provided by the United Nations' legal framework set out in the General Assembly's Declaration on the Elimination of Violence against Women by Resolution 48/104 of December 1993 (True, 2012). Articles 1 and 2 define violence against women as: 'Any act of gender-based violence that results in, or is likely to result in, physical, sexual, or psychological harm or suffering to women, including threats of such acts, coercion or arbitrary deprivation of liberty, whether occurring in public or in private life.' True states further that 'the UN definition embraces, but is not limited to, physical, sexual, psychological/emotional, and most recently, economic violence or exploitation occurring in the family or community and/or perpetrated or condoned by the state' (ibid.).

She further highlights that the violation of the right to life, liberty and security of the person shapes the enjoyment and fulfilment of all other human rights, including economic and social rights such as the right to work, health, social security, education, food, housing, water and land.

In Sudan, most of the forms and patterns of violent behaviour have been embedded politically, culturally and economically by the community, family and state. Specific forms of violence have been enforced by restrictive Islamic laws, such as stoning, flogging, forced veiling and restricted mobility in the public sphere. Other forms of violence against women include forced marriage, marital rape, domestic violence and FGM, as well as those related to the ongoing conflict, of which the state is an integral part, such as displacement, rape and sexual violence used as a weapon of war, abduction, ethnic violence, forced prostitution and trafficking, to mention just a few. Access to justice is complicated and almost impossible due to the system of impunity, especially among state actors (i.e. the police, security services, army and militias); the ambiguity of some articles in the 1991 Criminal Code; the stigma of violence, especially sexual violence; the lack of case documentation; and the lack of disaggregated data on violence against women.

### Socio-cultural norms and structural violence

Gender disparity is quite perceptible in Sudan, in both the North and South. Men are seen as active and dynamic while women are constructed as passive members of society. They are subordinate to men's power and are usually seen in a purely maternal capacity (Ahmad, 2014). There are many socio-economic and cultural factors supporting gender discrimination and inequality, and these in turn affect women's social, political and economic advancement. These factors are embedded in socialisation processes, in education, and everywhere in the public sphere. This institutionalised discrimination, which favours males over females within the family and the society at large, also leads many women to regard their role as limited to caring for children, obeying their husbands and becoming good housewives (ibid.).

## The family institution

It is imperative here to examine the role of the extended family as it relates to women's position and situation. Although as an institution it has undergone changes, the nature of these changes must be seen in relation to class and regional differences and it remains among the most dominant structures in Sudanese society (El Bakri, 1995). Within the extended family, sharp role distinctions between women and men continue to exist. Most social life and activities revolve around the family and are primarily the domain of women. Births, deaths, marriages and circumcision are the important celebrations and women must contribute either financially or by providing labour and being present. If they do not comply – especially working women – they will be subjected to ridicule or lose the family support on which they depend (ibid.). El Bakri concludes that the extended family in Sudan is not only the locus of women's oppression but also of their support. The extended family has fulfilled many important needs for women in Sudan; it is not suggested, however, that the extended family is a substitute for women's organisations (ibid.).

## The institution of marriage

Marriage is another crucial institution that thwarts the life of Sudanese women. It is considered necessary not only for its societal value but also for its impact on economic stabilisation (Gruenbaum, 2006). Marriage allows both women and men to gain access to the work of the other in the gendered division of labour, child bearing, social reproduction and social recognition and prestige (ibid.). In addition, marriage is the only legitimised way in which women can be sexually active and fulfil their own sexual needs.

Article 40, Clause 2 of the 1991 Personal Status Law set the minimum age of marriage as the age of discretion – ten years old – although Sudan had ratified the Convention on the Rights of the Child in 1990, which prohibits child marriage (Musawah, 2009). Also, Article 75 stipulates that 'the wife will be declared disobedient if she leaves the matrimonial home without legitimate justification, i.e. work outside or visit her parents without the husband's permission' (ibid.).

Given the background set out above, it is obvious that, throughout Sudan's history, women from the North and the South have had no chance to unite, build one nation or challenge their diversity and identity politics. This was made difficult and complex due to the ideologies and concepts leading to structural violence and othering on the basis of ethnicity, slavery, religion and language – us versus them, such as Arabs versus Africans, Islam versus Christianity and other traditional religions, or Arabic as a language and an identity in the North versus tribal languages, Juba, Arabic and/or English in the South.

### Institutional violence: Islamisation, state policies and legislation

Since 1989, the Islamist government has embarked on several policies to suppress the advancement of women in Sudan under the banner of the alleged demands of Islamic propriety. Their first step was the massive dismissal of women from public service, which affected almost 80 per cent of women in government offices, especially women in the legal and medical professions, the Ministry of Labour and journalism (Africa Watch, 1993). They were dismissed due to their political affiliations and secular ideologies, and all were replaced by Islamist cadres. In addition, women street vendors in the informal sector were violently attacked; it was stated that they made the city of Khartoum ugly (ibid.).

The regulatory measures that the Islamists pushed through during the early 1990s, using laws, policies, state regulations, decrees and orders, show their preoccupation with women's appearance, dress and conduct (Nageeb, 2004). These measures were specifically stressed by institutions such as mosques, the media and the school system and were implemented by public order courts, the police and security services (ibid.). Men as social and religious guardians are also entitled to correct women's conduct according to state regulations or based on Muslim men's 'correct' sense (ibid.).

In addition, the new military government added new elements to the conflict by aggressively imposing an Islamised programme in the South, naming it a jihad (holy war). Accordingly, they formed new 'Arab-only' militia groups named the Popular Defence, backed by the army (Nageeb, 2004).

Women supporters of the Islamist project supported the jihad by providing assets including personal gold and money and serving food for the mujahideen (Hale, 1996). Violence against women by the

Popular Defence, Sudanese army and the Sudan People's Liberation Army (the South Sudan group that fought for peace and equality) was not documented, and violence against women during the 1983–2005 period was not highlighted in international media or on the international agenda – unlike the case in Darfur, which was overwhelmed by international publicity relating to the widespread rape of women. However, this new formation was considered a threat to the social and cultural fabric of the non-Arab groups in Sudan, especially in other parts of the country, including Darfur, Abyei, the Nuba Mountains and southern Blue Nile (Kameir, 2012; Tonnessen, 2017).

I argue here that the force of Islamisation, with greater restrictions on women, did not come from a vacuum; in fact, the situation was ripe to derail women's contribution to the country's development and to strip them of the rights they had gained in the 1960s and 1970s. From the early 1980s, Sudan was reshaped by restrictive social, economic and political measures, with the introduction of sharia laws, known as September Laws, in 1983, which terminated the Addis Ababa peace agreement (1972–83) between North and South and triggered the war in the South. The restrictive measures included the compulsory wearing of the hijab, the requirement of male guardian approval for women travelling within and outside the country, and minimal access for women to equal benefits in areas such as housing: for example, regardless of whether a married woman is working, only her husband is entitled to receive the housing allowance, as he is the recognised breadwinner. This jeopardised women's access to some of their economic rights.

*Regulating women: employment bans, dress codes and*
*public order courts*

In September 2000, the governor of Khartoum issued a decree that restricted women's rights to employment, despite the fact that women's right to work had been achieved in the 1960s, as well as the right to equal pay, maternity leave and a pension by the early 1970s (Ahmad, 2014). The governor issued a decree banning women from working in hotels, restaurants and petrol stations with the recommendation that '[such] service providers hire those women in other places', and with clear directives to social affairs authorities, local government and the police and security forces 'to put this decision into immediate effect'. These instructions were circulated to all newspapers. The justification given by the governor was that this was 'in consideration of the State which sought the dignity of women and to situate her in the right place which they deserve as per the civilisation project of the nation and in line with our traditions and values of our religion' (ibid.). The justification undermined the position of those women who were the sole breadwinners in their families and highlights the Islamist reshaping of gender roles at the public level. The Women's Solidarity Group was formed to support the dismissed female workers and succeeded in taking the decree to the constitutional court, where it managed to freeze the law but not abolish it (ibid.).

The Public Order Law that was passed in Khartoum State in 1996, which is emblematic of the politicisation of ethno-religious identities (Arab-Islam), is also an authoritative statement on the status of minority cultures living under sharia law, as well as women (Abusharaf, 2009). This law was passed by the government to curb practices that it considered un-Islamic, and people who do not comply with it are taken to court. The law covers a range of activities affecting women's employment, enforcing Islamic dress (the hijab), and banning women's traditional wear (ibid.).

My own memories regarding the passing of the law are as follows:

I remembered when the law was issued in 1996, myself and a group of my friends were very angry, we felt that we had lost our agency to choose and decide for ourselves, not only what to wear. It was totally unacceptable, we refused to wear it [the hijab]; however, any time we wanted to walk out of our homes we were very fearful to be attacked or taken to court. For that we used to have a scarf in our purses; most women named it 'Just in Case'. Any time we left home we were never sure that we would be back to our homes; we lost our security and inner peace.

To ensure the implementation of this law, the government incorporated it with selected articles of the Criminal Code of 1991 and vested the Supreme Court, Court of Appeal and general criminal courts with full authority to imprison, fine, whip, confiscate from and enforce any punishment they saw fit on those who were non-compliant (Abusharaf, 2009). The articles from the Criminal Code of 1991 concern mainly offences of honour, reputation and public morality. The Act defines a range of offences related to what is generally understood to be the maintenance of 'public order'. This part identifies a series of crimes and penalties that regulate the interaction between men and women in public and private spheres. Section 152, 'Indecent and immoral acts', reads: 'Whoever commits, in a public place, an act, or conducts himself in an indecent, or immoral, dress, which causes annoyance to public feelings, shall be punished with whipping not exceeding 40 lashes, or with fine, or both' (ibid.).

In July 2009, Lubna Hussein, a journalist who worked with the UN in Khartoum, circulated publicly the story of her trial with the public order police. She was arrested with twelve other women from a restaurant in Khartoum and sentenced to forty lashes because of her indecent dress; she was wearing trousers. Her case, which later became known as the 'Pants Journalist' case, was widely depicted as an example of the subordination of Muslim women, especially by media in the global North (Fadlalla, 2011). In Sudan, following her resignation from her job with the UN, Lubna's case was picked up by women and human rights activists and politicians who seized the opportunity provided by it for the public to contest this oppressive law restricting women's public life. Although she was found guilty at her trial and sentenced to forty lashes, or a fine of 500 Sudanese pounds, or one month in prison, Lubna was not lashed. She refused to pay the fine and decided to be imprisoned for one month; however, the journalists' union paid the fine on her behalf and released her. This union is a non-elected government body (ibid.). At the trial, the police male witness who arrested her gave conflicting statements and described details of her body. As narrated by Fadlalla, 'as police officers, sworn to tell the truth, they had the right to gaze at Lubna's bodily attire and to graphically describe it to the public ... [offering] the general public an opportunity to peek closely to see the underwear, the belly button, and the bra'. The judge stated that 'the pants were tight, showing her thighs and underwear'. Fadlalla argues that 'the graphic description of Lubna's dress evokes feminist anthropologists' classic arguments that women's bodies serve as sites of conflicting political debates about morality, containment, social regulation, and public order law' (ibid.).

Despite the success of the campaign surrounding Lubna's case in shedding light on the Public Order Law in Sudan, and the national and international mobilisation during her trial, it turned out to be a failure. As stated by Fadlalla (2011): 'Lubna wrote a cynical counterargument commenting on how her class position and alliances had spared her the flogging and imprisonment.' Fadlalla continues that 'two weeks later, after Lubna's second trial, two female engineers arrested with her were sentenced to 20 lashes'. Lubna travelled extensively, talking about women's rights in Sudan, but she was never part of women's activism in Sudan. Sudanese women activists continued with their daily struggle to abolish the Public Order Law.

According to Nuba Reports (2017) on the public order courts, 70 per cent of the cases involved women. The Public Order Law has significantly impacted the lives of many women in Sudan, especially poor women and women in marginalised areas, as well as female students in schools and universities. Types of penalties imposed on women by the public order courts include physical punishment, fines and imprisonment (ibid.). The types of offences that take women and girls before the court are indecent dress, selling liquor and obscene acts (Figure 6.1). After South Sudan seceded in 2011, Khartoum lost 75 per cent of its oil revenue and the Sudanese government started to expand the number of public order courts across the country to aggressively increase revenue collection. A lawyer, Sabir Saeed, said that there are now twenty-two public order police courts in Khartoum alone and they are in almost every town across the country (ibid.).

### Violence, war and conflict

The North–South conflict was the main catalyst for the suffering and deteriorating position of women in South Sudan, the Nuba Mountains, southern Blue Nile, Abyei and Darfur. Over 1.9 million people were killed and 4 million forced to flee the South and seek refuge in the North

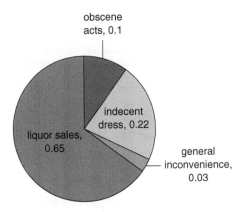

**Figure 6.1** Types of public order cases

or in neighbouring countries such as Kenya, Uganda and Ethiopia. Some even managed to reach Europe and North America. Women and children were the majority of displaced persons and refugees.

*South Sudanese women: displacement, marginalisation and war*

The internally displaced persons (IDPs) from South Sudan, both women and men, suffered multiple levels of discrimination, especially those who lived in the North. In addition to poverty, women in particular faced many cultural challenges, such as forced assimilation, including FGM in order to be culturally accepted to some extent (Abusharaf, 2009). The majority of the displaced women lacked many of the skills that were required to compete in the job market in northern Sudan. As a result, many worked in tea and food selling and brewing alcohol, which was prohibited along with sex work[2] by sharia law (ibid.). It was no surprise that the majority of women incarcerated in North Sudan prisons were from the South, the Nuba Mountains, southern Blue Nile, Abyei and Darfur. The law affected their economic contribution and put them at risk of flogging, fines and imprisonment (Clancy, 2012).

However, the suffering of women did not stop them from setting peace as a priority on their agenda. The South Sudanese refugees in Kenya and Uganda managed to organise and form groups including Sudan People's Liberation Movement/Army (SPLM\A) chapters (Ahmad, 2014). For the first time, women of the South fought in the front lines with men for the independence of South Sudan. Many women also managed to engage with the humanitarian aid agencies, registering women and making sure that families in refugee camps in Uganda and Kenya had enough food. Literacy classes were provided for women and their children with the help of the governments of Kenya and Uganda. The IDPs in the North were mostly settled around Khartoum, supported by UN agencies such as the World Food Programme, UNICEF and CARE. The role of the UN and other international aid organisations varied from food distribution to the building of schools and camps, awareness raising, sanitation, and so on (ibid.).

*Patterns of subjugation and violence in Darfur:*
*rape as a weapon of war*

Darfur had suffered a different level of conflict and discrimination from the 1980s onwards, mostly associated with underdevelopment and a lack of resources. However, in the current conflict, particularly between 2003 and 2005, women were increasingly subjected to mass rape and sexual violence (Fricke and Khair, 2007). More than 600,000 people were killed and over 2,000,000 were displaced. Amnesty International stated that the rape of women in Darfur was systematic and used as a weapon of war. A refugee woman living in west Darfur in May 2004 described the situation:

> I was sleeping when the attack took place. I was taken away by the attackers in khaki and civilian clothes along with dozens of other girls and had to walk for three hours. During the day we were beaten and the Janjawid (the government militia) told us 'you black women, we will exterminate you, you have no God.' We were taken to a place in the bush [where] the Janjawid raped us several times at night, for three days. We didn't receive food and almost no water. (Hashim, 2009)

Many victims of rape and their families are deeply traumatised, since rape specifically aims at terrorising and subjugating entire communities and affects their social fabric. In the conservative culture of Darfur, the stigma of rape is difficult to overcome – as a Fur woman remarked, 'No one would accept to marry a raped woman' (Human Rights Watch, cited in Hashim, 2009). Yet, sexual violence against women in Darfur has become woven into everyday life; this is poignantly underscored by a woman from north Darfur:

> When we leave the camp to fetch for fire wood we prefer to go as women rather than sending our men. When we go we only get raped but when our men go they get killed; we would rather get raped and come back. (Hashim, 2009)

The issue of rape in the Darfur conflict has drawn the attention of the international community and has been publicised in the international media, unlike the situation in southern Sudan. Not only has the government of Sudan denied the incidence of rape in Darfur, but some members of the ruling party claim that rape is part of Darfur's culture (Fricke and Khair, 2007). The late Magzoub Alkhalifa, governor of Darfur, alleged, for example, that 'Darfuri women are known for being promiscuous and shameless'. State denial of rape in Darfur is compounded by the fact that prosecuting rape cases in Sudan is exceedingly difficult and the courts place a greater burden of proof on women than on men due to unjust law, especially Article 149 of the Criminal Code of 1991, which defines rape as adultery (Hashim, 2009).

Alkhalifa's statement was no doubt related to the prejudices of many northern Arabised Sudanese from the centre about women in Darfur. Such prejudices conflict with their actual and recognised economic and socio-cultural standing. Darfuri women are known for their significant economic contributions and active participation in market and agricultural economies, particularly as handicraft sellers and in food and construction work. Women are the major economic providers in many parts of Darfur, and therefore they occupy public spheres. Their main role is to feed their families, and so they have larger fields in which they grow crops (millet and sorghum) and larger grain storage rooms than their husbands (Hashim, 2009). Men, on the other hand, have to provide only the amount of grain they need for their own consumption. This allows them to grow cash crops such as irrigated citrus fruits to trade, or to engage in wage labour, since they are expected to pay for anything that costs money such as clothes or utensils. In order for men to earn this money they spend a great deal of time outside their villages while women take care of daily life inside the village. Women are the de facto 'keepers of the land'. In practice, women need to have some income and men are not always around to provide when the need arises. This has led to the misconception among men in the North that Darfuri men are not responsible enough because they do not control their women (ibid.).

International organisations were the main source of reports and documentation of violence in Darfur, through the work of Médecins Sans Frontières (MSF-Holland), CARE, International Rescue Committee and some of the UN offices. They provided medical and psychological services to the victims of rape and most of their reports were made public, paving the way for the International Criminal Court (ICC) to issue an indictment against President al-Bashir in 2009. As a reaction to the ICC, the government expelled thirteen international and local organisations suspected of contributing to the ICC decision. This reaction created a huge vacuum in service provision for rape victims. In response to international pressure, the government of Sudan established a committee, mostly funded by the United Nations Population Fund (UNFPA) under the Ministry of Justice, to deal with violence against women in Darfur (Hashim, 2009).

Learning from the women of South Sudan, the Darfuri women showed an effective presence in peace negotiations and insisted that there should be real representation for women in all matters concerning their lives and their families.

## Women's resistance and organising in modern Sudan: failures and successes

Women's initial success in organising emerged from the anti-colonial and nationalist movement, in which independence and the sovereignty of the country were the main goals. Gender and women's rights were not their focus of activism (Ahmad, 2014). The modern Sudanese women's movement started in the late 1940s when women began forming organisations, mostly led by educated women. The year 1952 witnessed the founding of the Women's Union (WU) as part of the nationalist movement. The WU, despite its socialist ideology, sought to unite women in one organisation regardless of their political affiliations (Ali, 2015; Hall and Ismail, 1981; Badri, 2009; Hale, 1996). Like the nationalist movement, the WU was essentially urban, educated and middle class; southern and rural women remained on the extreme periphery of the movement. However, this was the trend in all anti-colonial movements during the 1950s and 1960s.

The interdependence of nationalism and feminism in Third World or global South countries highlighted by Jayawardena (1986, cited in Ahmad, 2014) confirmed the gains women could achieve by participating in nationalist struggles. Jayawardena analysed the idea that nationalism projects allowed women some space for resistance and strengthened both their capacity and self-confidence by granting them access to work and education. However, she maintained that in India and other countries in which the local bourgeoisie replaced imperialist rulers through a process of negotiation and gradual reforms, the women's struggle did not move beyond the sphere of limited reforms: that is, equality for women within legal processes, the right to vote, and the right to education and property. In Sudan, as in many other cases of women in the global South who were involved in an anti-colonial movement, the women in these nationalist movements did not address the basic question of women's subordination within the family and society (Ahmad, 2014).

Moreover, these reforms did not have the same effect on all women. Differences of ethnicity, religion and geographical location, especially in the case of Sudan, resulted in many women being deprived of the benefits of such reforms. Women in nationalist projects expressed modernity by practising their rights through suffrage, education and employment; however, rights within the family were left untouched. The WU was a clear example. When members were calling for political participation and the right to vote, this step was met with resistance from their Islamist sisters, who called it un-Islamic. This was the first split within the WU, resulting in the rise of a new women's organisation, the National Women's Front (NWF), which was established in the early 1960s as a wing of the Muslim Brotherhood, which has ruled Sudan since 1989 (Ahmad, 2014; El Bakri, 1995). To date, the women's movement remains divided largely between the socialist ideology of the WU and the political Islam of the NWF. Women organising in Sudan remain fragmented, falling between political parties and state feminism, and issues of violence against women, the family and sexuality have never become a priority (Ahmad, 2014; El Bakri, 1995).

Women's contribution to the nationalist movement is also connected to differences across gender, race, ethnicity and religion and their intersection. Certainly, only women who belong to the dominant nationalist project benefit from it. Women who are part of a minority nationalist project within the same geographical space (i.e. because they differ in ethnicity and religion) mostly suffer oppression at the hands of the dominant nationalist men and women. In Sudan, as mentioned earlier, nation building and the formation of the state often entailed fostering or imposing cultural hegemony, as demonstrated by the northern Sudanese elites enforcing Arabic and Islamic culture. This narrow definition of the state resulted in the North–South conflict in 1955–2005 (Ahmad, 2014).

The decade of the 1960s was the peak for the WU, as women gained the right to vote and stand for elections. In 1965, the first woman elected to parliament was the president of the WU. In 1968, women also gained the right to equal pay for equal work, training and promotion, and the abolition of monthly contracts for married women (Hall and Ismail, 1981; Badri, 2009: El Bakri, 1995, Ibrahim, 1996). Moreover, they succeeded in making all professional jobs available for women. Accordingly, women were able to enter the judiciary and become judges, even in personal law courts; they could serve as diplomats, in the armed forces and in the police, and they could work in hotels. They made demands, especially on the personal law, and succeeded in giving girls the right to be consulted before marriage and women the right to divorce in cases of abuse and when they choose not to continue in a marriage, provided they repay the dowry. They abolished the obedience law and allowed mothers custody of their sons until they reach the age of seventeen and of their daughters until marriage (Ibrahim, 1996). In cases of divorce, children were given the right to receive maintenance from their fathers, provided that it did not exceed half the father's income (ibid.). Although in the late 1970s and early 1980s some of the younger generation within the WU raised some concerns regarding violence against women, including FGM, domestic violence and forced marriage, this was met with resistance from the WU leadership (El Bakri, 1995).

Despite the split between the WU and NWF, they were both faced with 'state feminism' between 1971 and 1985 (Tonnessen, 2017). Some WU members joined the newly formed women's organisation the Sudanese Women's Union (SWU), which was mainly controlled by the state and monopolised interventions within the field of women's rights (ibid.). Unlike the WU, which was financially dependent on membership contributions, the SWU was fully supported by the state for all its financial needs. As stated by Khalid (1995), this period in the history of the women's movement 'witnessed many fundamental changes in social, political and economic relations, which more or less reflected state ideology'.

The regime known as the May Revolution (1969–85) ended a democratically elected government, replacing it with a one-party state. The WU was banned and went underground, together with the Communist Party, after an aborted coup in 1971 against the May Revolution (El Bakri, 1995). By the 1980s, the government was faced with many challenges, such as economic recession in the Middle East combined with famine in western Sudan and structural adjustment policies. It is worth mentioning that the regime succeeded in signing the first peace agreement with the South in 1972 in Addis Ababa, Ethiopia, thereby ending the conflict. However, conflict erupted again in 1983 due to the implementation of sharia laws in that year under the influence of the Islamists (Khalid, 1995). During this regime, improvements in educational services, especially in rural areas and in the South, expanded enormously. Moreover, women became ministers and judges and many reached middle-management ranks in civil service departments, confirming equal opportunity to access training and higher education (ibid.).

After the fall of the military government, the dismantling of government institutions – the SWU included – left a vacuum in the collective representation of women. The rise of political Islam attracted many young urban women. The most serious indicator of what El Bakri refers to as a crisis in the Sudanese women's movement was 'the inability of the existing women's organisations to deal with women's problems or attract enough women and transform themselves into a critical mass' (El Bakri, 1995).

After the uprising in 1985, the government failed to relieve the economic crisis, inflation continued to skyrocket and shortages of consumer goods 'were accompanied by a flourishing black market' (El Bakri, 1995). Islamic and other repressive laws were not abolished. The state of emergency was not lifted. There were no plans to end the conflict in the South. Women were not represented in any decision-making processes (ibid.). The Islamic laws of 1983 (the September laws) that set out several restrictions on women's legal status were not abrogated; instead, a new dress code was introduced for women working in government. Also, married working women in government were now entitled to two-thirds of male officials' housing allowance (ibid.); this was based on the belief that married women have a reduced financial responsibility since they have a husband who is the primary breadwinner. A women's committee was established in the Department of Passports and Immigration to enforce restrictions on women travelling abroad without being chaperoned by male relatives. The pretext for this was to stop travel by women who were going for sex work to the various oil-rich Arab countries and causing serious damage to Sudan's reputation abroad (ibid.).

After the fall of the May Revolution, the WU revived its activities and opened its doors to new membership. They announced that any woman, regardless of her political ideology, could be a member provided she did not have a bad reputation and had not been involved in the previous regime (El Bakri, 1995). Sudanese women's organisations made the women's agenda less important than their primary ideological affiliation – that is, political parties and the state, which are mostly male dominated.

The NWF emerged after the uprising as one of the strongest and most well-funded women's groups. Its ideological position is the same as that of the Muslim Brotherhood, with its main aim being to spread Islam and establish an Islamic nation. The NWF 'vigorously propagates images of the ideal Muslim woman and family' (El Bakri, 1995) through mass media. It also created a voluntary organisation, with its main recommendations, made when it was founded, to fight sex discrimination in employment; to call for an extension of maternity leave to six months (instead of two months) with full pay; to urge employers to provide transportation for their female workers; and to organise women in the informal sector (ibid.).

After the uprising in 1985, the army took over for one year, preparing the country for elections in 1986. A new government was elected, and during its rule (1986–89) Sudan signed and then ratified the International Covenant on Civil and Political Rights (ICCPR) and the International Covenant on Economic, Social and Cultural Rights (ICESCR). The Convention on the Elimination of All Forms of Discrimination Against Women (CEDAW) was not signed or ratified, however, as the women's agenda was not made a priority (El Bakri, 1995).

The women's movement was caught between state feminism and meagre political parties: for example, the Muslim Sisters, currently named the Sudanese Women's General Union (SWGU), is supported by the Islamist government. The SWGU's doctrine on women is based on the idea of gender equity but not equality – that is, women and men are not equal but have complementary roles and responsibilities due to their biological differences (Tonnessen, 2017). Therefore, women have to wear the hijab and nurture children to build an authentic Islamic (nation). The SWGU also states that men's sexual needs are prodigious, and therefore it approves of polygamy to enable men to fulfil their sexual needs. However, it also confirms that women are an integral part of the Islamic movement (Hale, 1996). This concurs with Moghadam's statement:

> One may hypothesise that in the earlier stage of the Islamist movement the influx of women in the workforce raised fears of competition with men, leading to calls for the re-domestication of women, as occurred in the Iranian Revolution. In the current stage with the labour force participation of women now a fait accompli, Islamists in Turkey, Iran, Egypt, Sudan and Yemen are not calling on women to withdraw from the labour force, indeed many of their female adherents are educated and employed, but they also insist on veiling and on spatial and functional segregation. (Moghadam, 1999)

This grants women rights in the public domain to participate in politics, work outside the home and receive an education, on condition that they behave piously and dress in a modest way. In this regard, the Muslim women's organisation turns out to be the strongest women's organisation, and government policy towards women is being maintained in the current period (from 1989 to date).

## New trends and shifts: women's non-governmental organisations

During preparations for the UN Fourth Conference on Women in Beijing in the mid-1990s, Sudanese women underwent a new shift, establishing women's organisations outside political parties and the state, paving the way for a new wave to emerge. They began considering issues such as violence against women, sexual violence, legal reforms (including of the personal law and the Criminal Code of 1991), legal aid, peace, citizenship rights, capacity building, women's political participation, women's rights awareness, the Protocol to the African Charter on Human and Peoples' Rights on the Rights of Women in Africa, the Convention on the Rights of the Child, Security Council Resolution 1325 and the millennium development goals (MDGs), to list a few (Hashim, 2009). The nature of activism changed markedly during the 1990s and 2000s, especially after the signing of the CPA in 2005, which witnessed an influx of donors and international organisations to support both North and South. Women's organisations started to receive training on gender concepts, women's rights, peace and violence against women (Ahmad, 2014). This has further helped to foster an interest in gender relations and bring women together to build alliances that allow them to achieve some of those rights (Tonnessen, 2017).

*Against all odds: southern Sudanese women's organisations*

The participation of South Sudanese women in the public sphere is a recent phenomenon. During 1960–70, women of the South were not able to venture into the political arena; men mainly occupied public spheres such as business and the army and assumed political positions. Women were usually relegated to the stereotypical role of nurturing and caring. However, after the signing of the Addis Ababa peace agreement in 1972, although women's visibility in politics was limited in comparison to the North, it was vivid in South Sudan. Moreover, some women from the South had joined the SWU during the May Revolution (Edward, 2011). The major breakthrough for southern women's political involvement and representation at government levels came between 2005 and 2011 following the signing of the CPA, which granted women 25 per cent representation in the Legislative Assembly. The former government of South Sudan witnessed an increased number of women at decision-making levels, as state governor, ministers, ambassadors and presidential adviser for gender.

However, women's political journey in the South did not occur without challenges, some of which arose from socio-cultural factors – education, ethnicity, class, and regional and family background. Practices such as forced and arranged marriage hindered women from pursuing their education and further affected their political participation and future careers. The late Dr John Garang, head of the SPLM/A, who died in a plane crash in August 2005, was the first South Sudanese leader to acknowledge women's role in the public sphere. Customary laws remain a real challenge in the lives of women in the South, making it difficult for women to escape the bondage of their ethnic/domestic role, which relegates women to second-class citizens (Edward, 2011).

### Successful attempts: Sudanese women building collectives

Women in the Islamic movement still strongly support government policies, including the Public Order Law. Despite this complex and challenging situation, some women's organisations have been able to strategise and build connections both locally and globally. Initiatives such as the 149 Alliance[3] campaign to reform the 1991 rape law, launched in 2008 with the support of Women Living Under Muslim Laws, succeeded in 2015 after many years of campaigning. However, access to justice for women remains challenging.

The Sudanese Women Empowerment for Peace was another collective, formed in 1997 by the Netherlands embassy in Khartoum and Nairobi to bridge the gap between women from the North, the South and the Nuba Mountains. This initiative brought women from Sudan and women in exile together to work for peace. They received intensive training that allowed some of the South Sudanese women to work in government. Despite their differences, these women managed to unite and work for peace, reaching a minimum agenda in 2000 at Maastricht. However, their contributions to the peace negotiation were trifling.

## Conclusion

It is difficult to talk about political economy and women's inequality in a context such as Sudan and South Sudan in isolation from global inequality and its neoliberal means and mechanisms. For both North and South Sudan, conflict was one of the main catalysts for the deteriorating position of Sudanese women as well as the key instigator of specific forms of gender-based violence. Legal discrimination – be it under Islamic laws or customary law – controls women's mobility and restricts their public life. This clearly shows that Islam is not the only tool used to discriminate against women. It is clear that social norms, the extended family, ethnic rules and marriage are more effective in imposing certain limitations on women. Whether Christian or Muslim, patriarchal norms have more power over women's social participation. These norms have taken different forms, such as forced and child marriages, the preference for males over females, and the stigma around issues of sexuality, sexual violence and reproductive rights, some of which have never featured in the women's movement agenda.

Throughout its history, Sudan has had a segmented women's movement. Generally not independent, it has fallen between political parties and state feminism. This did not allow a strong united movement to grow, and it remained a wing of the patriarchy, allowing limited rights and limiting women's accumulation of experiences and challenges. The pioneer women who led the movement worked for some women's rights, such as the right to work and to access education, equal pay for equal work and the right to political participation. However, the new wave of independent women's organisations is completely dependent on donor funding and faces a restrictive regime that controls women's freedom and autonomy. The pioneer women and the work they did is not being maintained by the new wave, although sometimes their shadow or the agenda of their political parties is still there in spirit.

In the era of transnational feminism, Sudanese women remain disconnected – they are not exposed to women's organisations in similar contexts to learn from them, such as women's mobilisation in Egypt, or the Iranian and Pakistani women's movements.

The governor of Khartoum's 2000 decree was frozen by the constitutional court, no other decree was issued, and women played a big role in resisting the public order police. The perception of the Islamists is pro-women, yet control over women's bodies, honour and morality is one of their central pillars. Women of the South have to be assured of the government's peace and security commitment. The national gender policy and reform of customary laws must be secured by building alliances and learning from the failure of the women's movement in the North. Women of both Sudan and South Sudan have to build a grassroots feminist movement, not just of elite women but of diverse and young women, and they have to conduct more research and networking.

## Notes

1  In respect to South Sudan, this chapter covers the South until independence in 2011 (2005–11) and does not include the eruption of the internal conflict in 2013.

2  Prostitution was not criminalised until 1983. During the Turko-Egyptian colonisation in the nineteenth century, prostitution and sex services for money were dominated by women of slave status. With the disruption of the market economy, female slaves were used as a commodity and self-enrichment by their lords. This activity was reduced by the British in the late nineteenth century through the abolition of slavery. During the British colonial period, prostitution was regulated and licensed, with regular medical inspections to protect the British troops. Later, they started regulating the consumption of alcohol in brothels, which spread and were tolerated in almost every town and village. Prostitutes were never part of the women's movement because they were considered immoral, yet they have long contributed to the economy. Even after independence, the British-regulated system continued and prostitutes paid taxes to the government. After the implementation of sharia, prostitution became criminalised, punishable by 100 lashes, fines or stoning, but I argue here that, whether criminalised or not, prostitution remained a source of revenue for the government. Prostitutes also engaged in collective action – historical records confirm that the women of Khartoum's red-light district celebrated Sudan Independence Day on 1 January 1956 by refusing services to white men for two days (Spaulding and Beswick, 2016).

3  The alliance was led by the Salmmah women's resource centre, which was shut down by the regime in 2014, the Sudanese Women Empowerment for Peace, Sudan Development Organisation, Al-Mutawinat Group, Alalag Centre for Media Services and Sudanese Environment Conservation Society, as well as Al-Amel Centre for Victims of Torture and Khartoum Centre for Human Rights, which were both shut down by the government in 2009.

# References

Abusharaf, R. 2009. 'Competing Masculinities: Probing Political Disputes as Acts of Violence against Women from Southern Sudan and Darfur' in Hassan, S. and Ray, C. (eds), *Darfur and the Crisis of Governance in Sudan: A Critical Reader*. New York: Cornell University Press.

AfDB. 2011. *The Political Economy of South Sudan: A Scoping Analytical Study*. Abidjan: African Development Bank (AfDB).

Africa Watch. 1993. 'Threat to Women's Status from Fundamentalist Regime in Sudan', *Women Living Under Muslim Laws Dossier* 11/12/13: 40–2.

Ahmad, M. 2014. 'The Women's Movement in Sudan from Nationalism to TransNationalism: Prospects for a Solidarity Movement'. PhD thesis, York University, Toronto.

Ali, N. 2015. *Gender, Race and Sudan's Exile Politics*. Lanham MD: Lexington Books.

Almosharaf, H. 2014. 'The Causes of Sudan's Recent Economic Decline', *IOSR: Journal of Economics and Finance* 2 (4): 26–40.

Badri, H. 2009. *Women's Movement in the Sudan*. Omdurman, Sudan: MOB Center for Sudanese Studies.

Brown, M. 2017. *Khartoum at Night: Fashion and Body Politics in Imperial Sudan*. Stanford: Stanford University Press.

BTI. 2018. *BTI 2018: Sudan Country Report*. Gütersloh: Bertelsmann Stiftung's Transformation Index (BTI).

Clancy, D. 2012. *Falling through the Cracks: Reflections on Customary Law and the Imprisonment of Women in South Sudan*. Kampala: Strategic Initiative for Women in the Horn of Africa (SIHA) Network.

Edward, J. K. 2011. 'Women and Political Participation in South Sudan', *Sudan Tribune*, 7 September, www.sudantribune.com/spip. php?page=imprimable&id_ article=40086 (accessed 6 May 2019).

El Bakri, Z. 1995. 'The Crisis in the Sudanese Women's Movement' in Wieringa, S. (ed.), *Subversive Women: Women's Movements in Africa, Asia, Latin America and the Caribbean*. London: Zed Books.

Elrayh, E. 2014. 'Women's Rights in the Constitutional Bill of Rights: Issues of Status, Equality and Non-discrimination' in *The Constitutional Protection of Human Rights in Sudan: Challenges and Future Perspectives*. London: REDRESS, https://reliefweb.int/sites/reliefweb. int/files/resources/140127FINAL%20 Sudan%20UoK%20Report.pdf (accessed 6 May 2019).

Fadlalla, A. 2011. 'State of Vulnerability and Humanitarian Visibility on the Verge of Sudan's Secession: Lubna's Pants and the Transnational Politics of Rights and Dissent', *Signs: Journal of Women in Culture and Society* 37 (1): 159–84.

Fricke, A. and Khair, A. 2007. *Laws without Justice: An Assessment of Sudanese Laws Affecting Survivors of Rape*. Washington DC: Refugee International.

Government of Sudan. 2012. *Sudan Household Health Survey 2010: Round 2*. Khartoum: Ministry of Health and Central Bureau of Statistics.

Gruenbaum, E. 2006. 'Sexuality Issues in the Movement to Abolish Female Genital Cutting in Sudan', *Medical Anthropology Quarterly* 20 (1): 121–38.

Hale, S. 1996. 'Gender Politics and Islamization in Sudan', *Comparative Studies of South Asia, Africa and the Middle East* 14 (2): 51–66.

Hall, M. and Ismail, B. 1981. *Sisters under the Sun: The Story of Sudanese Women*. London: Longman.

Hashim, F. 2009. 'Sudanese Civil Society Strategizing to End Sexual Violence against Women in Darfur' in Hassan, S. and Ray, C. (eds), *Darfur and the Crisis of Governance in Sudan: A Critical Reader*. New York: Cornell University Press.

Ibrahim, F. 1996. 'Sudanese Women's Union: Strategies for Emancipation and the Counter-movement', *Ufahamu* 24 (2–3).

Idris, A. 2013. *Identity, Citizenship, and Violence in Two Sudans*. New York: Palgrave Pivot.

IMF. 2013. 'Sudan: Interim Poverty Reduction Strategy Paper'. IMF Country Report 13/318. Washington DC: International Monetary Fund (IMF), www.imf.org/en/Publications/CR/Issues/2016/12/31/Sudan-Interim-Poverty-Reduction-Strategy-Paper-41025 (accessed 6 May 2019).

Kameir, E. 2012. *Perspectives on the Political Economy of South Sudan*. Abidjan: Fragile States Unit, African Development Bank.

Khalid, T. 1995. 'The State and the Sudanese Women's Union, 1971–1983: A Case Study' in Wieringa, S. (ed.), *Subversive Women: Women's Movements in Africa, Asia, Latin America and the Caribbean*. London: Zed Books.

Makuei, G., Abdollahian, M. and Marion, K. 2018. 'Optimal Profile Limits for Maternal Mortality Rate (MMR) in South Sudan', *BMC Pregnancy and Childbirth* 18: 278, https://doi.org/10.1186/s12884-018-1892-0 (accessed 6 May 2019).

Moghadam, V. 1999. 'Gender and Globalization: Female Labor and Women's Mobilization', *Journal of World-Systems Research* 5 (2): 366–89.

Musawah. 2009. *Home Truths: A Global Report on Equality in the Muslim Family*. Kuala Lumpur: Musawah, www.musawah.org/wp-content/uploads/2018/11/MusawahHomeTruths_En.pdf (accessed 6 May 2019).

Nageeb, S. 2004. *New Spaces and Old Frontiers*. Lanham MD: Lexington Books.

No Safe Place. 2017. *No Safe Place: A Lifetime of Violence for Conflict-affected Women and Girls in South Sudan*. London: What Works, www2.gwu.edu/~mcs/gwi/No_Safe_Place_Full_Report.pdf (accessed 6 May 2019).

Nuba Reports. 2017. 'Courts Target Poor Sudanese Women with Extortionate "Morality" Fines', Nuba Reports, 1 December, www.newsdeeply.com/womenandgirls/articles/2017/12/01/courts-target-poor-sudanese-women-with-extortionate-morality-fines (accessed 6 May 2019).

SIHA Network. 2015. *Third-class Citizens: A Paper on Women's Struggle for Equal Citizenship in Sudan*. Kampala: Strategic Initiative for Women in the Horn of Africa (SIHA) Network, www.sihanet.org/publications/third-class-citizens-women-and-citizenship-in-sudan/ (accessed 6 May 2019).

Spaulding, J. and Beswick, S. 2016. 'Sex, Bondage, and the Market: The Emergence of Prostitution in Northern Sudan, 1750–1950', *Journal of the History of Sexuality* 5 (4): 512–34.

Tonnessen, L. 2017. 'Enemies of the State: Curbing Women Activists Advocating Rape Reform in Sudan', *Journal of International Women's Studies* 18 (2): 148–55, http://vc.bridgew.edu/jiws/vol18/iss2/10 (accessed 6 May 2019).

True, J. 2010. 'The Political Economy of Violence against Women: A Feminist International Relations Perspective', *Australian Feminist Law Journal* 32 (1): 39–59.

True, J. 2012. *The Political Economy of Violence against Women*. Oxford and New York: Oxford University Press.

UNDP. 2015. *South Sudan: National Human Development Report 2015*. New York: United Nations Development Programme (UNDP), www.ss.undp.org/content/south_sudan/en/home/library/undp-global-reports/SSNHDR.html (accessed 6 May 2019).

UN-HABITAT. 2014. *Sudan's Report for United Nation's Third Conference on Housing and Sustainable Urban Development (Habitat III) 2016*. Khartoum: UN-HABITAT and Ministry of Environment, Forestry and Urban Development, http://habitat3.org/wp-content/uploads/Sudan-National-Report.pdf

# INDEX

Note: The following abbreviation has been used – *n* = note. Page numbers in *italic* refer to illustrations and tables.

# ZED

Zed is a platform for marginalised voices across the globe.

It is the world's largest publishing collective and a world leading example of alternative, non-hierarchical business practice.

It has no CEO, no MD and no bosses and is owned and managed by its workers who are all on equal pay.

It makes its content available in as many languages as possible.

It publishes content critical of oppressive power structures and regimes.

It publishes content that changes its readers' thinking.

It publishes content that other publishers won't and that the establishment finds threatening.

It has been subject to repeated acts of censorship by states and corporations.

It fights all forms of censorship.

It is financially and ideologically independent of any party, corporation, state or individual.

Its books are shared all over the world.

www.zedbooks.net
@ZedBooks